```
799.277358                        2789
              Cadieux            $24.95

North America's Unique Antelope
```

DATE DUE

IMPERIAL PUBLIC LIBRARY
P.O. BOX 307
IMPERIAL, TEXAS 79743

DEMCO

PRONGHORN,
NORTH AMERICA'S UNIQUE ANTELOPE

PRONGHORN, NORTH AMERICA'S UNIQUE ANTELOPE

The Practical Guide for Hunters

Charles L. Cadieux

*Photos by author
unless otherwise credited*

Stackpole Books

Copyright © 1986 by Stackpole Books

Published by
STACKPOLE BOOKS
Cameron and Kelker Streets
P.O. Box 1831
Harrisburg, PA   17105

All rights reserved, including the right to reproduce this book or portions thereof in any form or by any means, electronic or mechanical, including photocopying, recording, or by any information storage and retrieval system, without permission in writing from the publisher. All inquiries should be addressed to Stackpole Books, Cameron and Kelker Streets, P.O. Box 1831, Harrisburg, Pennsylvania 17105.

Printed in the U.S.A.

Library of Congress Cataloging-in-Publication Data

Cadieux, Charles L.
    Pronghorn, North America's unique antelope.

    1. Pronghorn antelope hunting.   I. Title.
SK305.P76C33   1986   799.2'77358   86-3691
ISBN 0-8117-1376-8

Contents

1	What Is a Pronghorn?	7
2	Aristocratic Family Tree	16
3	Pronghorn Numbers	21
4	State by State, Province by Province	24
5	The Impossible Dream	83
6	From Montana with Love	89
7	Pronghorn Habits	96
8	Pronghorns and Predators	115
9	Pronghorn Management	125
10	What Pronghorns Eat	133
11	A Strange and Wondrous Animal	141
12	Mortality Factors	155
13	Go Underground for Pronghorns	168
14	Where to Hunt	179

15	Rifle Selection	183
16	Decoying Antelope	189
17	Muzzleloaders	192
18	Hunting Equipment	196
19	Clothing for Hunters	199
20	Hunting Methods	202
21	Advice from the Experts	208
22	Pronghorns on the Table	223
23	Guide to Trophies	227
24	Bowhunting Pronghorns, *by Judd Cooney*	231
	Index	252

1

What Is a Pronghorn?

The first explorers of North America to write about the pronghorned antelope included Washington Irving. In 1836, he wrote:

"Their color is a light gray, or rather dun, slightly spotted with white; and they have small horns like those of a deer, which they never shed. Nothing can surpass the delicate and elegant finish of their limbs, in which lightness, elasticity, and strength are wonderfully combined. All the attitudes and movements of this beautiful animal are graceful and picturesque, and it is altogether a fit subject for the fanciful uses of the poet, as the oft sung gazelle of the east.

"Their habits are shy and capricious; they keep on the open plains, are quick to take alarm and bound away with a fleetness that defies pursuit. When thus skimming across a prairie in the autumn, their light gray or dun colour blends with the hue of the withered herbage, the swiftness of their motion baffles the eye and they almost seem unsubstantial forms, driven like gossamer before the wind.

"While they thus keep to the open plains and trust to their speed, they are safe; but they have a prurient curiosity that sometimes betrays them to their ruin. When they have scud for some distance and left their pursuer behind, they will suddenly stop and turn to gaze at the object of their alarm. If the pursuit is not followed up they will, after a time, yield to their inquisitive hankering and return to the place from whence they have been frightened."

That was a delightful description of a fascinating animal, but we have to quarrel with some of it. For instance, we've never seen a pronghorn that was colored gray.

The pronghorn is a creature of the wide open spaces. *Bureau of Land Management photo.*

We have noted almost every shade of red, brown, tan, and white, but never gray. Irving states categorically that these animals never shed their horns. We beg to differ, but then, more about that much later on in this book.

Another excellent observer, John J. Audubon, had this to say: "Observe now a flock of these beautiful animals; they are not afraid of man—they pause in their rapid course to gaze on the hunter, and stand with heads erect, their ears as well as their eyes directed toward him, and make a loud noise by stamping their forefeet on the hard earth; but suddenly they become aware that he is no friend of theirs, and away they bound like a flock of frightened sheep—but far more swiftly, even the kids running with extraordinary speed by the side of their parents—and now they turn around a steep hill and disappear, then perhaps come in view and once more stand and gaze at the intruder."

Once you've seen your first pronghorn, there is no mistaking one for any other species. His order is *Artiodactyla*, which means that he is a cloven hoofed mammal and has the main axis of the foot directly between the third and fourth digits (paraxonic).

His family is *Antilocapridae*, and he is the only living representative of this family, although there were other *Antilocapridae* along the evolutionary pathway, according to fossil remains. In fact, our pronghorn has been around for a very

What Is a Pronghorn?

long time. His fossilized remains, almost unchanged, are found all the way back in the Pleistocene and Miocene periods, possibly as far back as 10 to 25 million years ago.

The pronghorn's range in the Pleistocene era was evidently far greater than it is today, judging by fossil remains found in Wisconsin, Illinois, Nebraska, Florida, California, and Oregon. Our pronghorn survived the cataclysmic changes that accompanied the end of the Pleistocene. There are different theories for the disappearance of the "megafauna" (big animals of the Pleistocene). The most commonly accepted theory is that the advancing glaciers so cooled the world that these animals couldn't live. This theory has holes in it, of course. Why didn't these very mobile big animals move south ahead of the glaciers and find whatever climate they wanted? As anthropologist Dr. Frank C. Hibben of the University of New Mexico puts it, "Horses, camels, sloths, and antelopes all found slim pickings in their former habitats. But what was to prevent these animals from simply following the retreating ice to find just the type of vegetation and just the climate they desired? If Newport is cold in the winter, go to Florida. If Washington becomes too hot in the summer, go to Maine."

Why did glacial cold exterminate the woolly mammoth, perhaps one of the best insulated animals that ever lived?

Another theory is that the newly arrived hunter from Asia, man, killed off these naive beasts. The idea that a sparse handful of human hunters, armed with primitive weapons, could eliminate vast herds of big animals, is simply ridiculous. African natives, armed with better weapons, have not been able to exterminate big-game species in Africa, although they have lived with them for millennia longer than did the Bering Straits trespasser live with the megafauna of North America.

Another nagging question concerning both of these theories is this: The extermination of entire species occurred at roughly the same time—geologically speaking—on all continents. Did glaciers eliminate the huge bison from what is now Texas? Were the giant sloths unable to find food in Mesoamerica? Remember that the glaciers did not reach within 1000 miles of some of these megafauna habitats, yet the megafauna disappeared in a relatively short time, perhaps in a period of about 1000 years, which is like one tick of the geologist's clock.

The very worst of the glacial age was freezing our continent just 18,000 years ago, when North American temperatures averaged 18°F. colder than they do today. Obviously, glaciation caused catastrophic changes in the megafauna of North America, but during the "interglacials"—the periods between advancing ice sheets—boreal forest flourished over much of the area we now call the Great Plains. Imagine such forests covering the Dakotas, Iowa, Missouri, and Kansas. Surely that was not pronghorn pasture then. But for the past 8000 years, there has been no glaciation in the pronghorn pastures of North America.

Another disquieting bit of scientific information is that radiocarbon dating of megafauna fossils shows that the greatest part of the extinction took place *after* the last glaciation.

Rhinoceros and hippopotamus families all had their representatives on the North American continent, but they disappeared when the other, larger members of the genus *Antilocapridae* disappeared. Giant bison, camels, llamas, Irish elk, 100 species, almost all animals that weighed more than 100 pounds in adult weight—they all died out, and their ecological niches were not filled by smaller representatives of the same family, as has often happened along the evolutionary pathway that has shaped our present world's animals. But the moral to be learned here is not contingent upon finding the mortality factors involved. The moral is that, of all these hundreds of plains animals, only our pronghorn survived. He is, we repeat, the only surviving *Antilocapridae americana*. His was a successful, adaptable life-form.

When something is very successful, why change it?

How do we recognize this successful life-form? *Antilocapra americana* is the only hoofed animal that sheds its horns annually from a bony core. (Note I said the only hoofed animal that sheds its *horns* annually. Many animals shed antlers each year.) For more identification, our pronghorn has no dewclaws; chews its cud regurgitated from a complicated stomach system; has no upper incisor teeth, but only a pad of gristle that meets the incisor teeth to tear off its food. Want more? Its lachrymal bones do not touch the nasal bones.

Its small hooves are padded with a cartilaginous substance that reduces shocks to the skeleton and gives excellent footing, even upon slick rocks. This cartilage pad also makes it possible for the antelope to walk very quietly, but this is of dubious value for an animal that relies on speed for its defense and seldom tries to sneak

A fine looking pronghorn buck. Note how big the feet appear, contrasting with the slender leg bones. *Photo by Judd Cooney.*

This Wyoming buck and doe are the same age. Note size difference.

away, or to finesse its enemies in any way. The pronghorn simply outruns its enemies.

Pronghorns are smaller than average white-tailed or mule deer. A good-sized buck weighs in at 125 pounds, most average closer to 110, and does run nearly 20 pounds lighter than males.

Adult pronghorns stand approximately three feet high at the shoulders, and are about four feet long from chest to rump. One of the pronghorn's most striking features is the one that gives him his name. His horns are grown around a bony core, which is not shed each year. The horns rise nearly straight up from the crown of his head, then curve in toward each other. The points are usually lighter-colored than the rest of the horn. A couple of inches below the tips, each horn sports a "prong" that projects forward. We will talk more about that amazing horn development later on.

The other end of the antelope is also remarkable. The rump is covered with three-to-four-inch-long white hairs that usually lie supine and don't attract much attention. When the antelope senses danger, however, it can erect these long white hairs—which greatly enlarges the white area of the rump and which flashes a heliograph signal in the bright sunlight of the western plains. This alarm signal can be seen for many miles, and when it is repeated by a large bunch of animals on a bright sunny day, it is a striking display.

Compared to the whitetail or mule deer,

the pronghorn is a very vocal animal. It expresses alarm with a sharp, surprisingly loud, whistling snort, sort of a *Wheeeeoh*! When worried, it snorts in an entirely different way, and it can snort in frustration, also, as I found out when my photographic blind was between a pronghorn buck and the water he wanted to drink. They will also express anger, fear, or frustration by stamping with a front foot. The stamping often accompanies the whistling snort.

The pronghorn's senses of smell, sight, and hearing are all acute, with its eyesight meriting special notice. The old saying is that "By the time a man sees a pronghorn, the antelope has already read the writing on the Bull Durham sack tag hanging out of the man's shirt pocket." Put another way, the pronghorn's eyesight is probably equal to that of a man aided by 8x binoculars. In addition to the keenness of its vision, the eyeballs are placed well out from the bony socket—bulging eyes—which gives the animal a more-than-180-degree field of view with each eyeball. Just another reason why it is difficult to sneak up on a pronghorn.

Amazingly good eyes, plus exceptional speed of foot provide the antelope's main line of defense. The fact that the pronghorn relies on speed to escape, rather than on hiding, is what makes pronghorn hunting so interesting. If you are in an area populated with pronghorns, you'll see them, which is certainly not always true of deer hunting. Easy to see? Well, herein lies a paradox. The pronghorn is brightly colored, with a reddish-tan above and white underneath, with shiny erectile white rump hairs, with a black neck patch on both sides of the male's neck. The top three-quarters of the animal's body is generally tan, the neck has a black mane, and the underparts and that mirror rump are white. No other animal on the plains is so strikingly marked. BUT, and this is a very big BUT, this strikingly marked animal blends in with the drab colors of the clay banks and dry sage of the Wyoming plains. He is not all that easy to see.

Once he spies danger, the pronghorn sometimes stares at it with great patience. He may hold the pose, unmoving, for half an hour. On the other hand, he may come trotting closer to satisfy his well-known curiosity. But if the danger is recognizable and he decides that his presence is required somewhere else, the pronghorn can move off at remarkable speed. Six different reference books that I consulted on the matter of the highest speeds attainable by a running pronghorn gave me six different guesses; and that is all they are—guesses.

Note the protuberant eyes that give the pronghorn almost 360-degree vision. *Photo by Judd Cooney.*

They ranged from a low of 38 m.p.h. to a high of 70 m.p.h.

I'd like to throw in a personal observation on pronghorn speeds. I was driving on a smooth gravel road in Wyoming, traveling at a sedate 40 m.p.h. Looking out the window, I saw that a young pronghorn buck was pacing me, running parallel to the road, about 60 yards out in the field. I slowly increased the car's speed until my speedometer was registering an even 55. The buck pulled slightly ahead of me. As I decided to up the ante to 60 m.p.h., the buck put on a sudden spurt and crossed the road ahead of me. I would estimate his speed at the moment of crossing at 65 m.p.h. Although that animal was going all out, stretched out so that his "vest pocket was scooping up gravel," I had the feeling he could have gone faster if he had needed to.

Crossing the road ahead of a speeding car or railroad train is a characteristic trait of pronghorns that has been reported hundreds of times by competent observers. It tells us something about the personality of the pronghorn, for the crossover maneuver seems to be saying, "I'm faster than you, and I'll prove it!"

At first glance the pronghorn seems to be fragile, but this is definitely not the case. His hair is evidently loosely fastened to the skin, for he sheds it by great handfuls when touched. The fences he crawls under are often loaded with loose hairs pulled from that "easy shed" coat. His loose winter coat of hollow hairs is excellent protection against cold winds on the plains and prairies of the West. For at least 10 million years, he has withstood the vagaries of the western climate, existing in goodly numbers through blizzard and drought from southern Canada to Mexico. In 40 years of observing prong-

This fawn got its broken leg treated by sympathetic persons in the New Mexico Game and Fish Department. *New Mexico Game and Fish Department photo.*

horns I have come across remarkably few accidental deaths—with the exception of fences, which can be the pronghorn's undoing. Although he races over uneven terrain at breakneck speeds, he seldom if ever breaks his neck by falling. I have seen frantic animals bump into each other and fall as they raced away from danger, but the fallen animal got up and got going so quickly that you might have missed it if you weren't watching closely. Those pipe-stem-thin legs of the pronghorn are another surprise. Although they race across rough land, across rolling rocks and sliding gravel, they almost never break a leg. Those fragile leg bones have been laboratory tested, and it takes 45,300 pounds of pressure to crush them!

Antelope don't handle fences well. The common three-strand barbed wire fence doesn't slow them much. I've never seen them jump such a fence, but have watched in amazement as a whole herd went under such a fence on the dead run, without breaking stride. Each animal timed his own slide perfectly, went down on his belly and back up again on the other side so quickly that it seemed to be merely a dip in the smoothly flowing river of tan and white bodies. But woven wire fences stop them, and many antelope have died when a blizzard moved them up against such a fence and they did not know how to handle it. Pronghorn can jump, but they do not like to jump up and over things. They are capable of lateral jumps of as much as 20 feet, and commonly jump over small arroyos in their flight. When trapped (for restocking elsewhere) by conservation workers, I have seen them clear six-foot fencing in graceful leaps, but this is a great rarity. Usually a six-foot fence will do a good job of holding them, assuming there is no way through or under it.

They are definitely gregarious, herd animals that are seldom happy when alone. There are exceptions, of course, such as when the does go off by themselves to give birth to their young, and there are times when very old bucks will be driven from their harem and become recluses for the remainder of the rutting season. With those two exceptions, antelope are sociable critters and are usually found in bunches of from 20 to 100 on good ranges, and bunches of from 4 to 15 on areas where the pronghorn is not doing well.

What else can we tell you about pronghorns? Well, he is now the second-most-popular game animal in North America, trailing only the deer. He is the greatest success story in big-game management, coming back from near extinction to reach population crests that top half a million—although hunters take as many as 150,000 per year. Legal hunting is definitely a tool of good management where the pronghorn is concerned. The fact that the pronghorn can withstand heavy hunting pressure shouldn't surprise us either. Fossil evidence shows that the pronghorn was here on the plains of North America, along with the outsized bison, camels, megatheroids (giant sloths with a thyroid problem), cave bears, outsized lions, saber-tooth tigers, llamas, woolly mammoths, big giraffe-like animals, and herds of big-game animals of all kinds. When the first man came across the Bering Land Bridge from Asia, he found these tremendous herds of big game, and the hunter slaughtered them. Even today, scientists still find mastodons that have been frozen in the tundra for 10,000 years; some of these "freezer-burnt" gigantic packages of meat have contained flint spear points, proof that man, the hunter, did them in. Over the course of a few millennia, many of these big-game species were eliminated—but not the pronghorn. He is a survivor.

Probably the first white man to see the pronghorn antelope was with Francisco Vasquez Coronado, seeking the imagined treasures of the fabled cities of Cibola. Coronado traveled as far north as what is now Kansas way back in 1535, and he traversed the historic range of millions of pronghorns. It would be some three centuries later before the English-speaking world discovered the pronghorn, when Lewis and Clark wrote of seeing great numbers of these graceful, amazingly fleet animals.

The pronghorn is dependent upon public — rather than privately owned — land to a greater degree than any other big-game animal. Approximately half of all the nation's pronghorns live on federally owned land. More than 45 percent of these pronghorns live on land managed by the Bureau of Land Management, a part of the Department of the Interior.

In the chapters that follow, we will discuss many facets of this fascinating animal and its management.

2

Aristocratic Family Tree

One thing is certain: The pronghorned antelope of North America has been a successful life-form for a very long time. His is an ancient and proud family. The pronghorn evolved sometime during the Pleistocene Epoch, and evolved only in North America. Some paleontologists believe that an extinct deerlike species, *Cosoryx,* which evolved during the Tertiary Period, may have been the ancestral stock of the pronghorn. I won't worry about that; going back to the family tree in the Pleistocene is enough for me. But for those who worry about such things, Scharff in 1921 wrote the following: "The closely allied extinct genus *Merycosodus (Cosoryx)* made its first appearance in the Deep River deposits of Montana in middle or lower Miocene, and persisted until the Pliocene. During the latter period several new genera, viz.: *Capromeryz, Platatherium* and *Leptotherium,* branched off from the ancestral stock, and made their way into newly-opened areas. The last two occurred in recent beds in Brazil, the other in Nebraska. Thus the family *Antilocapridae* to which the recent pronghorn and all these fossils belong, originated in America and never left it."

We all know that *true* antelope are not found in the western hemisphere. But we have to agree with Wallace (1940) when he summed it up by calling the pronghorn, "an aristocrat among North American game animals, having existed on this continent since the Pleistocene or Glacial Epoch, or about 5,000,000 years. . . ." That's old enough for our purposes.

Subspecies

When taxonomists named five separate subspecies of pronghorn, back in the early days, it seems to me that they were stretching it a bit. The identifying differences between these five subspecies are very slight, in one case depending almost entirely upon the fact that the *A. a. sonorensis* is "somewhat paler" than the more numerous pronghorn to the north.

Not being able to quantify the phrase "somewhat paler," I do not know how pale a pronghorn has to be to qualify for the name of Sonoran pronghorn. *A. a. sonorensis* was named by the respected taxonomist E. A. Goldman, on the basis of two specimens! The differences between these two specimens is greater than the difference between *sonorensis* and *peninsularis*. Actually, Major Goldman had only one specimen to work with, for only the skull of the second specimen was in hand. Judging the "paleness" of the pelage of the one specimen is what gave him the description of "somewhat paler" in color. I have seen every possible shade of tan, white, beige, cream, oyster-white, off-white, brown, mocha, coffee, and brownish tan, to say nothing of cinnamon and rufous, all in one herd of pronghorns on the same afternoon, and that herd was in the center of their geographical range, near Upton, Wyoming.

Well, why don't we go back and collect 15 specimens of *A. a. sonorensis* from the type locality and see if they really are different enough to deserve the subspeciation assigned to them in 1945? Unfortunately, that would not be possible, for the pronghorn is extinct in the type locality that was 40 miles north of Rancho Costa Rica southwest of Hermosillo, Sonora, Mexico.

The skull and skin examined by Goldman in 1945, and which formed his basis for subspeciation nomenclature, was taken in 1932 — a long time ago. Biologists have recorded significant changes in morphological characteristics occurring in the 54 years since Goldman studied the small female he named *A. a. sonorensis*.

Goldman stated that the outstanding trait meriting the separate name was that of small size. Yet we have all seen greater differences in size among siblings than the difference noted in naming the Sonoran pronghorn.

The Sonoran pronghorn probably never existed as a separate subspecies. In any event, it does not exist today. Despite this, we have the endangered species program that declares that the Sonoran definitely is a subspecies and that it definitely is endangered. On April 4, 1985, John L. Spinks, Jr., chief of the Fish and Wildlife Service's Office of Endangered Species, wrote: "The Sonoran pronghorn is a separate subspecies." He further stated that: "Both the Sonoran pronghorn and the peninsular pronghorn are endangered (the latter occur in Baja California, Mexico)," and further, "Our best current estimates for the Sonoran pronghorn are that about 200–250 survive in Mexico and about 100 in Arizona."

The existence of this group of pronghorns in Arizona is documented regularly by the researchers of the Arizona Game and Fish Department. They keep a regular record of sightings, which has enabled them to draw a fairly dependable map of the area used by this pronghorn group.

The Arizona Game and Fish Department is the only agency currently trying to study the pronghorn antelope populations of the Arizona-Mexico border country. In their special report Number 10, *The Sonoran Pronghorn*, we find the following statement: "In any case, it appears that the recognition of *Antilocapra americana sonorensis* as a separate subspecies is unwarranted at this time." We agree heartily. The same publication goes on to discuss the question of assigning the Sonoran herds to a particular subspecies. After all, they have to belong somewhere. More about this later.

The Arizona Game and Fish Department has also done some work on the other endangered "subspecies," the Peninsular pronghorn. This group of pronghorns formerly shared a contiguous territory with the Sonoran group, but as the numbers of each group decreased, they became widely separated in distance. Today, the only known group of Peninsular pronghorns occurs in the hot desert sands south of Viscaino Bay on the west side of the Baja California peninsula. They have survived there simply because it is very difficult for humans to travel across the soft sands of the Desierto de Vizcaino, to cross the Sierra Placeres or Sierra Santa Clara Mountains, and because there is no good harbor on that stretch of the Baja Coast. A very inhospitable area, with some areas receiving less than four inches of precipitation per year, this land still holds enough food for the small group—estimated at fewer than the 200 that were known to be there in 1977. The Mexican Direccion General de la Fauna Silvestre censused 77 animals there in 1977 and postulated a herd of 200 from the evidence of 77. There is a good assumption that this has always been home to a family of pronghorns, simply because the area is known as the Llano de Berrendo, the plains of the antelope. These are the only pronghorns remaining on the Baja California peninsula. Their dying off has been predicted from 1963 to the present day, but as of now there seem to be a few animals hanging on to a precarious existence far from the disturbances of humans. This area is a very important one for wildlife—although it surely would not appear to be. The Bahia de Vizcaino is connected to Scammons Lagoon, where the great whales come to calve and to breed.

Both *A. a. sonorensis* and *A. a. peninsularis* are described as being paler in coloration than their northern counterparts. Perhaps it would be wiser, and more practical, to just remember that a pronghorn is a pronghorn is a pronghorn, regardless of how far south or north he lives, and then remember (or forget, it would not matter) that the southern groups are bleached by the Mexican sun, even as you and I are bleached (our hair, at least) when we spend long periods of time under the tropical sun.

Obviously, the chances for survival of these two southern groups could be improved by the infusion of new blood lines from healthier populations. For example—and although purists would scream at the "hybridization and dilution of the true subspecies"—I would like to see healthy individuals from southern New Mexico herds, or Texas herds, transplanted to the Desierto de Vizcaino, and I would like to see pronghorns from South Dakota or Wyoming moved to the inland populations of antelope in Chihuahua. Would the difference in climate and diet be too much for them? Who knows? But it would be worth the try, and Mexico would probably keep its pronghorn populations alive. As of today, one need only graph the (perhaps optimistic) reports of these discrete populations and look at the

Map shows original ranges of various subspecies of pronghorn: 1) *Antilocapra americana americana,* **2)** *Antilocapra americana mexicana,* **3)** *Antilocapra americana oregona,* **4)** *Antilocapra americana peninsularis,* **5)** *Antilocapra americana sonorensis.*

steep down trend of that graph. There is only one possible prediction: extermination.

Whether or not there ever were different subspecies of pronghorn in our recorded history, there is scant reason for recognizing true subspecies now. Ever since New Mexico began trapping and transplanting back in 1937, there has been a stirring and mixing of the gene pool of the pronghorn antelope on this continent. Surely this mixing has succeeded in blurring the already faint outlines of separate subspecies. When *A. a. americana* moved from Colorado, Wyoming, and Montana to Texas, he interbred with *A. a. mexicana*. When *mexicana* moved from Texas to Arizona, it is certainly possible that he diluted the gene pool of *sonorensis* or even *peninsularis*. Arguments for subspecies designation were weak in the beginning; they are impossible now that transplanting has moved genes to and from almost every state in the historic range. For our purposes in this book, there is only one pronghorn, *Antilocapra americana americana*. Long may he range the wide-open spaces of our continent!

3

Pronghorn Numbers

There were 40,000,000 pronghorns in North America when the first Europeans came to these shores.

In 1920, best estimates put the continental population at 14,000. Ninety-nine percent of the herd was gone.

In 1986, the continental population hovers near the 600,000 mark.

These spectacular fluctuations have been a hallmark of pronghorn antelope history. Severe fluctuations still occur, due mainly to hard winters, but modern wildlife management has learned how to smooth out the hills and valleys on that numbers graph. According to Jim Yoakum (one of the nation's top authorities on the pronghorned antelope), the 1924 population stood at 1300 in Canada, 2400 in Mexico, and 26,700 in the United States. Yoakum further estimated that in the years between 1924 and 1976, the Canadian population moved up from 1300 to 22,300, for a gain of 21,000 animals; the United States herds moved up from 26,700 to 406,400, an increase of 379,700, but that the Mexican herd had dropped from 2400 to 1000.

Reasons for the first great population change—the drop from 40 million to 14,000 in the years between 1776 and 1920—can easily be charged against the displacement of the herds by humans. But the reasons are more subtle and more complex than first glance would indicate. Reasons for the decline of pronghorns prior to 1920 can be assessed against:

1. Unrestricted shooting for food and for market. Remember that there was no law against shooting a pronghorn any time you wanted to. At times, the carnage must have been terrific. Although the

story of the antelope kill in Clarendon, Texas, during the winter of 1881 might have grown as the years went by, it was reliably reported that the people of that area found a large herd of pronghorns trapped in a corner of a fence during a blizzard. Taking advantage of the readily available meat supply, the Texans were reported to have killed 1500 in one day. The same report, out of Texas, tells us that it was a time-killing pastime for the young gentlemen of the city on the Canadian River to drive their buckboards out in the country on a Sunday and see how many pronghorns they could kill with pistols. Reportedly, kills of 40 pronghorns per party were not unusual. This type of activity was probably not limited to Texas, either. Even after protective legislation was enacted, it was usually not enforced. Illegal shooting has always been a problem with pronghorn protection.

2. Elimination of prime foods on pronghorn range due to overgrazing by cattle and, worse, by sheep.

3. Fencing of what had once been unrestricted open range, which stopped seasonal migrations and which prevented the antelope from using ancestral ranges.

4. Elimination of sage from arid lands, which were then turned to irrigation. The irrigated land produced great crops in some instances, but antelope were left out of that scheme of things. Croplands were not antelope-producing lands.

5. In the southernmost parts of their range, there was a great change in vegetation types. Mesquite, not indigenous to the western hemisphere, was brought into Mexico with the influx of cattle from Spain. Mesquite marched inexorably northward, despite millions of dollars worth of effort to "chain it down," to eradicate it, to get rid of it in some way.

Texas, especially, has large areas of what were once prime pronghorn pasture, but which are now mesquite jungles. (Callahan, Shackleford, and Haskell counties are prime examples.) Although mesquite is utilized to some extent by pronghorns as food, they will not often be found in dense stands of tree-sized vegetation. This vegetation change, which also took place in northern Mexico, transpired in the years from 1890 through 1940. It is doubtful that mesquite has extended its range since 1940.

It is tempting to lay some of the blame upon predation, especially by coyotes, and on drought and/or hard winters. But we must remember that the antelope co-existed with the coyote for millions of years and that the pronghorn lived through drought and hard winters over those same millions of years. However, that, too, is a simplification. Restricted ranges made the pronghorn more vulnerable to predators and to the vicissitudes of the weather. Perhaps 2000 years ago the antelope combatted drought by migrating to greener pastures, by concentrating near the few remaining water supplies. Today, fencing and croplands stand in the way of such migration, which accentuates the results of drought. The same thing is true of predation. In centuries past, the pronghorn doe was able to choose a birthing place far from the herd, if she wished to. In that secluded spot she dropped her fawns and they escaped the coyote for the first five days of their lives. After those critical first five days, the fawn could—and did—outrun the coyote. Today, the doe seeking a good spot to drop her fawn is apt to have her choices severely restricted by fences and by agricultural practices, by railways and by highways. The coyote has an easier job of finding the newborn fawns, because they must of necessity be concentrated on smaller ranges.

Now, the catastrophic slide in numbers from 1776 to 1924 ended, and the antelope began a spectacular increase in numbers. What are the reasons for the increase?

1. Man discovered that he couldn't make a living farming in many areas of the Great Basin states—and consequently abandoned those ill-advised ventures. The range returned to a semblance of its original state, and the antelope came back.

2. Protective legislation brought the plight of the pronghorn to public attention, and there was a great shift in public sentiment away from the "pioneer" mentality and toward a conservation ethic.

3. Enforcement of game laws had a good effect, but this was minimal when compared with the improvement brought about by the change in public attitude.

4. Trapping and transplanting, originated by the State Game and Fish Department of New Mexico in 1936–37, placed breeding stock into prime habitat, thus setting the stage for a population increase. It should also be noted that this transplanting was beneficial in another way. Some endangered species have suffered greatly as a result of line inbreeding. In other words, as the total population dwindles, there arises a danger of closely related individuals breeding. Trapping and transplanting brought genes from Montana to Arizona, from Colorado to Utah and from Wyoming to almost every state west of the Mississippi. This had a lot to do with maintaining the vigor of the herds, and preventing line inbreeding.

5. The introduction of Compound 1080 into the arsenal of coyote-killing methods caused the greatest single decrease in coyote numbers ever recorded. This allowed improved fawn survival and spurred a great increase in pronghorn numbers.

6. Intelligent game management, including regulated hunting of pronghorns, did much to maintain healthy pronghorn populations across the western range.

During the most spectacular years of this population increase—from 1924, when Edward Nelson made his "low ebb" population count, until 1976, when the herds seemed to be reaching the maximum sustainable populations over much of their range—during the time when pronghorns increased from 14,000 to half a million—regulated hunting removed almost two million pronghorns from the equation!

The low ebb in numbers, about 14,000 in 1920, left pronghorns with nowhere to go but up, and up they went. The first real census—rather than an informed guesstimate—was performed by Nelson in 1922–1924, and it reached the total of 26,700 animals. A decade later the figure was up to 130,000. In 1944 it was up to 246,000; 360,000 in 1954; and 406,400 in 1976. In 1985, Wyoming alone boasted an estimated population of more than 400,000!

In the next chapter, we will take a more detailed, state-by-state and province-by-province look at the ups and downs of the pronghorn population since the coming of the first Europeans to this continent.

4

State by State, Province by Province

Saskatchewan

For up-to-date information on the antelope herds of Saskatchewan, and for a brief account of the history of pronghorn population fluctuations in that province, we turned to Mr. Marlon Killaby, research biologist stationed at Swift Current.

Biologist Killaby reports that the pronghorn population of Saskatchewan fell as low as 4300 animals in July 1974, as a result of a severe winter that decimated herds of other game animals as well as the pronghorn. Pointing up our thesis that the pronghorn has remarkable recuperative powers, Killaby reports that the 1984 July population was estimated at 11,000!

His figures on recent population dynamics of the Saskatchewan herd show:

1980	6183 pronghorns
1981	6491 pronghorns
1982	8466 pronghorns
1983	8339 pronghorns
1984	11,000 pronghorns

The winter of 1984–1985 was relatively mild in the prairie province, and Mr. Killaby expected and saw a modest increase in the July population of 1985.

From other sources, I find that the pronghorn once used all of Saskatchewan south of what Canadians refer to as the parklands, in pre-white man times. However, since the settlement of the province by Europeans, the range has been severely restricted to the extreme southwestern corner. However, Mr. Killaby reports an expansion of this "normal" range in the present period of increasing populations. He reports that small herds have moved north and east along the perimeter of their "normal" range and have taken over quite a large chunk of the province. It is believed that most of these small herds migrate to the breaks of the Saskatchewan River to winter. If we compare the winter conditions in this northern herd of pronghorns with the summer temperatures encountered by the Llano del Berrendo herd on the Baja Peninsula in Mexico, we must conclude that the pronghorn is a remarkably adaptable beast, surviving a temperature range that can vary from 115°F. on the Baja to perhaps −55°F. in some Canadian environments. That's a spread of 170°F.

The hunter kill and success percentage in recent years is shown in the accompanying table.

Kid : Doe Ratios, 1965–84

Year	Ratio (per 100 does)	Year	Ratio
1965	54	1975	64
1966	85	1976	81
1967	82	1977	65
1968	74	1978	74
1969	87	1979	90
1970	77	1980	68
1971	70	1981	69
1972	60	1982	51
1973	68	1983	85
1974	56	1984	56

Hunter Kill and Success Rate, 1968–84

Year	Harvest	Success Rate
1968	2652	—
1969	2141	—
1970	3464	—
1971	3097	—
1972	2433	—
1973	2241	—
1974	closed as a result of bad winter.	
1975	1237	—
1976	1383	—
1977	1387	84.7%
1978	1345	85.9%
1979	1723	87.2%
1980	1650	79.0%
1981	1856	83.1%
1982	2090	81.2%
1983	2010	80.0%
1984	1985	79.1%

Mr. Killaby reports that antelope do cause local problems with agricultural interests in Saskatchewan. This is a result of grazing and pawing of fall rye and winter wheat crops. He reports that this damage can be locally acute if it occurs before freezing hardens the ground and protects the root systems. He sounds a warning that increased planting of these crops — fall rye and winter wheat — may result in an escalation of crop damage reports as the herds expand into agricultural regions.

Saskatchewan research, shown in the accompanying table, gives us a report of kid : doe ratio histories since 1965. Saskatchewan biologist Marlon Killaby sums up the future of the pronghorn in that province:

"In my opinion the continued existence of viable antelope populations in Saskatchewan revolves around two major factors: a) the quantity and quality of winter ranges and b) climatic conditions. Climate, that is, winter snow characteristics and spring storms at fawning time is the prevalent influence owing to our northern range limit for this species.

"Expanses of native grasslands still exist for summer range and should persist in the short term. Even in areas of rapid conversion to agricultural cultivation antelope herds appear to hold their own if the right mix of native and cultivation is maintained. However, the degradation or loss of winter range in Saskatchewan and Montana (where a number of our herds migrate) limits the ability of antelope to sustain their current status when exposed to our harsh climate." (Personal communication to me dated April 12, 1985.)

Alberta

One of the finest big-game areas in North America, Alberta supports a good population of pronghorns. In 1980, Alberta estimated 18,640 animals; in 1981, the number went up to 20,700. Biologists credited the increase of that period to the fact that they had enjoyed two mild winters in succession, with resultant reduction in winter mortality and a higher birth rate of fawns.

Alberta has held two separate hunting seasons in the same year in the past. One is a trophy season, with only bucks sporting horns of five inches or more being legal game. The other season—non-trophy—allows the taking of does and of bucks with horns less than five inches in length. The 1980 season was the first time that females and young males could be legally hunted in Alberta since 1975.

At present, there is no separate archery season for pronghorns in Alberta.

Pronghorn numbers have fluctuated widely in Alberta as in most other states and provinces. Alberta records a low of only about 1000 animals after the severe winter of 1906, an increase to 24,000 in 1964, and back down to 8500 after the severe winter of 1964–1965. Slowly recuperating herds were again knocked back in the 1977–1978 winter, sagging to about 7400. Since that time, a series of milder winters has allowed the herds to build up to about 22,000 as of this writing.

The roller-coaster history of pronghorn populations in Alberta emphasizes the fact that this is on the northern limit of the animal's range, and that winters will always be the limiting factor on their populations.

Pronghorns migrate between Alberta and the United States, and between Alberta and neighboring Saskatchewan. Today, biologists estimate that about 15,000 winter in the province. A hunter is allowed to apply for a pronghorn permit every third year. Still, with that limitation, Alberta gets about 7000 applications each year, a number that far exceeds the allowable harvest. Realistically, Alberta sets a goal of maintaining a herd containing between 10,000 and 18,000 animals.

Nonresidents may apply for a trophy antelope license in Alberta. Trophy definition in Alberta, by law, means carrying horns of at least five inches in length. Nonresidents, as well as residents, may only apply for a permit every third year. But remember that Alberta law defines a citizen of the United States not as a nonresident, but as a nonresident alien—and there are no pronghorn permits for nonresident aliens.

Manitoba

There was a great expanse of tall grass prairie in southern Manitoba that was once home to a goodly number of pronghorns. Samuel Uskiw of the Department of Natural Resources tells me that the historic range ran from the U.S. border north to Carberry and the Little Saskatchewan River and east to the Red River. The greatest numbers occurred on the Souris Plains and the Brandon Hills.

Hunting for food caused the disappearance of the Manitoba pronghorns by

1882, and since that year the only antelopes to grace the grasslands of Manitoba have been stragglers coming in over the North Dakota or Saskatchewan borders. Today the pronghorn situation in Manitoba can be summed up in one word — gone.

Montana

Montana consistently ranks in the top three states as far as pronghorn population is concerned. Fourth largest of the 50 states, Montana has lots of room and suitable habitat for antelope — and the prepioneer days herd probably numbered two and a half million animals! Their decline in numbers seemed to have started later than in many other parts of the pronghorn pastures, and they were recorded as being very numerous as late as 1896. However, conversion of rangeland to cropland, encroachment of humans on their ancestral range, overshooting, and fences all cooperated to drop pronghorn numbers all the way down to 3000 by 1924!

About 75 percent of Montana was considered as antelope range before the settlers came, with only the forested higher country of western Montana being without antelope. Fortunately for the pronghorn, the conversion of rangeland to cropland ground to a halt in the dust bowl of the Dirty 30s. Then drought forced settlers to abandon marginal lands by the thousands, allowing these areas to revert to native plants. This caused a reversal in antelope fortunes as the pronghorns reclaimed what had once been theirs. In 1945-50, a transplanting program moved 3554 antelope into 33 areas where none had existed. In other areas, supplemental transplants were made to existing small herds. As a result of these efforts, antelope now flourish over the southeastern two-thirds of the state.

The natural process of pronghorns reclaiming abandoned farmlands continued apace, enforcement of game laws was strengthened, and the transplanting program had a good effect. By 1965, the pronghorn count in Montana had risen to about 75,000.

A Montana educational pamphlet states it accurately: "Optimum antelope habitat consists of open, rolling sagebrush-grasslands relatively free of human encroachment. Sagebrush and weeds are items essential in the year around pronghorn diet. Much of the original antelope habitat was destroyed during the first two decades of this century when thousands of acres of native Montana prairies were overgrazed or cultivated. While some antelope were taken for food by homesteaders, the alteration of native prairie to cultivated farmlands was another reason for the population low reached by 1924. With the great drought of the 1930's homesteaders left by the hundreds. The abandoned, cultivated fields gradually reverted to vegetation more favorable to antelope. The early stages of vegetation succession, comprised mostly of weeds, were used heavily by antelope. With the additional food and space, antelope populations steadily increased with only temporary setbacks due to severe winters in 1948-49 and 1964-65."

The factors contributing to the increase in Montana's pronghorns occurred despite sport hunting when populations would support that hunting. Prior to 1872 there was absolutely no legal protection for pronghorns. From 1872 to 1894 there was a closed season from August 1 to February 15 each year. From 1895 to 1902 an annual bag limit of eight was established and the hunting season was open September through November. Closed seasons were the rule from 1903 through 1934. In 1935 a 30-day permit season was opened in Carter and Powder River counties, and in 1936 the season was opened in Choteau County. Another period of totally closed seasons ran from 1935 through 1942. A regulated permit season was opened in 1943 and has been continued on an annual basis ever since. Hunters in Montana now harvest more antelope than any other big-game animal except deer. The harvest has been high, as has hunter success, illustrated in the accompanying table.

Hunter Success in Montana, 1943–83

Year	No. Permits	Pronghorns Killed*	Success Rate
1943	750	553	73%
1944	650	540	83%
1945	1575	1400	89%
1946	2424	2300	95%
1947	2854	2800	98%
1948	2652	2800	106%
1949	3932	3800	97%
1950	8345	7700	92%
1951	9272	8171	88%
1952	18,622	18,096	97%
1953	23,677	19,145	81%
1954	20,866	17,737	85%
1955	39,055	26,000	67%
1956	25,923	22,818	88%
1957	25,820	14,400	65%
1958	19,850	14,000	69%
1959	21,148	15,658	81%
1960	20,820	14,981	79%
1961	27,103	19,278	79%
1962	32,164	22,937	79%
1963	31,346	22,238	80%
1964	37,109	26,982	79%
1965	27,886	18,630	73%
1966	21,770	13,900	71%
1967	19,993	12,599	70%
1968	18,358	11,500	71%
1969	23,167	14,543	73%
1970		17,487	
1971		18,403	
1972		15,488	
1973		19,303	
1974		18,810	
1975		17,298	
1976		16,292	
1977		18,528	
1978		13,471	
1979		10,039	
1980		12,016	
1981		14,954	
1982		20,830	
1983		26,438	

* More than one animal allowed in some areas, in some years.

A disturbing situation exists at the Charles M. Russell National Wildlife Refuge. Here, legislation that set up the refuge in 1936 used the following wording: "Natural forage resources therein shall be *first* utilized for the purpose of sustaining in a healthy condition a maximum of four hundred thousand (400,000) sharptailed grouse and one thousand and five hundred (1,500) antelope, the primary species...." (Emphasis supplied by Cadieux.)

The intent of Congress has been subverted badly here. The natural forage has NOT been utilized for the benefit of grouse and pronghorns. Far from it. The natural forage has been used to feed domestic livestock, grazing on what should be a wildlife refuge, for the benefit of politically important ranch interests. This is not what Congress intended. With a state the size of Montana, one would think that the pronghorn could be allowed a few acres of his own; that is what Congress intended. But today the available forage is allotted about 60 percent for domestic livestock and only 40 percent to wildlife!

Although wildlife biologists state that the 1500 goal for pronghorns could easily be met on the habitat in those parts of the refuge lying within Garfield and McCone counties, not even that portion of their inheritance from Congress has been given to the pronghorn. In fact, when the pronghorn population did reach its projected goal of 1500, there followed one hard winter and most of the pronghorn population starved to death!

At the time when this book went to press, the pronghorn herd had again built up to 1500 animals. But the overgrazing by domestic livestock still continues, and the future for that herd is not bright.

Back in the 1970s refuge personnel began a campaign to return use of the refuge lands to the rightful owners — the pronghorns. But ranchers sued in court and blocked everything. They've succeeded in blocking it for so long that the original Draft Environmental Impact Statement is now so badly out of date that the Fish and Wildlife Service has developed another Draft Environmental Impact Statement. This DEIS examines five alternative courses of action. They are:

1. Continuation of the present management program (no action). This "do-nothing" program has proved a disaster for the native species, a bonanza for the livestock interests.
2. An enhanced wildlife program, favored by the F & W S.
3. Intensive wildlife management (which should be the course of action, as it was the course of action envisioned by the Congress in setting up the Charlie Russell).
4. Multiple Use.
5. Elimination of livestock. I believe that total elimination of livestock would not be wise. In some cases, cattle grazing can actually improve pronghorn forage stands. However, I strongly favor the elimination of all sheep grazing on the lands set aside for pronghorns. The two interests are not compatible. In Texas research, combining sheep and pronghorns results in starvation of the pronghorns.

It is difficult to argue in favor of pronghorns in Montana, a state that has plenty of pronghorns elsewhere, and where the rancher has all of the political clout. However, the fact remains that the Charlie Russell was meant for grouse and pronghorns, not for beef and mutton production.

It is certainly 10 years past the time of decision for the argument over the forage plants on Charlie Russell. Local ranch interests have delayed it for 10 years. Now is the time to decide — and decide in favor of the pronghorns, as Congress intended.

North Dakota

I grew up in North Dakota and saw my first pronghorns on the wide prairies and rolling plains of the western third of the state. I have a vivid memory of the very first time I ever saw antelope. I was riding the (then) Northern Pacific train out near the North Dakota — Montana border. I was coming east, returning from a trip to my favorite uncle's home. The sun was just rising after a night blessed with rain. My eyes beheld two unbelievable sights. Roads built of scoria appeared shiny, blood-red in the morning sun. I marvelled at those roads, never having seen them in their washed beauty before. But more exciting, I watched a herd of some 13 pronghorns that were pacing the train, running easily and looking at the train as they ran.

Perhaps I had seen antelope before, I cannot remember, but those brilliantly colored, tan and brown and white and black animals were less than 100 yards away from the train, and were brightly lit by the morning sun. I thought they were the most beautiful things I had ever seen.

That must have been around 1926 or 1927, and North Dakota's pronghorn stocks were very few, for this was near the low point of populations all across the pronghorn range. I summarized the state's antelope situation in an article that appeared in the January 1954 issue of *North Dakota Outdoors*:

"The story in North Dakota is a strange one. Antelope hunting was stopped by the North Dakota legislature in 1899, after the herds, which once rivalled the bison in numbers, had been reduced to a pitiful remnant. For over half a century no antelope was shot legally in North Dakota. For the first forty years of this century, the herd did not increase in numbers. Depending upon the severity of the winter, a small band drifted back and forth between states, down near where North and South Dakota meet the Wyoming border. A smaller group, fairly constant in numbers, made its home in McKenzie County. After forty years without significant increase in numbers, a full scale program of coyote control was started in the western part of the state. The small relative of the wolf is the greatest single danger to the antelope. Although unable to handle the adult animal except in extreme cases, the coyote preys heavily on the kids during the first days of their life. When the coyote began to dwindle in number, the antelope numbers began to mushroom.

"Noting the consistent increase in the pronghorn herd, North Dakota opened its first season in half a century on the antelope. It was also the first permit season held in North Dakota. This was in 1951.

"Despite the removal of approximately 975 antelope in 1951, the herd still increased in size, so a second permit season was held in 1952, with 1,100 permits being used. Again the success percent ran above 95.

"The season was not opened in 1953, because it was intended to trap some of the surplus animals from the areas of over concentration and spread them out in other suitable areas in North Dakota. This trapping will begin in January of 1954. At that time, an attempt will be made to corral and remove the animals which have encroached too heavily on cropland."

Lewis and Clark found great numbers of antelope, which they called "goats," when they came to North Dakota in 1804. They reported great numbers near the mouth of the Cannonball River where it flows into the Missouri, and watched as the Indians killed many with guns and even with sticks . . . after driving the antelope into the river itself.

In August 1806, Alexander Henry reported numerous herds of "cabbrie" on his way from the Mouse River to Fort Union. In 1833, Maximilian said the "cabri" lived the whole year in the immediate vicinity of Fort Clark. He also reported that the herds migrated westward to seek the protection of the mountains against winter storms and that they returned in great numbers each spring. According to Maximilian, the Missouri River was no barrier to the eastward movement of the antelope, as he witnessed large herds of antelope swimming eastward to the better pastures of the east-river country.

In 1873 J. A. Allen reported that antelope were the most abundant game animals from Fort Abraham Lincoln west to the Little Missouri River. He said they were constantly in sight and were noteworthy for their speed and grace. Allen also reported that a fatal epizootic had raged among the antelope in the entire area between the Yellowstone and Missouri rivers, killing as many as three-fourths of the herd. He found their carcasses littering the ground for more than 100 miles, but said that the fatal disease — whatever it was — had not crossed either the Yellowstone or Missouri. He saw 10 dead for every live antelope on that sad occasion.

Antelope numbers fell catastrophically in the last decades of the nineteenth century. In 1877 a herd estimated at 3000 was seen between Valley City and my home town of Jamestown. But in 1892 it was worthy of mention in the newspapers when an observer reported seeing eight antelope near Valley City. The last antelope were killed near Canby in 1892. Antelope were common near Crosby, in the northwest part of the state, up until 1903, but no more were reported after 1906.

By 1915 it is probable that the antelope had been eliminated from the area east and north of the Missouri River. In the rough, badlands-type country south and west of the Big Muddy, the antelope clung to a few areas — mostly unsuited to farming, and thus not as densely settled by homesteaders.

Teddy Roosevelt, who chronicled his ranching-hunting days in the Little Missouri country, reported that he had no trouble killing antelope for camp meat whenever he wanted to. This in the 1880s; the antelope continued to dwindle in numbers until 1916, when it could be said that they had disappeared from almost all areas of the state.

In 1925, E.W. Nelson gave the following report on antelope numbers:

60 antelope in northwestern Dunn County and into McKenzie County.

9 antelope in southwestern McKenzie County.

75 animals formed the largest band in the state, ranging through central Golden Valley and Billings counties. Most of these were on the 11,000-acre William McCarthy Ranch, where they were given complete protection from hunting.

55 antelope were reported in the Badlands of the Little Missouri River in Slope County.

26 antelope were reported from southwestern Bowman County.

If my arithmetic is correct, that adds up to about 225 antelope in the entire state. Obviously, with poor communications and great distances involved, there could have been another 500 unreported in the state. But it seems fairly certain that the low point of antelope numbers showed fewer than 1000 in North Dakota.

Writing in 1925, pioneer biologist Vernon Bailey summed up the situation with the North Dakota herd as follows (North American Fauna, No. 49, Bureau of Biological Survey): "The few antelope still inhabiting the roughest and least-settled parts of the Badlands would doubtless, if taken in time, for the nucleus of a herd that might rescue the species from being wiped out in the state, if not out of existence. If rough land of little value except for forest production and grazing were properly fenced so that the antelope would not stray to unprotected areas, and if coyotes could be trapped to a harmless minimum and sheep scab kept out, it would seem that antelope would increase as rapidly as any herd of sheep."

Trapping and transplanting of antelope played a part in the increase and relocation of North Dakota's antelope herds, as is discussed in the chapter on restocking. However, the 1925 prediction made by Bailey—that antelope would greatly increase in numbers if coyotes were trapped down to a harmless minimum—actually came true when Compound 1080 (sodium monofluoracetate) actually did reduce coyote numbers to a harmless minimum in the late 1940s and early 1950s.

Antelope are exceptionally winter-hardy animals, despite their somewhat delicate appearance. Their coat is made up of hollow hairs and seems to provide excellent insulation against the bitter cold that is a hallmark of northern winters. However, ice and snow can do a real number on antelope herds, if the available food supply is covered.

James McKenzie summed up the continuing story of North Dakota antelope in an article in *North Dakota Outdoors* in August 1963. The headline read, "225 to 10,000 in 40 years."

The 1950 antelope census showed 2492 animals in North Dakota. The 1951 census showed 3878 antelope. With the exception of 1953, there has been a permit season every year from the original one until 1963. A total of 20,000 hunters killed 19,400 antelope during those 11 years; and five bowhunting seasons killed another 25 animals.

Despite this kill, antelope numbers went from 225 in 1926 to 10,000 in 1963. Hunting pressure, within reason, does not endanger antelope populations—although it does serve as a management tool to keep populations within the carrying capacity of the land.

But other factors, not controllable, also affect total antelope numbers. North Dakotas herd went up to as high as 14,726 animals, but fell again to 8000-plus in 1976. Blame for this huge fluctuation is laid directly on "hard winters" by James McKenzie. In a speech given to an antelope management workshop in 1970, McKenzie stated:

"The population trend spiraled upward through the remaining 1950s and early 1960s until it peaked out at more than 14,000 animals in 1964. During this period (1951 through 1964) 13 hunting seasons were held, a total of nearly 27,000 permits were issued and a harvest of about 25,000 animals was realized." I have chopped off this historical account at the end of the fall hunting season, 1964, for a very good reason. The following month, November, the snows came.

"The winter of 1964–65 will long be remembered for its severity, with frequent blizzards; deep crusted snows; low temperatures over prolonged periods; and with the effects of a combination of these factors upon both domestic and wildlife stocks in North Dakota.

"That winter may be characterized by its impact on the primary pronghorn antelope range because that is where the most devastating conditions developed.

"I have averaged the climatological data from seven reporting stations in the southwestern part of North Dakota as a basis for my attempt to describe conditions as they existed from November 15, 1964 through March 31, 1965. During that 137-day period there were 75 days when the minimum temperature was 0°F. or colder; there were 10 days when the maximum temperature was never above 0°F; and there were an additional 93 days when the maximum was below 32°F.

"It is well to emphasize the fact that there were 34 days during this period when the temperature did rise above 32°F. These days of thawing trends were fairly evenly distributed through seven distinct periods of the winter. In other words, seven times during the winter thawing 'peaks' did occur, but in each instance they were followed by severe 'troughs' of extremely cold temperatures extending over periods of several days. These are 'crusting' conditions.

"The average temperature for the winter of 1964–1965 was 8.3°F. below the seasonal normal of 18.7°F., and it varied from 14.2°F. below normal in December to 2.9°F. below normal in February. Significantly, the average temperature for March was 12.4°F. below normal. As we say in North Dakota, we had a cold snap.

"Precipitation records by months showed November, December and January to be above normal and February and March to be below normal. This means that most of the snow that fell on the antelope grounds stayed on the ground for the entire 137-day period. The reported snow depth at the reporting stations bears out this contention, as the average snow depth on November 27 was six inches and it was still six inches on March 30. It never dropped below four inches and it ranged up to 17 inches in depth.

"Keep in mind that this snow had thawed and then froze into seven distinct crusts or strata. There was literally an impenetrable layer of ice over much of the pronghorn range in North Dakota.

"Finally, there is one climatological ingredient that isn't recorded other than in a general way—wind velocity. When the wind chill factor is considered, wind velocity assumes major importance in a discussion of this nature. For instance, with the temperature at −20°F. and a wind speed of 25 m.p.h., the wind chill is the same as when the temperature is −65°F. and the wind speed is 5 m.p.h. To a pronghorn attempting to winter on an exposed hillside in North Dakota, the seriousness of the wind chill factor is hardly a moot possibility. . . . The July 1964 population was in excess of 14,000 animals. The July 1965 survey revealed that this figure had been reduced to 6151 animals on the same area censused a year previously, a reduction of 56.8 percent. . . ."

Jim went on to point out that reproduction was greatly reduced in the spring of 1965, because the does were not in good condition. To further point out how serious the situation was, Jim found antelope hair and antelope flesh in the viscera of winter-killed antelope!

This meant that the starving antelope had even tried to cannibalize their dead brethren, seeking protein in any form to fill hungry bellies.

From 1965 to 1968 there was a period of herd rebuilding in North Dakota. Restricted permits numbered 7132 hunters who bagged 6025, yet populations rose to 8250 animals counted in 1968.

However, Old Man Winter took another swipe at the North Dakota antelope herd in the winter of 1968–1969. This was virtually a replay of the disastrous 1964–1965 experience. Results were equally bad, with the total census falling 23 percent to 6320 animals. Happily, reproduction stayed up in 1969, or the decline would have been even worse. McKenzie hazards the informed guess that the less drastic drop in reproduction in the second winter storm year was due to the fact that the herd was in better condition going into the winter—perhaps as a result of the culling effect of the 1964 winter.

Pronghorn antelope management in my native state of North Dakota has been enlightened, and professional. Given a continuation of this sound management, and given a freedom of political influence on that management, the future of the pronghorn antelope in North Dakota seems to be bright. However, there are great areas of this state that could support antelope, yet do not. The reasons are: (1) landowner resistance to having potential crop-eating antelope stocked on their lands; (2) absence of suitable, permanent watering areas; and (3) illegal hunting of antelope, especially near Indian Reservations.

South Dakota

Today, South Dakota is usually in third place in pronghorn numbers, following only Wyoming and Montana. The state has always had a pronghorn population, but came perilously close to exterminating them—as did all western states—in the period following settlement and leading up to 1935.

Prior to 1800, probably 700,000 pronghorns roamed the prairies of South Dakota, rivalling the bison in numbers. In 1841, Maximilian reported wintering antelope west of the Missouri River, along the Cheyenne River. He said that they would swim the Big Muddy in the spring to return to summer pastures in the Coteau des Prairie. In 1879, the Yankton, South Dakota, newspaper reported antelope as plentiful on the prairies east of the James River. However, by 1909 the last antelope had disappeared from pastures east of the Missouri. There was really no physical barrier to antelope retaking their ancestral range east of the river, but that same river, in both Dakotas, marked a demarcation between primarily rangeland on the west side and primarily cropland on the east side.

Protection got a late start in South Dakota in 1911 when the legislature enacted legislation to protect the antelope from extermination. Prior to enactment of this law, it had been legal to shoot as many as five pronghorns per year.

South Dakota's human population has shown but slight increase since 1900. The state has never been densely settled. There were no large cities to provide a demand for the market hunter to supply. Given the estimates that there were as many pronghorns as bison, it is difficult to imagine that the market hunters—who eliminated the bison—could have decimated the huge herds in the period from 1890 to 1911.

Other factors were probably at work. J. H. Allen reported a fatal epizootic had devastated pronghorn numbers between the Yellowstone and Missouri rivers, killing an estimated 75 to 90 percent. This epizootic may have reached down to reduce the South Dakota herds as well. There was a terrible blizzard in 1893 and antelope always suffer population losses in extremely bad winters. However, the antelope have always survived those blizzard winters in numbers sufficient to allow them to recoup their population losses in a couple of years.

The late Wendell Bever, a good friend of mine, was chief of big game in the South Dakota Game, Fish and Parks Commission in the 1950s. Wendell had an interesting theory about the catastrophic loss of pronghorns in pioneer days. He thought that humans destroyed the pronghorn's

Successful hunter with good antelope buck. *South Dakota Game, Fish and Parks photo.*

ability to move through winter snows when they removed the bison from South Dakota ranges. He reasoned that the pronghorn was able to move in deep snows because the bison moved ahead of him, sort of breaking the trail. I have the greatest respect for Wendell's astuteness and knew him as a skilled, trained observer of wildlife. Therefore, I put a lot of credence in this possible explanation of pronghorn losses. The bison and pronghorn had been sympatric for centuries, and the pronghorn nearly accompanied the bison into extermination.

The much-quoted census made by Edward W. Nelson, chief of the biological survey, placed the 1924 South Dakota population at only 680 animals scattered in 11 bands across 12 western counties of South Dakota.

Legal protection for antelope in 1911 did nothing to slow the decline in numbers. And the creation of an antelope refuge in Harding County in 1921 had no noticeable effect. But in 1937, it became apparent that the pronghorns were on the increase. In the words of a South Dakota report, "Better law enforcement, and perhaps predator control resulted in the first appreciable increase in antelope numbers." Another quote from the same source says that "since the population was still quite small, management was simply a matter of law enforcement and predator control."

By 1941, biologists were able to census 10,000 pronghorns in Butte and Harding counties, and estimated 1000 more in the other west river counties, for a statewide total of 11,000. By 1965, 23 counties west of the river all held antelope herds, and transplants had been released in seven east river counties. By 1965, the total statewide population had reached 28,000. Despite restocking aimed at increasing the range of the antelope, the center of population remained in Harding, Butte, Perkins and Meade counties, which held 75 percent of South Dakota's pronghorns in 1965.

Hunting under regulated permit began in 1942, with 500 permits being issued. Hunting has continued to the present day, and is an accepted tool of wildlife management.

The accompanying table shows the growth of South Dakota's pronghorn herd under wise management.

Growth of South Dakota Herd, 1941–84

Year	Population Estimate	Legal Kill
1941	10,000	480
1942	unknown	—
1943	7973	976
1944	5370	480
1945	6721	closed
1946	9442	609
1947	14,800	1875
1948	13,000	2371
1949	7425	closed
1950	10,920	759
1951	14,356	3151
1952	16,608	7880
1953	15,090	4750
1954	16,756	5196
1955	16,664	4281
1956	19,374	5616
1957	16,885	3885
1958	16,235	2900
1959	20,272	4950
1960	23,330	6037
1961	27,480	7990
1962	26,382	6152
1963	27,658	7280
1964	24,566	6050
1965	27,286	6776
1966	20,954	4244
1967	23,400	4847
1968	22,142	2419
1969	23,595	2880
1970	25,100	3807
1971	34,690	5452
1972	34,894	6370
1973	33,128	6831
1974	41,358	8542
1975	43,083	10,331
1976	33,505	6722
1977	40,390	7592
1978	28,425	4714
1979	18,333	2473
1980	25,402	4408
1981	37,227	6530
1982	54,060	11,104
1983	67,281	14,727
1984	61,640	16,999

Note: 1983 was the first year that nonresidents were allowed to hunt pronghorns in South Dakota, and 1984 was the first time that more than one tag was issued per hunter, which is a real indication that South Dakota has more antelope than antelope hunters.

A few observations about the causes of South Dakota's resurgence in pronghorn numbers might be in order here. South Dakota regional supervisor Warren Jackson comments in an article prepared for the *South Dakota Conservation Digest* in 1971 that, "Substantial increases in pronghorns in the late 1930's and 1940's are attributed to improved law enforcement, an important tool in modern game management. Predator control may have contributed to the population recovery as well."

Because I spent many years in law enforcement work, it is pleasant for me to see credit given to law enforcement. Because I spent even more years in predator control work, it is even more pleasant, and more unusual, to see credit given to predator control.

Western South Dakota has a long record of supporting coyote control programs. Ranchers who provided homes for pronghorns also paid for the coyote control work that went on over those same pastures. South Dakota stock growers bought and paid for the airplanes that were used by federal coyote hunters. Walden Lemm, of Spearfish, was a pioneer in this work and accounted for thousands of coyotes in his years of piloting the planes that hunted down the coyotes. It is almost impossible to quantify results of predator control work, but it is difficult not to see the connection between reduction in coyote numbers and improved fawn survival of pronghorns in western South Dakota.

Another fortuitous circumstance surrounding the resurgent pronghorn in South Dakota was the appearance on the state wildlife management stage of such men as Wendell Bever, who went on to become director of Oklahoma's department, and Fred Priewert, who became director in Iowa and a host of others. Innovative thinking, supplied by trained biologists, along with the development of a good rapport with the rancher-landowner — these were the keys to the human end of the pronghorn equation in South Dakota.

Pronghorn numbers have not grown to expected potential on the Indian reservations such as the Standing Rock and Cheyenne reservations in the north and the Pine Ridge and Rosebud reservations in the south. The State Game, Fish and Parks Department in 1971 delicately stated the reason as, "Existing tribal laws are not compatible with successful pronghorn management." Remembering my own experiences in trying to successfully prosecute Indians for game law violations in both of the Dakotas, I would put it more bluntly: "Indians historically have paid mighty little attention to game laws."

Taking a hard look at the fact that South Dakota opened the first modern-day season in 1942 with 500 permits, and noting that hunters now kill an average of more than 10,000 per year, while watching the herds increase and multiply to the point where only Wyoming and Montana have more pronghorns, it is obvious that South Dakota is doing something right!

The future of South Dakota's herds may depend upon habitat improvement in wintering areas. Grazing competition from domestic livestock has reduced plant density and distribution for desirable (to pronghorns) plants. And, as is always true in the Dakotas, a series of bad winters could reduce the herds drastically, as it has done in the past.

Nebraska

In general, all of Nebraska was within the historic range of the pronghorn. In general, Nebraska's pronghorn population was decimated by the same factors that almost eliminated the pronghorn over the rest of the range. Some people believe that the extirpation of the buffalo, which usually lived in the same areas with the pronghorn, had a serious effect upon pronghorn numbers. Evidently the grass-eating buffalo cleared the way for the forb-eating pronghorn. From a low of 10 bands totalling 187 pronghorns in 1925, the pronghorn put on a sustained battle to avoid extinction.

The history of the comeback in Nebraska is typical of that recorded in other western states. First, toothless legislation was enacted and not enforced. Actions such as the 1873 law making it unlawful to kill pronghorns in Nebraska between January 1 and September 1 were symbolic but of no practical effect. In 1897, there was another ceremonial bit of legislation, which shortened the open season to that period from November 1 to January 1. Finally, in 1907, the season was closed entirely, and this did have a small beneficial effect.

It was almost too late. In 1925, remember, the Nebraska pronghorn population had sagged to 187 individuals. A long period of recovery brought pronghorn populations to 3500 in western Nebraska by 1955. Hunting seasons have been held every year since 1953, with the exception of 1958, when populations did not warrant even a bucks-only season.

A Nebraska Game and Parks Commission publication describes the pronghorn range thusly: "The major antelope range is broken by three escarpments and several rivers and creeks in an east–west direction. The Pierre Hills, commonly referred to as the badlands in Nebraska, extend south from the South Dakota state line in the northwest part of the state. The Pierre Hills then rise abruptly to meet the Pine Ridge escarpment which slopes gently southward to the Box Butte table land and on to the North Platte Valley. South of the river, the Wildcat Hills escarpment drops into the Pumpkin Creek Valley and confronts the Cheyenne escarpment and its tableland."

Much of this area boasts an annual precipitation of about 15 inches in the west, and grades upward to 23 inches in the eastern part of the range.

This prime antelope area is characterized by vegetative cover consisting of sparse grass (blue grama, needle and thread, western wheatgrass, and buffalo grass) cover interspersed with a lot of prickly pear cactus. There is a good supply of sagebrush, which seems to be a *sine qua non* for the pronghorn. A good variety of other forbs is found through this area. It would seem to be prime antelope grounds.

A great area of Nebraska is composed of the Sand Hills—a particularly attractive area to any wildlifer. Knowing that this area could support far more antelope than it had, the state department signed up cooperating ranchers on 1.7 million acres of the 20,000 square mile Sand Hills and began transplanting wild-trapped antelope into that area. The restocking took place from 1958 through 1962, and 1077 pronghorns were released at 20 sites. Pronghorns are gregarious, however, and they promptly congregated into larger herds than were anticipated in the original stocking pattern. Because there were many individuals in one herd, depredations upon alfalfa fields proved too much to take for the ranchers in the Sand Hills, and they called for relief. Limited hunting seasons started in 1964. A total of 3238 Nebraskans have participated in the antelope harvest in the Sand Hills, so the transplanting effort is judged worthwhile.

Pronghorns are firmly established in those parts of Nebraska butting up against Wyoming and South Dakota.

Since 1953, a total of 19,182 antelope have been harvested by 23,719 rifle hunters. Hunter success over the years has varied from 74 to 88 percent, with 81 percent being the average. There have also been archery seasons, and in the past 11 years, bowmen have killed 142 pronghorns.

Hunter kill for the past 11 years is summarized here. Obviously, the antelope herds are being harvested at or near the maximum sustained yield level, supporting seasons that harvest a good portion of the annual increase without destroying the herd's ability to reproduce itself.

Nebraska Harvest, 1974–84

Year	Firearm Kill	Archery Kill	Total Kill
1974	1305	12	1317
1975	1463	7	1470
1976	1352	14	1366
1977	1325	10	1335
1978	1131	6	1137
1979	541	14	555
1980	710	6	716
1981	664	16	680
1982	701	18	719
1983	885	21	906
1984	940	18	958

It is also obvious that the terrain and vegetative cover of the Sand Hills could support a much larger herd of pronghorns. However, the well-being of more antelope in the Sand Hills region must be predicated upon the good will of the rancher. Given today's economic climate on the ranch front, the rancher cannot be expected to carry more pronghorns if it means carrying fewer head of cattle or mowing fewer acres of alfalfa.

Idaho

Former Fish and Game Director Tom Murray described the early history of Idaho's pronghorns in these words:

"The sagebrush plains were the ancestral home of large herds of antelope from Weiser to Teton Basin. Foothills and mountain valleys afforded good spring, summer and fall ranges, and the sweet and white sage flats interspersed with shadscale provided abundant winter forage.

"The largest herd was located on the north side of the lava flow from Craters of the Moon to Henry's Lake and from the buttes north to Salmon City. The second largest herd was in the Raft River area west to Salmon Falls Creek. There were sizeable herds all along the lower Snake River with the biggest concentration from the Bruneau River west to Reynolds Creek and from Clover Creek to the Indian Creek drainage north of the Snake River. Sizable concentrations once ranged in the Nyssa-Payette area on both sides of the Snake River.

"With the advent of civilization, migration routes up and down the main stem of the Snake were broken by trading posts, ferries and stage stops.

"When the colonizers moved in with their flocks, fences, canals and plows, the river-to-foothill-to-benchland migration routes were checkerboarded. As a result the herds split up into small segments with portions of the critical ranges growing luxuriant crops under irrigation.

"The most critical period for the entire antelope population was from 1900 to 1922. The enlarged Homestead Act, the Carey Act and other land acts together with marked population increases saw practically all of the flat surface areas homesteaded or preempted by the control of springs and water holes."

This familiar story depicts the catastrophic decline in numbers that was so common all over the 11 western states. Idaho had no magic prescription for reducing the impact of *Homo sapiens* upon the numbers of *Antilocapra americana*. In 1912 the Fish and Game Department reported that "very few antelope were to be found in southern Owyhee County and in portions of Blaine and Lemhi Counties. Of the thousands of these animals that formerly roamed the Snake River Valley only a few remain."

Fences were almost the last straw in Idaho, where access to water was jealously guarded over much of the southern half of the state. Settlers took up most of the former range and the antelope neared extinction in Idaho. But man's misfortune turned out to be good luck for the pronghorn. The nadir in population counts was probably 1922, when the informed estimate stood at 1500 animals! But 1922 through 1935 was an uncommonly dry period. Small farms and ranches "dried off" of the pronghorn range, and the fences disappeared or fell into disrepair as people became disillusioned and left the land. Sage, which had been perceived as an enemy for farmer and rancher alike, slowly began to make a comeback in Idaho, and as the sage flourished, so did the pronghorn, for reasons we are just now beginning to understand.

Widespread transplanting efforts took place in 1949–1950, with 607 animals going to new homes, greatly improving the chance for population increases. By 1954 the Idaho herd was estimated to contain 13,200 animals, which is close to the levels maintained from that year until the present.

Management of Idaho pronghorns is done on a scientific basis, starting with the all-important population aerial surveys in 1939. Landmark studies of Idaho antelope by biologist Robert Folker pointed up the fact that sagebrush was an important winter food, as well as a priceless habitat for does about to give birth.

Idaho's leading manager of pronghorns, Robert Autenreith, notes that sagebrush continued to be considered as being worthless and that sagebrush eradication was successful over a large part of Idaho's ranges — ranges used by cattle and pronghorn alike. Most of the area from which sagebrush was eradicated was planted to crested wheatgrass. Domestic livestock benefited; pronghorns definitely did not.

Continuing research on Idaho's pronghorns seeks to quantify the dangers posed by fences in the winter, and to determine the relative fawning success of pronghorns with and without tall sage habitat. It is obvious from earlier results that fawn survival is lessened when does cannot find suitable areas of tall sage in which to secrete the newborn young.

Idaho uses the helicopter to accurately assess pronghorn populations each August, and this information is vital to intelligent management of the herd through hunter harvest.

The results of this hunter harvest since 1951 are summarized in the accompanying table.

Further research in Idaho will provide answers to the following questions:

1. How many pronghorns can be sustained on presently available ranges?
2. Does hunting during pronghorn breeding season have any effect — good or bad — upon pronghorn reproduction?
3. Can pronghorn herds be managed to preclude disastrous results if further land

Idaho Harvest, 1951-84

Year	Bucks	Does	Fawns	Total Killed
1951	818	513	8	1339
1952	730	570	92	1520
1953	680	514	56	1250
1954	579	275	116	970
1955	445	253	124	822
1956	476	281	162	919
1957	unknown	unknown		1006
1958	505	314		822
1959	unknown	unknown		700
1960	437	264		701
1961	unknown	unknown		799
1962	339	210		549
1963	390	223		613
1964	541	295		836
1965	647	330		977
1966	692	406		1098
1967	788	497		1285
1968	842	447		1289
1969	969	494		1463
1970	1004	529		1533
1971	1016	432		1448
1972	973	492		1465
1973	812	397		1209
1974	895	379		1274
1975	841	350		1191
1976	605	259		864
1977	815	267		1082
1978	866	330		1196
1979	1018	300		1318
1980	1112	286		1398
1981	1478	359		1837
1982	1639	324		1963
1983	1731	588		2319
1984	1578	475		2053

area withdrawals reduce the management base?

4. Can predator control increase pronghorn neonatal survival? If so, is it cost effective?

The answers to these questions are very important, evidenced by the figures compiled for the all-important equation of "fawns per 100 does." The ratios are given in the accompanying table.

Fawn: Doe Ratio, 1973–82

Year	No. Fawns Per 100 Does
1973	49
1974	62
1975	48
1976	56
1977	55
1978	63
1979	65
1980	52
1981	58
1982	47

Idaho attempted to answer the question of whether or not predation was the primary limiting factor in pronghorn populations through a study carried on 40 miles south of Challis, Idaho, on lands managed by the Bureau of Land Management. Of 60 antelope fawns equipped with radio transmitters in the 1978–1980 study, 36 were newborn, 15 were less than 48 hours old, and nine were less than 10 days old.

To quote from the Idaho research report, "Predator kills accounted for a 50 percent loss of transmittered fawns in 1978, 44 percent in 1979 and 29 percent in 1980. Contact was lost on a total of 11 fawns due to probable transmitter malfunctions." In other words, it is possible that some, or all, of the fawns with which radio contact was lost, were also lost to predation.

Surprisingly, the researchers were able to attribute the loss of eight fawns to golden eagles and only seven to coyotes.

Answers to these questions are all-important to Idaho sportsmen, if the Idaho Fish and Game Department is to realize the sportsmen's long-term goals and objectives. As of mid-1985, these objectives were to increase the population only slightly from the 1981 figure of 20,460 to a 1990 population of 21,800, but to increase the harvest from 1895 in 1981 to 2533 in 1990. They also hope to make the pronghorn easier to bag, evidently, for the 1981 figure for "hunter days per animal bagged" was 5.1 and the 1990 estimate is only 3.2 days per animal bagged.

Idaho's published objectives also include maintaining the buck:doe ratio in August to 30:100 or above.

Perhaps the most important objective is stated in the three-word sentence "Enhance antelope habitat." Right on! But how to do this is a question not answered in three words, unfortunately.

The research done by Autenreith et al in the Challis area brought to light very interesting information concerning the importance of good sagebrush cover to protect newborn pronghorn fawns. One preliminary conclusion is that production averages (despite predation) align rather closely with the total canopy coverage of bedding sites. This indicates, to my layman's eye, that habitat improvement may be vitally important in ensuring neonatal fawn survival, which means increased recruitment of the year class into the adult pronghorn herd, and increased total numbers, which means increased hunting opportunity for all.

This facet of the pronghorn population picture is beautifully explained by Robert E. Autenreith:

"With these comparisons, we begin to more fully understand each antelope population in terms of current status and trend. The Road Creek population summers on range that has been abused since the 1860s by cattle, sheep, goats and horses both domestic and feral. The result has been a reduction and in many areas almost an elimination of the understory. The population was exposed to relatively heavy hunting pressure which reduced the total population to a low level. The predator population focused on the fawning area during the fawning peak and due to the high seeability of bedded fawns (who often sit up and look around) killed a disproportionate number which ensured a continually depressed population.

"Management action in this case was to close the season to hunting, reduce the feral horse population, and initiate a range improvement program through a BLM sponsored stewardship committee. With an improvement in range condition, the camouflage and visual screens system which has functioned for eons should serve again to increase the survivability of the Road Creek fawns during the vulnerability period."

Author's note: If anyone has said it better, we've not yet read it.

Oregon

Oregon maintains a steady population of pronghorns, never very large, and never falling to disaster levels. The controlled hunts in 1984 were typical of the situation there. In 1984, 2040 permits were issued, resulting in a kill of 982. Strangely enough, only 1774 of the 2040 permits were used, a much lower percentage than is usually found in antelope hunts. Perhaps this reflects the fact that most of Oregon's human population is in the western quarter of the state, and most of the antelope are well to the east. It may also reflect the fact that the Oregon big-game hunter may be spoiled by excellent hunting on other species of big game, especially deer, elk, and bear.

During this 1984 hunt, there were 140 antlerless (?) permits issued for the Ochoco and Murderer's Creek hunts, resulting in a take of 50 antlerless (?) does. We suspect that the use of the term "antlerless" is a carryover from deer hunts, but we do remember that does also grow horns, not antlers, as well as the antelope bucks.

The 1984 take also included six pronghorns taken during the muzzleloader season held on W. Fort Rock, where the bag limit of one antelope was sought by 46 hunters, who scored at a 13 percent success rate.

The fact that the pronghorn is a difficult target for the bowman was underscored by the two archery seasons held on the Gerber Reservoir herd's home grounds. A total of 450 permits were issued, 272 bowmen actually hunted, and they killed a total of four pronghorns — for a success ratio of about one and one half percent.

The biggest kills were made in the Malheur River (78), Steens Mountain (87), Beatys Butte (98) and Juniper herds (56). The highest success ratio, 88 percent, was encountered on the Hart Mountain Refuge, where 20 permits issued resulted in 17 hunters afield who took 15 bucks.

Similar results were experienced in 1983, when a total of 1523 permits issued put 1484 hunters in the field, resulted in a kill of 953 for an overall success ratio of 64 percent. Bowmen did slightly better than in 1984, killing a total of five pronghorns for 272 hunters afield.

It is obvious that Oregon bases the number of permits issued on the buck: doe ratio found in the spring counts, and this has proved to be a good management tool in other states. If the bucks-only hunts do not seem to keep populations within the carrying capacity of the range, Oregon does not hesitate to open the season on does. However, there has been slight need for that technique over the past two decades.

For example, the 1984 census showed a total of 4602 antelope—713 bucks, 3210 does, and 679 classified as fawns, on the various game-management units. From this preliminary data, the department authorized the issuance of 2040 permits, resulting in a total kill of 982. Subtract the antlerless (sic) kill and you have a well-managed herd, but one which is not apt to develop many trophy heads, simply because bucks are cropped every year and not allowed to become old and heavy-horned.

The Hart Mountain National Wildlife Refuge in Oregon shelters a herd of pronghorns whose numbers have fluctuated from a five-year average in 1965–1969 of only 432 animals to the 1983 total of 1538. These figures are for the Hart Mountain Biological Unit, which includes other lands outside of the refuge boundaries. The 1983 count showed a significant departure from the long-term average population, as shown in the accompanying table.

Hart Mt. Unit Averages

5 yr. Averages	No. of Pronghorns on Hart Mt. Biological Unit
1955–59	685
1960–64	635
1965–1969 (note 1)	432
1970–1974	481
1975–79	632
1980	1066
1981	1356
1982	938
1983	1538

Note: Predator control was discontinued after 1967.

To quote from a refuge report:

"The 1983 summer composition count classified a record 1,538 pronghorn within the Hart Mountain Biological Unit, with 799 animals using the refuge and 739 immediately south of the refuge. Kid–doe ratios reflected 23 : 100 on the refuge and 28 : 100 off.

"Kids per 100 doe ratios reflect an interesting phenomenon which seems to occur in wet years—the farther herds get from wintering grounds, the lower the ratio of kids/does. This past year, the lower elevation country off the refuge was in excellent condition following above average precipitation and a mild spring. This year's count may suggest antelope simply did not need to travel as far to find suitable habitat for kidding. The later season build up on Hart Mountain may indicate a higher percentage of non-breeding juveniles.

"During the last dry spell (1977–1978) the opposite was witnessed with only 48 antelope counted south of the refuge and over 600 on the refuge."

Another Hart Mountain Wildlife Refuge report gives us some insight into the coyote situation. The observer in a census airplane made these comments about coyotes as seen from the air: "In the north refuge area we counted 10 coyotes . . . one was being chased by a herd of 15 antelope; another by a lone doe antelope. On the top of the mountain we saw one coyote. In the south refuge area we saw 5 coyotes . . . one was being chased by a small herd of antelope. South of the refuge we saw only 3 coyotes. The area south of the refuge is as big or bigger than the north refuge area. It is also about three times as large as the south refuge area. Yet we saw three to five times the number of coyotes per square mile on the refuge than off. The kid/doe ratio on the north refuge area was only 11 . . . off the refuge it was 28. The south refuge area had a ratio of 24. The lower ratio on the north part of the refuge could be caused by heavier predation on the kids by coyotes. But another factor could be the longer migration distances required for pregnant does."

Hunting is used as a management tool on the Hart Mountain Refuge, of course, and the results of the permit hunts are listed in the accompanying table.

Hart Mt. Hunting Results

Year	Hunters	Pronghorns Killed
1968	10	9
1969	16	15
1970	15	15
1971	14	11
1972	15	15
1973	16	13
1974	15	14
1975	15	11
1976	16	16
1977	15	15
1978	15	15
1979	14	13
1980	15	14
1981	18	18
1982	16	15
1983	18	16
1984	17	15

Nevada

The pronghorn antelope management in Nevada is skillfully described by George K. Tsukamoto, so we will quote directly from a Nevada publication as follows:

"The North American population of pronghorn antelope *(Antelocapra americana)* experienced sharp declines during the 1800's, culminating in lower population levels in the 1930's compared to their former abundance and wide distribution. . . . Prior to 1947 pronghorn management in Nevada was but a token effort. With the establishment of the Department of Fish and Game in 1947 and with the availability of funds from Federal Aid in Wildlife Restoration (Pittman-Robertson Act of 1937) greater effort has been expended to gather biological information which is necessary to determine the annual status and trends of the pronghorn populations of the state.

"Nelson (1925) conservatively estimates that 35 to 40 million pronghorn inhabited North America prior to the arrival of white man. Seton (1929) estimated 40 million antelope in the western United States alone near the year 1800. . . .

"By 1918 the United States population had dwindled to its lowest point in history with an estimated 13,000 animals."

The first mention of pronghorns by a white man came in 1829, when Peter Skene Ogden noted that his hunters killed three antelope near Wells, Nevada. In 1904, Zenus Leonard recorded the scarcity of game when the Joseph Walker expedition entered the Great Basin desert areas. He found the country very poor in game except for some bighorn sheep, some antelope, and rabbits.

The Homestead Act of 1862 greatly accelerated the fencing of antelope ranges and the conversion of rangeland to cultivated acres. Nevada boasts a very large percentage of semi-arid lands, and settlers chose the few river valleys and existing fertile valleys for their homes, thus effectively ousting the pronghorn from the best part of its ancestral range.

But worst of all was the overgrazing by cattle and sheep, which started with the

A group of pronghorns drinking at a water hole on the Charles Sheldon Antelope Refuge, Nevada. *Photo by E. J. Greenwalt.*

introduction of cattle by Joseph Walker in 1834. The Mormon pioneers brought cattle and sheep with them, and the discovery of the Comstock Lode in 1859 and the rush to grab land that followed, dealt the pronghorn several severe blows. Bigger populations of miners brought increased demand for meat, and livestock numbers mushroomed. In 1867, estimates placed the cattle population at 36,000, sheep at 24,000, and horses at 5000 in Nevada. By 1880, these populations had grown to 250,000 cattle, 259,000 sheep, and 34,000 horses. By 1910, an estimated 100,000 wild horses roamed Nevada ranges. This competition for scant available forage was too much for the pronghorn, and it almost disappeared by 1922.

The 1917 legislature closed the pronghorn hunting season until 1921. In 1931, the Charles Sheldon Antelope Refuge was created through the efforts of a Mr. E. R. Sans (more about him later on in this chapter), and in 1936 536,956 acres were withdrawn from the public domain to create the Charles Sheldon Antelope Range, whose primary purpose was to protect pronghorns.

Nelson showed 4253 pronghorns in 11 herds when he made his 1922 census.

Seton reported 13,000 to 15,000 pronghorns for Nevada in 1926, and Allen estimated 12,700 in 1939 (see accompanying table).

Nevada Pronghorn Population, 1937–84

Year	Estimated Population	Total Kill
1937	12,700	
1938	12,700	
1939	16,719	
1940	20,604	
1941	21,455	
1942	not known	
1943	20,525	253
1944	not known	137
1945	not known	120
1946	8700	386
1947	9000	371
1948	7000	closed
1949	3500	closed
1950	4265	125
1951	2074	278
1952	4013	closed
1953	4000	133
1954	4000	160
1955	3800	173
1956	3500	53
1957	3500	69
1958	3500	126
1959	3500	135
1960	2255	146
1961	3175	211
1962	3000	152
1963	3175	182
1964	3175	204
1965	3175	185
1966	3175	191
1967	3000	151
1968	3000	193
1969	3000	209
1970	3000	258
1971		286
1972		293
1973		281
1974		272
1975		212
1976		250
1977		354
1978		324
1979		332
1980		419
1981		468
1982		507
1983		
1984		446

Note: This tabulation is for rifle hunts only.

When the historic Nelson survey was conducted in 1922–1924, Nevada was listed as home to 4253 pronghorns. This was a relatively high count when you remember that in the same year, the premier pronghorn state of Wyoming claimed only 7000 head. During the intervening years, Nevada's herds have grown but slightly while Wyoming has burgeoned to a figure near the 400,000 mark. Why the big difference?

To answer that question, we must keep two things in mind: One, Nevada is out on the periphery of the pronghorn pasture, while Wyoming is its center; and two, Nevada ranges are primarily desert—true desert and high mountains, neither of which are optimum pronghorn habitat. Nevada's good pronghorn pastures do not occur in large contiguous acreages, but are rather small and disjointed. Wyoming, on the other hand, has the nearly perfect mixture of forbs and shrubs that the pronghorn prefers. In addition, Wyoming pronghorn habitats are large and contiguous, a never-ending place for pronghorns to prosper. In Wyoming, the stage was set for a wonderful upswing; in Nevada, the situation was precarious at best and remained that way.

The Charles Sheldon Antelope Range, mentioned earlier in this discussion of Nevada's pronghorn herds, carries a healthy pronghorn herd. Aerial counts in summer are conducted with the Nevada department's helicopter, which allows for very accurate censusing. The aerial counts for the past five years for which data are available are summarized in the accompanying table.

Nevada Kid: Doe Ratio, 1980–84

Year	Total Counted	Kids/100 Does
1980	1355	28
1981	1577	44
1982	1558	13
1983	1623	23
1984	1608	12

The Sheldon NWR 1984 Annual Report lists the results (see accompanying table) of the pronghorn hunts held annually on the refuge. This represents a 94 percent success rate over the 18 years for which records are presented.

It seems that the men engaged in predator control work (killing coyotes) were the first to become convinced that the coyote was the main threat to pronghorn herds that were trying to stage a comeback on less and less suitable habitats. In 1920, Mr. E. R. Sans, in charge of predator control work in Nevada, saw his first pronghorn, and immediately started a lifelong effort to help the plains speedsters. He had a vision of a wildlife refuge, set up to protect the pronghorn from overhunting. Inasmuch as there were no game laws at all protecting the pronghorn in any way in Nevada of the year 1920, Sans had his work cut out for him. He met with the

Sheldon NWR Hunting Results, 1967–84

Year	No. Hunters	Animals Killed	Success Ratio
1967	10	10	100
1968	10	10	100
1969	20	20	100
1970	20	17	85
1971	19	18	95
1972	20	17	85
1973	20	20	100
1974	20	19	95
1975	20	19	95
1976	24	24	100
1977	25	24	96
1978	30	28	93
1979	30	25	83
1980	29	29	100
1981	30	29	97
1982	31	27	87
1983	30	30	100
1984	40	37	92

county commissioners of Washoe County and persuaded them to set a closed season for pronghorns. In 1921, he convinced the Humboldt County commissioners to do the same. In 1921 he met with Nevada Game and Fish Commission to set a closed season, statewide, for pronghorns. Sans was then instrumental in getting a law passed that authorized the governor of the state to set aside lands for the protection of wild game. The Washoe County Commissioners set aside 400 square miles of their land as an antelope refuge. Governor James C. Scrugham issued a proclamation setting aside 11 areas. One was the area previously set aside by Washoe County and another covered the major portion of what was to become the Charles Sheldon Range and Sheldon Antelope Refuge.

In 1923, Sans got orders from E. W.

Nelson of the Biological Survey office in Sacramento to hire enough men to capture 40 pronghorns. The pronghorns were captured and Sans cared for them in his own backyard until they were shipped out. They went to Grand Canyon, the National Bison Range in Montana, and to a wildlife reservation in Nebraska.

In May 1925 Sans again found himself with 17 antelope fawns in his backyard, these destined for the national zoo in Washington and for a zoo in Detroit, Michigan.

Sans kept trying to get his employer, the Bureau of Biological Survey (forerunner of today's Bureau of Sport Fisheries and Wildlife), to help establish a refuge for antelope. He finally convinced E. A.

An important date for Nevada and Oregon pronghorns—June 19, 1931. E. R. (Daddy) Sans, left, and Paul J. Redington, Chief of the Bureau of Biological Survey, erect a sign on the boundary of the Sheldon refuge. *USF&WS photo.*

Golden, head of that organization, and Golden made his recommendation to purchase and withdraw land for the refuge. But there was no action on his recommendation. Sans wrote to Gilbert Pearson, president of the Audubon Society, and that got the ball rolling. Pearson got his board of directors to commit $10,000 to start the refuge. He also got the Boone and Crockett Club to commit to another $10,000, provided that the refuge be named for one of their better-known members, Charles Sheldon. Then the Department of Agriculture recommended that public domain land within eight miles of the refuge core be withdrawn and dedicated to the refuge purpose. This was done and the refuge became an actuality.

One of Sans' employees on the new refuge was a young man named Ernie Greenwalt. He went on to become one of the best-known and most respected refuge managers in the entire system. His son, Lynn Greenwalt, was born on the Sheldon Refuge. Lynn later went on to become the director of the Fish and Wildlife Service, a post he held for eight years prior to 1981.

Ernest J. Greenwalt wrote in December 1958: "E. R. Sans held the title of first refuge manager at the Sheldon. During the eight years I was in residence there, Sans was my immediate supervisor and as an absentee landlord looked after the goings on from his perch as Predator and Rodent Control Leader in Nevada with his offices in Reno. The Sheldon was certainly his baby. He had the vision of doing something for the antelope in northern Nevada and it was Sans who worked tirelessly behind the scenes until he got the job done and the refuge established."

E. R. Sans died on December 20, 1958. He was a true friend of the pronghorned antelope.

California

Before the first of the conquistadors saw California, it is quite possible that the pronghorn was the most numerous big game animal in what is now our most populous state. California now has the largest human population of any state, but its antelope population has shrunk to a tiny fraction of what was in the 19th Century.

At one time, pronghorns were found all over the Golden State, with the exception of the high mountains, the heavily forested areas, and some lands along the northernmost Pacific shore. Today the pronghorn is found in the northeastern corner of the state, and nowhere else.

The catastrophic decline of the California pronghorn began when gold was discovered at Sutters Mill. The gold rush of 1849 led to a great demand for meat, and the market hunters went to work on the pronghorn herds. The fertile valleys of California attracted more permanent residents than did the gold rush, and by 1923 the pronghorn had dropped from an estimated population of half a million to about 1000 animals, and this remnant population hung on only in the northeastern corner of the state.

In the 50 years before 1925, California lost more than 400,000 pronghorns. In the 50 years since 1925, California was able to build the herd up to about 7000 animals — a nice 700 percent increase, but hardly comparable to the glory that once was California's pronghorn herd. It is doubtful if there will be further increases in California's pronghorn population, simply because the exploding human population and the expansion of crop farming into more and more remote areas has exerted pressures against the pronghorn herds, leading to a management system that has to take into account crop depredation. If fear of crop depredation is uppermost, expansion of pronghorn populations into new habitats is unlikely.

Recent winter census of California pronghorn populations has shown the usual fluctuations common across much of the western United States. The four counties of Lassen, Modoc, Shasta, and Siskiyou hold almost all of the state's pronghorns, as shown in the accompanying table.

California Pronghorn Distribution, 1951–85

Year	Lassen	Modoc	Shasta	Siskiyou	Total
1951	1901	2635	0	0	4536
1952	848	1434	0	0	2282
1953	811	1167	22	125	2125
1954	573	1097	30	150	1850
1955	573	1142	31	217	1975
1956	744	1397	0	197	2338
1957	708	1042	26	197	1973
1958	576	1353	21	215	2165
1959	589	1124	24	180	1917
1960	568	1068	16	128	1780
1961	501	1280	18	110	1909
1962	600	1620	13	36	2269
1963	694	1531	18	132	2375
1964	746	1672	23	177	2618
1965	834	1454	121	59	2468
1966	1017	1479	30	209	2735
1967	1040	1251	23	223	2537
1968	884	1469	0	254	2607
1969	1031	1595	0	244	2870
1970	1031	1800	37	115	2983
1971	1412	2147	2	239	3800
1972	1383	2109	0	272	3764
1973	1262	2734	0	361	4357
1974	1615	2767	0	365	4747
1975	1252	2506	22	329	4109
1976	1491	2943	0	435	4869
1977	1420	2818	43	627	4908
1978	1974	3245	1	652	5872
1979	1590	2894	0	614	5098
1980	2094	3944	0	872	6910
1981	2020	3823	68	994	6905
1982					6984
1983					7123
1984					6807
1985					6509

With the exception of a small herd (the Mono Herd) located on the California-Nevada line south of Highway 395, the pronghorn population is almost entirely confined to the area east of the Cascade and Sierra Nevada mountains from Lassen County north. This is mostly lava country, flat over much of the range. Average annual rainfall measures from eight to 20 inches. Temperatures fluctuate from a January low of 20°F. up to July highs of as much as 70°F. Even with this limited range, the California pronghorns show considerable shifting between winter and summer pastures. Some migrating pronghorns in California have moved more than 70 miles between summer and winter habitats, but this movement is extreme. What is important in this regard is the fact that migration corridors are imprinted on the herds and any blocking of these corridors can spell the end of that particular herd.

The Mono herd is ranging on land administered by the BLM (70 percent) and Forest Service (30 percent). Forty individuals were transplanted to this herd in 1982. Most of this herd winters in Nevada, on BLM land.

California wintering habitat consists of black sage and big sage, but also shows bitterbrush in limited areas. Rabbitbrush, saltbush, tumbling mustard, and cheatgrass are common. Summer ranges do not exhibit as uniform a vegetative cover as do the winter ranges. Perennial grasses, dry land carex, annual forbs, and sage are dominant, but there are summer ranges dominated by juniper/sage habitats, along with sage/grassland habitats and—sadly—cultivated croplands that are used by summering pronghorns.

Pronghorns range over three and one half million acres of California, and two thirds of this is public land managed by either the BLM or the U.S. Forest Service.

After a long period of complete legal protection, a permit season was opened in 1942. Five hundred permits were issued and 405 pronghorns killed. Seasons were held intermittently from 1942 until 1964, and annually since 1964. Numbers killed are illustrated in the accompanying table.

California Hunting Results, 1942–84

Year	No. of Permits	No. of Pronghorns Killed
1942	500	405
1943	500	362
1944	500	322
1945	500	307
1949	500	349
1951	416	280
1959	171	120
1964	240	183
1965	240	141
1966	265	179
1967	250	156
1968	260	189
1969	270	204
1970	300	241
1971	400	303
1972	380	301
1973	385	305
1974	410	284
1975	225	170
1976	375	306
1977	325	271
1978	400	352
1979	374	329
1980	489	390
1981	515	450
1982	701	525
1983	601	448
1984	594	439

Note: 1980 kill included 15 does and 1 bow season kill.

California management includes censusing and harvest regulation by individual herds, rather than by areas, and this is indicative of the intelligent handling of the resource. Management plans include provision of watering spots where the absence of water prevents the pronghorn herd from moving into otherwise suitable habitat.

Although the pronghorn herd in California is in no danger of disappearing, it is also certain that the pronghorn populations will not be allowed to increase to any great extent because such increases would lead to serious crop depredation. California pronghorns are familiar with alfalfa and they like it.

Utah

It is thought that the pronghorn antelope occupied almost all of Utah, except the higher elevations and thickly forested areas, in the time before the coming of the first Europeans. They remained numerous until settlement began in 1847. From that time forward, the antelope herds were decimated by meat hunting. They were gradually extirpated from many regions of the state, and finally reached a low of perhaps 670 animals when Nelson made his nationwide—or at least Westwide—survey in 1922. At that time, antelope were found only in the arid deserts of the state, eking out an existence on lands that no one wanted because they were not arable.

The legislature extended nominal protection to the pronghorn in 1898, although no effort was made to enforce the law protecting the pronghorn. From 1922 through 1947, no appreciable increase in numbers was noted, although a limited permit season was allowed in 1945 in Daggett County, to crop some of the mature males from a healthy population.

Since 1964, Utah has done a good job of repopulating former pronghorn ranges by means of trapping and transplanting. Montana provided the first animals for transplant—129 pronghorns from around Gardiner and Chinook—which were released at Parker Mountain. The list of transplants is shown in the accompanying table.

It is interesting to note that the stocking of the Parker Mountain area was so successful that the Utah Division of Wildlife Resources was able to use it as a source of planting stock, and took 848 pronghorns from Parker Mountain by means of trapping and transplanting in the important developmental years of 1975 through 1982. In addition, the state issued 137 permits for the hunting of antelope on Parker Mountain in the 1984 season.

It is also worthy of note that Utah received stock from Montana, Wyoming, and Colorado, and furnished stock to Arizona. Truly, there was excellent cooperation between western states during the rebuilding years of the pronghorn herds.

Utah's pronghorn antelope population has risen to above the 6000 mark as a result of conservative management. Even with an estimated population above 6000, Utah regulations permitted the harvest of 463 antelope in 1983, which is a kill of only 7 percent of the available herd. In 1985 (personal communication from L. Ray Remund, Utah Chief of Communications), Utah estimated its pronghorn population to be above the 10,000 mark.

Pronghorns have been hunted legally in Utah since 1945, with the exceptions of 1948 and 1951 to 1953, when no hunts were held. The kill never rose above 100 animals—although it reached 99 in 1960 and 93 in 1967—until 1968 and has never dropped below that figure since. In fact, the 1977 kill was 208 and the 1978 kill was

Montana Pronghorn Transplants

Date	Where From	Released	No.
12-64	Gardner, MT	Parker Mtn.	20
1-15-65	Chinook, MT	Parker Mtn.	109
9-23-70	Sybille, WY	Clark Bench	22
1-15-71	Lusk, WY	Hatch Point	84
		Myton Bench	71
11-22-71	Lucerne Valley	Myton Bench	30
		Art Smith (USU)	6
		East Clark Bench	105
		Hatch Point	88
2-12-72	Clay Basin	Clay Basin	16
		Icelander Wash	150
12-17-75	Parker Mtn.	Johns Valley	75
		Puddle Valley	70
1-20-79	Parker Mtn.	Johns Valley	77
12-5-79	Parker Mtn.	Puddle Valley	72
12-81	Snowville	Pilot Mtn.	31
1-82	Parker Mtn.	Pilot Mtn.	55
		Clarks Valley	40
12-82	Parker Mtn.	House Rock, Arizona	49
		East Bench-Book Cliffs	22
		Hogle Zoo	6
		Pilot Mtn.	145
12-82	Snowville	Clarks Valley	125
		Pilot Mtn.	24
1-83	Maybell, CO	East Bench-Book Cliffs	114
		Myton Bench	136
12-83	Parker Mtn.	Cisco	150
		12 Mile Wash	42
		Cedar City	45

276. Surely this points to a conservative harvest of pronghorns in the Beehive State.

Latest figures on pronghorn harvest in Utah are shown in the accompanying table.

Arizona

Arizona estimated its antelope population at roughly 7500 head in early 1984. The herds range over roughly 21,300 square miles of the state, excluding those on Indian reservations. According to the

Utah Hunting Results, 1979–83

Year	Permits	Does Killed	Bucks Killed	Total
1979	320	0	270	270
1980	314	2	280	282
1981	357	0	323	323
1982	446	35	365	400
1983	502	38	425	463

Department of Game and Fish, 29 percent of the pronghorns are found on private lands, 23 percent on national forests, 21 percent on state land, and 13 percent on BLM-controlled lands. The remaining 14 percent are on military reservations, national wildlife refuges, and national parks.

In northern Arizona, the pronghorn uses widely different habitats—pinon/juniper/grassland—shortgrass prairie/salt desert scrub—sagebrush/grassland—chapparal/grassland, mountain grassland, and even some in the ponderosa pine forests. In southern Arizona, they range in desert grasslands, with a small population of the Sonoran subspecies living in Sonoran desert scrub.

Arizona reports that some of the pronghorn herds have declined drastically since standardized aerial surveys were begun in the late 1940s. They point out that the fawn:doe ratios have declined in many herds since predator (for which read coyote) control by means of Compound 1080 was banned in 1972.

The antelope is a valued resource for big-game hunters in Arizona. An average of 1100 firearm permits are issued each year, and these hunters take an average of 800 pronghorns, or about 1/12 of the herd. Certainly this is a conservative harvest. Interest in pronghorn hunting continues to grow with the number of permit applicants rising each year. Bowhunters account for only six pronghorns per year, on the average.

While many state game departments seem reluctant to even consider the possibility that coyote predation is a limiting factor on their pronghorn herds, Arizona has faced the problem directly. A milestone study was conducted on the Anderson Mesa herd of pronghorns, forcing Arizona to the obvious conclusion that: ". . . (1) coyote predation can be a major mortality factor for neonatal pronghorn fawns, (2) coyote predation can depress a pronghorn population or keep a population from increasing by severely reducing recruitment; and (3) that reduction of coyote density will result in increased pronghorn density if habitat is adequate to support the increase. It is entirely probable that coyote predation is also a major factor in the chronic low fawn survival seen during the last decade in Unit 1, Unit 10 and others. However, it is also probable that coyote predation in other Units differs from Anderson Mesa in degree rather than in ecological and behavioral mechanisms. The basic problem now is lack of economical methods for reducing coyote density."

Another fascinating piece of research done by Arizona points up the fact that fawns are much less apt to survive today, without coyote control by Compound 1080, than they were in the days when Compound 1080 was used. The results are shown in the accompanying table.

From the evidence shown in the table, it should be apparent that pronghorn does produce more fawns and raise them to the point where they can be counted in the state's herd, when they do not lose so many neonatal fawns to coyotes. Or, at least, coyote control by the use of toxi-

Fawn Survival Rates

Game Management Unit No.	Mean Fawn : Doe Ratio		Percent Change
	1961–1970	1973–1982	
1	57.7	24.9	−56.8%
2	46.9	30.5	−35.0%
3	43.7	41.5	−5.0%
4	53.8	32.6	−39.4%
5	41.4	27.3	−34.1%
6A	50.9	47.1	−7.5%
7	41.1	32.2	−21.7%
8	44.6	41.4	−7.2%
9	29.5	27.9	−5.4%
10	42.1	20.8	−50.6%
17	43.6	37.2	−14.7%
18A	33.8	28.6	−15.4%
18B	51.3	37.4	−27.1%
19A	49.7	38.0	−23.5%
19B	52.3	45.6	−12.8%
21	47.0	55.1	+17.2%
31–32	37.6	44.8	+19.1%
35	50.8	43.6	−14.2%

cants (for which read Compound 1080) did result in greatly increased percentage of fawn survival in the pronghorn herds studied in Arizona.

History of hunter pronghorn kill in Arizona is shown in the accompanying table.

In addition to this harvest by the gun, bowhunters killed 13 in 1978; 19 in 1979; 21 in 1980; 13 in 1981; 15 in 1982; and 24 in 1983, for a total of 105 bowkilled pronghorns in Arizona in six open seasons.

New Mexico

Perhaps New Mexico's biggest claim to fame in wildlife management is that it was the state which originated the trapping and transplanting of antelope from overcrowded ranges to understocked ranges. This movement of antelope played a major role in the surprising comeback of the herds in the period following the nadir year of 1926.

The credit for this innovation should go to Elliott S. Barker, one of the giants of wildlife management, who was leading the New Mexico Game and Fish Department in the Dirty 30s. He shares credit with Paul Russell, who was placed in charge of the experimental operations and who carried them through to a successful conclusion. In Paul Russell's words:

"In the spring of 1936, State Game Warden Elliott S. Barker advised me that my duties might include proving the feasibility of trapping and transplanting antelope. This would depend upon future authorization from the State Game Commission. . . ; the real challenge came when Mr. Barker told me of authorization

Arizona Pronghorn Kill, 1960-83

Year	Permits Issued	Hunters Afield	Bucks Taken	Doe or Fawn Taken	Total	Percent Success
1960	1200	1174	722	0	722	62%
1961	1411	1373	687	68	755	55%
1962	1215	1173	559	53	612	52%
1963	1281	1259	690	39	729	58%
1964	1413	1377	716	128	844	61%
1965	1303	1273	672	26	698	55%
1966	1230	1198	570	28	598	50%
1967	1416	1371	693	35	728	53%
1968	835	817	367	2	369	45%
1969	835	815	410	0	410	50%
1970	1149	1128	601	28	629	56%
1971	924	905	565	0	565	63%
1972	1037	1007	518	0	518	51%
1973	1264	1247	656	21	677	54%
1974	1308	1262	723	31	754	60%
1975	1278	1220	675	18	693	57%
1976	1067	1006	534	0	534	53%
1977	1089	1017	591	1	592	58%
1978	880	849	415	0	415	49%
1979	844	810	427	0	427	53%
1980	708	683	444	0	444	65%
1981	730	713	407	0	407	57%
1982	835	814	506	0	506	62%
1983	879	839	534	0	534	64%

to proceed with the experiment in December of 1936."

The commission had authorized the expenditure of $500 for experimental trapping, and if this proved successful and if the antelope mortality was not prohibitive, an additional $4500 would be made available. This was a first in wildlife management.

The experiment started with the full cooperation of a few landowners. This cooperation extended to the lending of wire to make wing walls, providing of good riding horses to be used by herders, even to the full cooperation of the ranchers themselves in the operation—they actually rode herd on the antelope, using their own horses to start the herds moving toward the traps. The list of ranchers who helped includes, but is not limited to, G. W. Evans, John W. Gist, Milt Craig, and Earl Scott (both of whom represented new car dealers and provided vehicles for the chase), and Bill Benton and Slim Nichols.

The site of the first attempt was on the San Augustine Plains near Magdalena, New Mexico. A wing-wall trap was set up in a slight depression, which hid it from view until the antelope were nearly into it. Paul Russell stresses that he took into account the natural escape route of the antelope, and that it was not a case of "driving" the antelope. Driving would imply superior speed on the part of the horsemen and vehicles attempting to do the herding. Rather than trying to drive the animals, Russell and his crew attempted to move the animals in a leisurely manner, gradually increasing the speed until the animals actually bolted into the trap.

Inexperience ruined the first attempt. The antelope entered the wing walls, but saw the danger and reversed their field. They ran right at the oncoming cars and riders and succeeded in crashing through the ranks.

Quoting Paul Russell again:

"The score was several bruised antelope, including one that ran into a car, a man knocked down by the momentum of an escaping antelope; a big buck roped by Slim Nichols; and some valuable experience."

As a result of that failure, Russell started using an antelope gate that closed off the escape route behind the fleeing antelope. This allowed the animals a chance to cool down and become less frightened before they were eased into the holding pen itself. Other modifications in procedure led to the first successful catch on April 5, 1937, when the gates were closed behind a herd of wild adult pronghorns. They were released before nightfall that same day on the La Jencia ranch northeast of Magdalena. The era of trap and transplant was officially underway.

Handling the antelope once they are caged has always been a problem. In this first successful operation in 1937, Cowboy-Rancher Jess Addington tried his hand first. Figuring that a pronghorn couldn't be any rougher than a steer, he stepped into the catch pen and was greeted by a doe that lunged for the light of the opening. He caught a hoof in the chest, which knocked him down. But Jess hung on and wrestled the doe into the holding crate. Ranch-raised H. B. Birmingham, Jr. entered the catch pen next and demonstrated what was to become standard operating procedure in antelope wrestling.

Standing to one side, H. B. let the doe start past him, then grabbed an ear with his left hand. Slamming his hip against the animal, he reached over and grasped the right flank with his right hand. Thus suspended off the ground, the antelope was unable to fight, because its strong back legs had no purchase. The antelope kicked frantically, but was easily carried out of the pen and into a crate. This method carries the weight of the animal on the captor's hip and upper thigh, and takes away the antelope's purchase on solid ground, thus robbing it of most of its effective strength. Paul Russell reported later that he suffered a severe bilateral hernia when a well-meaning but ill-advised observer grabbed the hind legs of an animal while Russell was holding it. Given that solid purchase it almost tore free, and the injury resulted.

By April 16, 1937, the feasibility of this method had been proved. Twenty-nine animals had been released on distant ranges: 15 on the La Jencia Ranch, nine on Floyd Lee's ranch, and five on the J. V. Ranch east of Carrizozo, where there supposedly were other antelope.

Needless to say, the commission accepted proof of success and released the rest of the $4500, which enabled Russell and cooperators to improve the traps. They substituted rope mesh walls for steel mesh walls, which ended that portion of mortality caused by antelope hitting the steel wall at high speed. This resulted in

Even at extreme telephoto range, it is apparent that these three bucks all sport excellent trophy racks. This photograph was taken on the Fort Wingate Ordnance Depot in New Mexico. Only bowhunting is permitted here, which allows some bucks to elude hunters long enough to grow trophy racks.

broken legs, loss of hair and hide, and occasionally (when the spring action of the wall threw the antelope over backwards) in broken pelvic bones, which necessitated putting the injured animal out of its misery.

Each trapping attempt taught the New Mexico innovators something new about handling the antelope. To sum it up, we go again to the words of Paul Russell: "The 1938 antelope trapping operations started in December 1937 and ended in April 1938. During that time (1) Cord netting was used and proved efficient antelope trap pen material. (2) Well padded individual crates, in three sizes, were proven practical for hauling live antelope long distances. (3) Teamwork of skilled horsemen was adapted to, and proven effective in capturing large numbers of antelope. (4) The first professional photographs were made of trapped antelope. (5) Moving pictures of antelope trapping, transplanting and release scenes were made. (6) Two hundred and fifty wild antelope including all age classes of both sexes, from short yearling upward, were released with no obviously critical injuries, on new ranges."

Two-hundred-and-thirty-eight of these 250 were released in New Mexico. The other 12 went to the Wichita Mountains

Author Cadieux with good buck taken in northeastern New Mexico.

Wildlife Refuge in Oklahoma in return for a dozen elk.

Elliott S. Barker showed motion pictures of the entire operation at the 1938 meeting of the International Association of Game Fish and Conservation Commissioners in Asheville, North Carolina, and this started other states to thinking about the possibilities of expanding the occupied range of the pronghorn in their own borders.

Texas sent Warden Tom S. Redford and Regional Game Manager Dr. Lee W. Fisher to study New Mexico's antelope trapping methods. Texas had good success in trapping and relocating antelope that very same spring of 1939. Texas began the use of airplanes to help move the herds into the traps.

C. W. Sheffner and Gale Thomas came from Wyoming to observe the New Mexico operation in March 1941 and Kautz and Banta of the Colorado Game and Fish Department in November 1941. In late November 1941, Pittman Robertson funds were first authorized for trapping and transplanting antelope in New Mexico.

World War II stopped this work, as it stopped so many other worthwhile projects, in 1943. By that time New Mexico had transplanted more than 1500 antelope. This was before the creation of Los Alamos County, and the State Game and Fish Department could boast of having antelope in every one of the 31 counties in the state.

Trapping resumed after the war, and by 1956 the total of New Mexico antelope translocated had risen to 4400. In addition, Texas, Wyoming, Montana, Colorado, Arizona, and other states had used the system developed by T. Paul Russell in New Mexico.

Details on New Mexico's pioneering trapping operations are summarized in the accompanying table.

In 1956, another transplant was undertaken with the San Juan County Game Protective Association, in which 161 animals were trapped with a 6.8 percent mortality and 132 released in New Mexico.

By 1956, New Mexico had transplanted 4219 within the state and sent 171 out of state. The antelope that went to Oklahoma were traded for 40 elk, which became the foundation of the San Antonio Mountain and Mt. Taylor herds, and for more than 4000 pheasants.

Since 1956, New Mexico has trapped and transplanted to good effect. Regular

New Mexico Trapping Data, 1937–56

Year Ending June 30	Total Trapped	Fatalities — % of Trapped	Released in N.M.
1937	?	?	29
1938	?	?	238
1939	?	?	208
1940	439	5.99	385
1941	294	8.81	261
1942	322	4.66	307
1943	83	6.02	78
1946	14	0	14
1948	723	6.09	679
1949	582	2.06	488
1951	10	0	10
1952	392	1.79	318
1953	341	3.22	265*
1954	181	2.21	169
1955	436	3.21	409
1956	369	3.52	229†

* 49 traded for 4900 pheasants
† Trade with Oklahoma

seasons, tightly regulated, have resulted in a sustained-yield harvest but few trophy animals. The best hunting is in the northeast corner of the state, with the area near Roswell, in the southeast, running a close second. New Mexico is doing a good job of managing its pronghorns, but there is a very great unoccupied range in the Land of Enchantment, and there is potential for increased populations.

Colorado

Colorado usually ranks in the top four states in numbers of pronghorns. But the herds that occupy the flat, dry eastern one half of Colorado are but a tiny remnant of the estimated two million that roamed the state when the first white men came to the region.

All observers stated that the pronghorn probably outnumbered the bison on the western plains, and Seton—a very qualified observer—puts their 1800 population estimate at 40 million. Two million of these roamed Colorado! Completely unprotected by any law, the pronghorn was slaughtered by market hunters who sold the carcasses for less than a dime apiece in 1868. This is not exaggerated, as actual records show that wagonloads were shot on the eastern plains and sold in Denver at three carcasses for "two bits," the 25-cent coin being the smallest in common circulation at that time.

Cadieux with buck taken in northeastern New Mexico. Rifle is a homemade 30–06 on a Springfield action with a 2X–7X variable scope.

Pronghorns were observed by the thousands in North Park, in extreme northeastern Colorado, during the summer of 1876. Market hunters, lured by the (then) going price of $1 per carcass, moved into North Park in 1890. For all intents and purposes, they wiped out the pronghorn in North Park, although two or three lasted for a few years longer.

The Colorado General Assembly, in its first session in 1877, mentioned the pronghorn as a protected species and prohibited the practice of "coursing" pronghorns with dogs. But there was a great difference between passing a law and enforcing that law. There were no game wardens in those days and most regulations were observed more in the breach than in compliance.

In 1891, the legislature set a yearly bag limit of five pronghorns per hunter. In 1897, the legislature set up the Department of Forestry, Game and Fish and set a bag limit on the pronghorns of one animal per year. It also set an open season from September 1 to October 15. However, to show that they weren't really serious, the legislature enacted the provision that antelope could be taken at any other time of the year if a "reasonable necessity existed."

Naturally, with this callous attitude, the antelope had little chance of surviving.

If the photographer is patient and the pronghorns have not been hunted for years, close-range photography is sometimes possible. This Fort Wingate pronghorn, on land where only bowhunting is allowed, comes close to the staff photographer for New Mexico Game and Fish Department.

Taking advantage of its innate curiosity, hunters lured pronghorns into easy range and shot them. The two million found in 1868 decreased to an estimated 25,000 in 1898. Alarmed, the legislature closed the season in 1899 and "all ensuing years."

By 1918, the national population had gone down to perhaps 13,000 and certainly less than 1000 of these lived in Colorado. In 1921, the Colorado Antelope Refuge was set up in the extreme northeast corner of Larimer County. Its 110 acres helped to protect a small remnant herd.

When Nelson made his famed 1922–1924 survey of antelope numbers, he placed the national total at 30,326 and allocated 1233 of these to Colorado.

As in most other western states, trapping and transplanting of antelope from stocked to understocked ranges resulted in a good build-up of antelope numbers. Protection of resident herds by landowners also played a great part in the resurgence of antelope numbers that began after World War II.

By 1945, Colorado tabulated 6595 antelope, issued 1120 permits, and actually killed 834 pronghorns. By 1950, the kill had risen to 2148; in 1953, to 4456. Despite the fluctuations that plagued all pronghorn herds across their range, the trend has been steadily upward in Colorado, and the state now has a herd that numbered 58,000 in 1983 and now supports liberalized hunting seasons that harvest as many as 9394 pronghorns in a single year's season.

This is a remarkable comeback for the pronghorn, which hit a low of 1000 in 1918. When we remember that this increase took place while hunting seasons were enjoyed by more and more hunters each year, it is obvious that the pronghorn responds to protection and management,

Diane Cooney, a fine huntress in her own right, with a nice pronghorn taken in Colorado. *Photo by Judd Cooney.*

and that harvesting of the surplus by the hunter is a good part of wise management.

Texas

Although the 97th meridian is generally considered the eastern boundary of the pronghorn's historic range, pronghorns were reported from as far east as Henrietta in Texas, and from as far south as Alice in the southern part of the state. There is good historic evidence that pronghorns occupied more than 70 percent of Texas before the coming of Europeans. However, most of these animals were found in the Trans-Pecos area and in the High Plains of the Panhandle.

The antelope did quite well in Texas until settlement of the western parts of the state began to intensify in 1880. By 1890, the pronghorn was in serious trouble. Following the pattern seen elsewhere across their range, the antelope herds in Texas dwindled from perhaps two million to a low of 2407 in Nelson's survey of 1922–1924. A total of 692 was counted in the Trans-Pecos, along with smaller herds in the Lower Plains and Panhandle. In addition, a small herd clung to a precarious existence in Jim Hogg County in deep south Texas. After 1880, the era of the open range was dying, and fencing grew apace, with disastrous effects upon antelope, which found themselves fenced away from water supplies. Over the millennia in which antelope had been sympatric with buffalo, the *grazing* buffalo actually improved forage conditions for the *browsing*, forb-loving pronghorn. But overgrazing by cattle and sheep ruined the range for all ungulates, and the pronghorn suffered.

Texas' human population rose from half a million to four and one half million people in 1921, causing competition between man's needs and the needs of wildlife, and the pronghorn suffered. Market hunting continued at a record pace, and antelope carcasses were shipped to eastern markets by the railroad carload. Naturally, the pronghorn suffered.

All during the period of catastrophic decline—circa 1880 to 1924—the pronghorn was thought to compete with domestic livestock for forage crops. Ignorance of the pronghorn's food habits led to his systematic destruction by ranchers who wanted to save grass for their own cattle. The pronghorn suffered, of course. Other mortality factors included drought, from which west Texas is never very far removed. In the prolonged drought of 1964–1965, about 60 percent of the Marfa Flat pronghorn herd died. According to Schmidly's *The Mammals of Trans Pecos Texas*, the only forage left alive over much of the area was blackbrush, creosote bush, and snakeweed. Deaths were blamed on malnutrition and blackbush toxicity. Another contributing factor was the introduction of large numbers of sheep into west Texas. Sheep compete with pronghorns for food, and when sheep overgraze dry lands—such as those of Trans Pecos Texas—the damage can be long-lasting.

Excessive hunting was the primary cause of the decline in Texas. This is surprising when we consider the historic belief in Texas that trespassers are not welcomed. "Shoot first and ask questions later" was the watchword in treating trespass upon privately owned land in Texas—and almost all of the state is privately owned.

However, when a few ranchers decided to protect their remaining pronghorn herds, the antelope began a slow and steady increase. The closed season that the legislature had enacted as early as 1903 was now enforced, more by the landowner than by enforcement personnel of the state, who were in very short supply. Charging a cash fee for the privilege of trespassing on private land for the purpose of hunting became an established custom in Texas, long before it did in other western and southwestern states. Because antelope were looked upon as a cash crop in some parts of the antelope range in Texas, the pronghorn was protected by the landowners—to ensure their own income. In a private communication to me, Charles K. Winkler, Texas Big Game Program Director, wrote: "Generally the

Texas landowner regards antelope as a cash crop, particularly in the Trans-Pecos region. A few landowners in the Panhandle complain of crop depredation but rarely does anyone want the antelope on their property exterminated or removed. About 20 percent of the landowners who receive permits do not allow hunting but I think in most cases these are ranchers that only receive one or two permits which they reserve for their personal use and, for some reason, don't use the permits."

Texas reports give credit for the population increase to two factors: Increased protection by landowners and increased emphasis on the control of predatory animals, especially the coyote, which evidently dined heavily on newborn pronghorns.

At present Texas pronghorn herds can be divided into three ranges: the Trans-Pecos, which is home for about two thirds of the state's antelope, and the Panhandle and Lower Plains Regions, which halve the other one third of the state's population. Even with the good condition of today's Texas pronghorns, they only occupy about 25 percent of their historic range.

The 1986 populations in the Panhandle and Lower Plains areas are threatened even today by changes in agricultural practices that transform uninterrupted grazing land into cropland. Deep well irrigation has made this conversion of rangeland to crop possible, but depletion of underground aquifers is already limiting the rate at which irrigation can be brought to west Texas. As it becomes economically infeasible to water these lands, many of them will probably revert to range, with positive effects upon the antelope herds.

Texas was one of the first states to observe New Mexico's pioneer trapping and transplanting efforts, and the first to add the airplane as a tool with which to drive antelope into the traps.

In 1939, Texans did their first trapping, using the trap developed by Russell in New Mexico. That first attempt corralled 257 pronghorns, which were released into 21 different sites across the historic antelope range. Through the years 1939-1956, Texas restocked approximately 4000 antelope into areas of suitable habitat. Restocking was stopped in 1956, and limited permit hunting was begun. In 1972, antelope restocking was resumed, and in two years another 1100 pronghorns had been moved to suitable habitat in the Trans-Pecos and Lower Plains regions. By 1977, eight of these newly transplanted herds were big enough to support hunting. In 1979, Texas went back into the restocking business with 81 antelope being transferred from Wyoming to Texas. A total of 350 pronghorns were obtained from Colorado during 1980-1982. Transplanting was also a two-way street, as 51 pronghorns were trapped in Texas and traded to Arizona for bighorn sheep. Average cost per pronghorn trapped in Texas was estimated to be $249.

Texas has had a limited permit season on antelope every year since 1955. Wise management has allowed the Texas herds to prosper, and they now have a population estimated at 18,000. There is considerable unoccupied rangeland in Texas—unoccupied by pronghorns, that is. The future for the pronghorn seems bright, and the potential habitat is there to support another 30,000 animals, according to some estimates.

An interesting facet of the pronghorn management picture in Texas is that of rancher conservatism. A 1982 status report by the Texas Parks and Wildlife Department comments: "Permit utilization during the last five years has remained fixed at around 65 percent due to rancher conservatism. This partial utilization of permits has prevented the maximum harvest of surplus antelope, but it has allowed the production of some trophy-sized bucks and resulted in a post hunting season sex ratio of approximately 2.5 does per buck."

Landowner antipathy toward doe harvest — which in Texas is referred to as the killing of mother deer or antelope — has been a complicating factor for Texas wildlife managers for many decades. Texas ranchers accepted doe permits — whether for white-tailed deer or for antelope — then substituted their own judgment for that of the biologist by tearing up the doe permits, effectively reducing the harvest of female animals.

There is also a greater demand for trophy animals in Texas than in most of the pronghorn's range, so the production of larger horns on mature bucks is a desired end, while the maximizing of the harvest does not seem to be important for many landowners in Texas. As has often been said, "Texas is different!"

Tiny remnant populations of pronghorns that hung on in areas distant from the usual known range of the pronghorn is always a touch-and-go situation. Texas is no exception in this regard. There had been a tiny remnant herd in Jim Hogg County in south Texas up until 1983. The state added Colorado wild-trapped pronghorns to this herd on the Alta Vista Ranch and on the nearby La Rucis Ranch — sort of a transfusion of new blood — but it failed. No antelope have been reported from Jim Hogg County for three years now. Another remnant herd, on the sprawling King Ranch, no longer exists, according to a private communication to me from Charles K. Winkler, who directs the Big Game Program for Texas.

Drought conditions in west Texas have perhaps been the greatest limiting factor on pronghorn herds. Both 1984 and 1985 were years of higher than average precipitation on the Texas pronghorn pastures, and that resulted in increased fawn production. The pronghorn situation in Texas looks good at present, with estimates of total population riding around the 15,000 level.

Mainland Mexico

Senor Jose C. Trevino, of Mexico's Departmentado Fauna Silvestre, Chihuahua, and Sanford D. Schemnitz, of New Mexico State University, presented a report at the 10th Biennial Pronghorn Workshop in Dickinson, North Dakota, in 1982. Their summation is perhaps the best information available, so we quote from it quite extensively here:

"The first record describing pronghorn in Mexico was published in 1723 in Torquemada's *Monarquia Indiana* in which a hunt honoring Viceroy Antonio de Mendoza in 1540 is described. The author stated that 600 deer and 'berrendos' were killed, and those 'berrendos' did not occur in Spain, and that they 'not only ran but flew.' Fray Augustin Morfi saw antelope near Durango City in 1777 and reported that 'they abound in the provinces.' The Englishman George F. Ruxton referred repeatedly to the many antelope between Durango and Chihuahua City in 1849. Lumholtz found that pronghorn were abundant near Casas Grandes, Chihuahua, in 1891. However, during the late 1800s, after the Apaches and Comanches had been extirpated from the north and normal settlement had been resumed, the antelope were rapidly depleted and by the end of the century they had become scarce. Mearns (1907) wrote that pronghorned antelope were rare in the southwest, where they had ranged in the thousands 25 years before.

"In 1925 Nelson reported an estimated population of 2,395 pronghorns for Mexico with the following distribution: Coahuila 600, Chihuahua 700, Sonora 595 and Baja California 500. As part of the widespread interest in the antelope decline in Mexico, a special closed season was declared in 1922 by President Obregon, and hunting has not been allowed since.

"Grinnell (in Sheldon 1925) reported that pronghorn were abundant in Chihuahua, and ranged in small bands along the Mexican Central Railroad, diminishing in numbers toward the south. The southernmost band was located 60 km west of Chihuahua. Antelope were more abundant in eastern Chihuahua, where Grinnell roughly estimated their numbers at several thousand. Also he stated that pronghorn hunting was prohibited on ranches owned by Americans and Englishmen.

"Information about pronghorn distribution and numbers in Chihuahua had been given in the past by various workers. However, their reports were based only upon reported sighting and did not include any intensive terrestrial or aerial surveys.

"During the summer of 1976, pronghorn herds were located by means of automobile survey. Once the herd was located, it was counted and sex ratio and old-young ratio determined by means of aerial observation using fixed wing aircraft.

"Herds located in 1976, were studied in 1977. Ten separate herds were located and counted. The results are shown in the accompanying table. The authors report that this tabulation does not include two additional herds of antelope, 30 at El Oso and Iglesias and 32 at Doce de Octubre observed in the fall of 1978."

Several comments are perhaps in order here. First, the reporters stated that antelope hunting was stopped in 1922, and that there has been no hunting since. This is legally correct, but in actual practice, the opposite has been true. We must remember that game law enforcement is

Pronghorn Distribution in Mexico, Summer 1976

Area	Males	Does	Fawns	Total
El Berrendo	9	23	2	34
El Cuervo	10	21	4	35
Villa Ahumada	2	6	0	8
Montezuma	27	39	4	71
El Sueco	55	131	18	204
Tres Castillos	13	25	3	41
Coyame	33	44	17	94
Julimes	5	10	1	16
Benavides	4	14	3	21
Camargo	11	22	4	37
Totals	169	336	56	561

SOURCE: Report of 10th Biennial Pronghorn Workshop, 1982.

almost nonexistent in Mexico. A country worried about the possibility of revolution against the government—perhaps brought on by a burgeoning human population outstripping its food supply—does not have the time or resources to allot to wildlife conservation. Even the aerial census reported by Trevino and Schemnitz was financed by United States Foundations.

Secondly, the research report refers to Chihuahua, the largest state in Mexico—only. When we throw in consideration of the antelope herds on the Baja California peninsula, we come to another matter entirely. Here, most authority has been concentrated in the hands of the military. Even though the civilian government in Mexico City says that hunting is illegal, the commanding generals in the Baja have often issued "permits" to foreign hunters. Ashamedly, we must admit that most of these hunters have come from the United States.

In another part of the report, Trevino and Schemnitz state that antelope hunting has been stopped on ranches owned by Americans or Englishmen. This, of course, says nothing about the possibility of hunting continuing on the much greater acreages owned by Mexicans. It also says nothing about the fate of antelope in Coahuila and Chihuahua in the wake of expropriation, whereby foreign-owned ranchos were broken up and given to the landless peon. In almost every case of expropriation, the new owners ate the antelope.

It is easy to criticize Mexico for its handling of its wildlife resources. It is easy, and it is wrong. When you find yourself faced with the problem of seeing your children go hungry, or shooting a pronghorn, are you sure what your reaction will be? When you worry about feeding millions, do you have time for counting berrendos in a far-off pasture in Chihuahua?

Baja California

Until you have seen it, there is really no way to describe the inhospitable region known as the central part of the Baja California peninsula. A land of hot sands, scant rainfall, and blazing heat through nine months of the year, the Baja was once known in our country by its reputation as a torture test for automobiles. Now that the Baja road has tamed that test, recreational vehicles of all kinds regularly traverse the Baja road without fear. However, they treat it with respect, for it is a fierce, hard, unforgiving place.

On the Pacific side, a huge estuary, known as Scammons Lagoon, is home to the great whales for a couple of months each year. Here they come to give birth and to breed again, putting on a great display of acrobatics as they go through their exciting time.

Very near to the Lagoon is a remnant population of pronghorns, assigned to the rare and endangered subspecies that taxonomists call the Peninsular pronghorn *(Antilocapra americana peninsularis)*. Biologists often refer to this subspecies as the "most distinctly different" of the five subspecies currently recognized. One startling difference in life history is that the Peninsular pronghorns drop their fawns in late January and early February, long before their cousins up north. Undoubtedly this is an adaptation designed to produce the fawns at a time when temperatures and rains will offer a better chance of survival. In addition, they spread the fawning period out over a period of nearly a month, as opposed to their northern counterparts who usually get all the fawning done in about 10 days.

Because of their endangered status, these animals have been watched closely by the Arizona Game and Fish Department and by the U.S. Fish and Wildlife Service. David E. Brown of the Arizona department tells me that there are between 40 and 80 head of this rare pronghorn in this isolated backwater of man's world. On my only trip to that area, I glassed five head, distorted by the dancing heat waves. I could not make out their sex. Although their environment is a harsh one, they benefit from the fact that man comes there but seldom. Anyone approaching across the flat, salty soils and scant saltbush and cactus undergrowth can be seen by the pronghorns for miles, although it is hard to make out the details of any object shimmering in the summer heat waves.

Despite the protection offered by environment and isolation, the population trend of this isolated group has been steadily downward for the past 20 years. Evidently much of the blame for this decrease can be laid to the increase in human numbers. More and more people are moving into the area near the Vizcaino Desert, as the government attempts to settle agricultural workers wherever there is a possibility of irrigating crops. More and better roads are coming, and this is almost certain to sound the death knell for this remote, isolated pronghorn population.

Mexican officials give "increased poaching and coyote-caused mortality" as the twin reasons for the decline. It is impossible to quantify the human poaching aspect, but the coyote mortality has been quantified by personnel of the Denver Wildlife Research facility. They have operated scent stations that give them an index of coyote numbers. They've found extremely high counts, with the very highest coming in the exact spots where the remnant herd of pronghorns is found. This is no coincidence, of course.

U.S. Fish and Wildlife personnel have given instructions to Mexican workers, teaching them how to operate steel traps and M-44 coyote getters (spring-actuated mechanisms that discharge cyanide directly into the coyote's mouth when he attempts to take the scent-impregnated top of the getter). While it is true that these archaic coyote-control measures will kill some coyotes, the situation here is desperate. It would seem that it would be wise to allow the U.S. experts to teach the placement of Compound 1080 baits, in order to effect a high-percentage kill of coyotes in a wider area, thus giving the endangered species a chance. It is no time to discuss the niceties of whether or not 1080 should be used. While we talk, the Peninsular pronghorn may be extirpated. The U.S. personnel who worked in the Vizcaino Desert recommended the use of "single bait" 1080 poisonings. To the best of my knowledge, their recommendation never went any farther than the paper it was written upon. The American experts also recommended the aerial hunting of coyotes in this flat, wide-open area, where fixed-wing aircraft would be very effective. Citing the fact that there would be no need for the more expensive helicopter, the Americans put in a good word for aerial hunting. The perennial shortage of both funds and planes in Mexico's more isolated areas will undoubtedly preclude adoption of that recommendation. Any talk of preserving this population by removal of a large part of the big coyote population should take into account the fact that control measures would have to be conducted over a very large area. To control coyotes only at the scene of the pronghorn's battle for survival would be ineffective, because other coyotes would continue to fill the vacuum created by removal of local coyotes.

Contingency plans have been drawn up to capture a great percentage of the endangered herd, remove them to a safer habitat (protected by the big salt company that operates in the area of Scammons Lagoon), and raise them in captivity until numbers are sufficiently large to allow reintroduction into the same wild that has proved too much for them today. I believe that this is radical surgery. Surely it would disrupt the natural scheme of things far more than would the systematic use of Compound 1080 baits. In addition, trapping animals in the heat of the Baja might prove fatal to a large percentage of these rare animals. It really would seem fruitless to produce pronghorns for reintroduction into an environment where they had previously failed to make a go of it. Would it not be better to improve the environment, and then replace the endangered species? A variation of this capture and propagate suggestion is that fawns could be captured when dropped and then reared in captivity, safeguarded from coyotes, until they reach 3 to 4 months old and are (relatively) immune from coyote attack. Then they could be released into the wild.

The steady decline in numbers was documented by United States scientists who conducted aerial surveys and ground counts. The population was set at "less than 80" in the 1984 counts. In January of 1985, a total of 70 pronghorns was counted.

It can only be expected that this will continue and that the *peninsularis* subspecies will be but a memory in the future. The question still remains as to whether or not this ever should have been called a true subspecies.

However, we should remember that it makes no difference whether we say *peninsularis* and *sonorensis* became extinct, or if we say the two southernmost isolated groups of pronghorns became extinct. Either way, we will be expressing a loss, and the world will be the poorer for this loss.

Wyoming

Geographically, Wyoming was probably the center of the historic range of the pronghorned antelope. Today, Wyoming is the center of the modern-day range, although that range has been severely reduced since the day when 40 million pronghorns outnumbered the bison from the edge of the tree country west of the Mississippi almost all the way to the Pacific, and roamed freely from Sinaloa and Coahuila to Saskatchewan and Alberta.

In many parts of the country where bison and pronghorn were sympatric, the bison was an important part of the ecosystem, being the heavy grazer who made it possible for the forbs and brush to exist without being choked out by climax succession grass. But in a great section of south-central Wyoming, the pronghorn prospered on lands that were unproductive for almost any other form of herbivore. Here the pronghorn didn't need help from the bison to keep the grass mowed down; climate took over that job.

It is doubtful if the Indian inhabitants of the Wyoming area ever preyed heavily on the pronghorn. It was perhaps easier to kill a bison than it was to arrow a pronghorn, considering the wary, elusive nature of that speedster. This changed when the white man's needs brought the market hunter to Wyoming. In the decades before 1880, market hunting systematically reduced the pronghorn numbers in Wyoming at a fearful rate. In 1881, more than 55,000 antelope hides were shipped down the Yellowstone River to St. Louis. The last bison was killed in Wyoming in 1889, and the pronghorn was in bad shape.

In 1869, the legislature prohibited the sale of antelope between February 1 and August 1. As was the rule in those days, there was no effort made to enforce that law. In 1875, the hunting season was set for August through January. Again, no enforcement.

In 1902, Wyoming set limits as follows: two deer, two elk, three antelope, and one bighorn sheep for each $1 hunting license. If you hunted only in your own county, you didn't need a license at all.

In 1909, the antelope season was closed and remained closed until 1915.

In 1924, Nelson's nationwide census showed Wyoming's population at only 7000 pronghorns. Today, Wyoming publications dispute that low figure, stating that they had 14,000 in 1924, and that it rose rapidly to 20,000 in 1926 and up to 35,000 head in 1936.

In 1950, Wyoming estimated that it had 76,000 antelope, and credited that increase in numbers to the fact that World War II had made it hard for the hunter to go afield. Most men of prime hunting age were in the military service, and ammunition was in short supply for almost all popular calibers.

Obviously, Wyoming is special as far as antelope are concerned. The reasons are many and varied, but it is mostly a matter of undisturbed habitat. The pronghorns have been greatly reduced where croplands can be farmed economically, as in the extreme southeastern corner of the big, wide-open state. Wyoming has no big cities, and few medium-sized ones. The human population has remained relatively constant over the past 40 years, although that has been changing recently thanks to the coming of coal surface mining in Wyoming.

The terrain of Wyoming is better suited to ranching than to crop farming, and the rainfall is not sufficient to allow for dryland farming. This favors antelope.

Since the Wyoming Game and Fish Department was charged with management of the state's renewable game resources in 1927, that department has gone out of its way to make the pronghorn an asset to the landowner, rather than a liability. Cognizant of the fact that ranchers control the legislature, the State Game and Fish Department has set up a system whereby the landowner profits from the harvest of each and every antelope taken from his land.

Today, pronghorns range over 90 percent of Wyoming—in fact, all but the eastern half of Goshen and Laramie counties. The other parts of Wyoming all hold antelope, except for the higher elevations where there is forest cover. Elevation alone doesn't seem to bar the adaptable pronghorn, for I have seen them above 8000 feet many times in many places, but they do not take well to a habitat where they cannot see for long distances. Confined in a forested area, the pronghorn becomes paranoid and sees an enemy behind every bush. In truth, the presence of bushes makes it easy for a predator to sneak to within short distances of an antelope, and the pronghorn knows that his safety lies in the wide-open spaces.

The common sage seems to be the pronghorn's insurance policy, and Wyoming has lots of sage. Sagebrush eradication projects that open the range for forage grasses make money for the cattleman but spell trouble for the pronghorn. Today, the well-managed pronghorn herds in Wyoming seem to be assured of a good future. The catastrophic losses to winter blizzards are the only real danger for the biggest pronghorn herd in the nation. If we remember that the pronghorn has co-existed with the blizzard ever since the Miocene age, and has never been eliminated, we have little cause for concern. The status of Wyoming's antelope herds is reflected in the generous seasons and high sustained yield of their harvest over the past 30 years.

From a scanning of the table, it should be apparent that if you want to kill an antelope, Wyoming is the place to do it. Since it became the norm for landowners to charge for the privilege of hunting on their lands, Wyoming residents have shifted their hunting efforts more and more to publicly owned land—and there is lots of it in Wyoming. This has actually resulted in making more hunting opportunities available to the nonresident hunter who seldom minds coming up with the fee for hunting rights. The fact that the landowner makes more money from a nonresident hunting on his land than he does for a resident hunting on his land has made the nonresident very popular in some areas of Wyoming.

In addition to the tremendous value of the hunting opportunities that Wyoming has provided, we must remember that Wyoming has been most generous in providing seed stock for transplants into many other states. There is hardly an area of today's antelope range that does not sport pronghorns whose ancestors came from Wyoming.

Pronghorn, thy home is Wyoming!

Wyoming Hunter Success Rates

Year	No. Killed	% Success
1953	34,909	88%
1954	30,776	90%
1955	33,090	89%
1956	23,013	88%
1957	25,708	86%
1958	23,910	86%
1959	26,542	84%
1960	31,674	88%
1961	34,873	86%
1962	37,444	86%
1963	35,590	85%
1964	28,945	77%
1965	23,944	85%
1966	23,872	75%
1967	23,375	77%
1968	25,247	78%
1969	28,171	87%
1970	31,125	86%
1971	34,595	86%
1972	34,499	83%
1973	36,924	89%
1974	42,534	90%
1975	51,491	84%
1976	58,480	87%
1977	58,858	88%
1978	58,132	87%
1979	44,616	83%
1980	47,994	84%
1981	67,801	88%
1982	79,515	87%
1983	98,680	92%

Oklahoma

Although all of the prairie and plains country of Oklahoma was historic range for the pronghorn, it can now claim only a small part of Texas County (in Oklahoma) and the western one half of Cimarron County, which is the tip of the Oklahoma Panhandle.

State by State, Province by Province

When settlement almost eliminated the pronghorn from the West, it did a very good job of eliminating the pronghorn in Oklahoma. The "base line" count used by Nelson in 1924 was only 20 animals for the entire state of Oklahoma. Over the past 20 years, Oklahoma pronghorn populations have varied between 300 and 500 animals. Herds move in and out of Oklahoma from the Texas Panhandle, according to long-time friend Dean Graham, Chief of Information for the Oklahoma Department of Wildlife Conservation.

Back in 1966, things were looking up for the Oklahoma pronghorn herd. Noting that as many as 100 male animals could be removed from the herd without affecting reproduction in any way, the big-game biologists recommended an open hunting season. When Oklahomans applied for permits in the 1966 season, they were applying for the first legal pronghorn hunt since statehood. The recommendation was for 100 permits to be issued — 70 in Cimarron County and 30 in Texas County. The historic season was scheduled for September 15–17, 1966. During the three-day season, 54 animals were taken by 80 hunters for a 68.7 success percentage. Because the season had been closed for so many years, there was considerable optimism on the part of trophy hunters who felt that there might be a world-record buck waiting for them in western Oklahoma. Landowner cooperation during the hunt was excellent and many ranchers either led or directed hunters to the best hunting areas.

In 1967, 80 hunters went afield in Cimarron County and killed 24 animals for a success ratio of only 30 percent; and in Texas County, 30 hunters killed 11 animals for a success ratio of only 36.6 percent.

In 1968, 70 permits were issued in Cimarron County and 50 in Texas County. Total kill was only 30 buck antelope, and the average size was reported to be smaller than in previous seasons. In Cimarron County, only 14 kills were reported compared to 25 in 1967 and 38 in 1966. In his report of the season results, big-game biologist Cy Curtis noted "the pronghorn herds will not withstand annual hunts." The department did not recommend an open season in 1969 and one was not held.

In 1972, limited permit seasons were again held in Cimarron and Texas counties. In Cimarron, 60 hunters took 27 antelope and in Texas County, 19 hunters took seven pronghorns.

A part of the Oklahoma story is the history of antelope stocking on the Wichita Mountains Wildlife Refuge, a sprawling area administered by the U.S. Fish and Wildlife Service, mainly for the propagation of bison destined for slaughter. Historic writings show that the area near the refuge once carried a normal population of pronghorns, and, in fact, pronghorns were definitely present on the refuge area itself. During the catastrophic decline in numbers that affected all pronghorn herds on the continent, the herd on and near the refuge was eliminated.

The Boone and Crockett Club supplied the first transplanting stock, when four bucks and seven does were moved to the refuge from Yellowstone Park in 1910 and 1911. No luck! The herd diminished rapidly and left only one very lonesome doe from 1917 to 1921.

Another attempt was made in 1921, when the American Bison Society obtained 10 fawns from Alberta, and got six more the next year. This nucleus expanded to 34 head by 1927. Then troubles reared their heads: According to office records on the refuge, heavy tick infestations, hemmorhagic septicemia and actinomycosis were all mentioned as causes, along with coyote depredation. The herd was gone in 1931, although heroic measures were adopted to try to prevent the losses to disease and parasitism.

Another attempt was made in 1937, this time with four fawns (three bucks and one doe) captured in Oklahoma. None lived more than six months.

In March 1938, four bucks and eight does came from New Mexico. In 1940, four bucks and 18 does came from New Mexico. These seemed to prosper and the count rose to 71 in 1943. In 1949, the population had dropped to 39 animals.

Refuge figures show a definite correlation between coyote removal and pronghorn fawn survival—and the resultant increase in pronghorn populations. Respected research biologist Helmut K. Buechner has a hard time admitting this, however. In his excellent report, he shows us that: "The first good fawn production was in 1949, when 22 fawns were counted. During the 1948–1949 season, 117 coyotes were removed with cyanide guns, in addition three Compound 1080 stations appear to have been exceptionally effective. All of the horse meat was consumed and early spring inspection showed little coyote sign."

True scientist that he is, Mr. Buechner refused to make a categorical statement that there was a connection between coyote removal and herd increases. He states: "Whether these are true cause and effect relationships cannot be decided with the evidence at hand, since no controls existed. Possibly biological factors such as disease, malnutrition, improper diet, adverse weather, inadequate low quality range, and the principle of inversity, together with their influence on reproduction, are more potent regulators of antelope populations than coyotes."

Whether or not we accept what appears to be obvious—that coyotes reduced the Wichita Mountains pronghorn populations—the fact remains that several attempts at reintroducing the pronghorn to this (once) native range of the pronghorn have failed. There are no pronghorns on the refuge as of this writing, nor are there any plans to reintroduce them. One of the refuge personnel penned a note on the front of the research data that they kindly supplied to me. It read, "The last antelope died in 1968. Poaching may have been a serious factor." The addenda were not signed.

Kansas

In 1540, Spanish explorer Coronado wrote of great herds of "ciervos, remedados de blanco" in the area which is now Kansas. The translation is simply, "stags, patched with white." From this description and other writings, we know that he referred to the pronghorn. Indeed, it would have been surprising if the lush tall grass prairies of Kansas had not been home to a large pronghorn population. It was almost three centuries later when Zebulon Pike (1806) passed through the Kansas area and again noted that antelope were common.

In 1874, J. A. Allen documented the slide in pronghorn populations that followed the national trend. He observed that: "In 1871, pronghorn were common as far east as the middle of the state and formerly ranged much farther eastward. Not observed in winter much to the eastward of the Colorado boundary. . . . although tolerably frequent in northwestern Kansas in summer, they are far less numerous here than in eastern Colorado, or on the plains of southern Wyoming."

This early quotation is memorable for illustrating two salient points. One, Kansas pronghorns have always drifted back and forth over the state boundaries into eastern Colorado, and, to a lesser extent, northward over the border into Nebraska. Secondly, he pointed up the pre-eminent position of Wyoming in the pronghorn picture. That has continued to this day, of course.

In 1905, Lantz wrote: "Pronghorn were fast disappearing. A recent law protects these animals, but the law is ignored by many of the settlers in western Kansas. A few small herds have been reported to me within the last year . . . in the extreme western counties of the state. . . . There seems to be little hope that the antelope will not become completely extinct . . . (in Kansas) . . . within a decade."

By 1912, it was thought that the only antelope in the state were three seen in Stanton County. But remember that Kansas shared herds, during migrations, with Nebraska and Colorado.

When Nelson made his "first ever" census of antelope in 1924, he found only eight pronghorns, and these were in Morton County. But remember that census was not an exact science, and remember also that antelope travel great distances when not blocked by fences. There was reliable evidence that a herd of seven spent the winter on the Bill Mull farm of Ashland, Clark County, in 1926. Others were reported south of Syracuse in Hamilton County. Tiny bands of antelope have a hard time existing. First of all, the absence of females of breeding age causes the young bucks to roam great distances, which greatly increases their mortality rate. Secondly, the small population comprises a tiny gene pool, and line inbreeding is inevitable.

Private citizens tried a few releases of antelope from Montana (and other states) in the intervening years, but these efforts were sporadic, poorly planned, and too small to be effective.

In July 1962, the Kansas Game and Fish Commission conducted a survey which reported that there were 56 pronghorns in Sherman and Wallace counties. It was decided to transplant to increase these herds. In 1964, 84 pronghorns were brought from Montana and released in these counties. At least 13 died during, or shortly after, the travel phase of the operation. In January 1966, another 61 pronghorns were introduced from Colorado—with 53 stocked in Barber County and eight going to the Maxwell Game Refuge in McPherson County. This was, as it usually is, a barter deal, with Kansas trading 50 white-tailed deer and 125 lesser prairie chickens to Colorado for 100 antelope. In 1967, 50 pronghorns from Nebraska were released in Ellsworth County and another 33 were released in Edwards County. For reasons not yet known, this group dispersed widely, two traveling as much as 90 miles from the release site.

By 1969, it was apparent that only the Wallace and Sherman county releases were succeeding. This points up the fact that pronghorns had succeeded in staying alive in those two counties for a long time, evidencing the better habitat found there. That herd also spread east into Logan County. In 1975, the census of this herd showed a total of 673 pronghorns. In the same year, there were 54 pronghorns in and near Barber County.

The gradual buildup of the Kansas herd allowed a limited hunting season in 1974.

Despite regular hunting seasons, the well-managed herd grew to 845 animals by the winter of 1978.

One large group of pronghorns was trapped on the Sioux Army depot in Nebraska and brought to Kansas. Semi-tame, these antelope did not succeed in establishing themselves in their new home. This, of course, invited the comparison between wild-trapped turkeys or pheasants and their game-farm-raised counterparts. The wild individuals possess characteristics that cannot be fostered in the domestic game farm atmosphere. Wild-trapped stock has proved itself infinitely better in almost every species considered for transplanting.

In 1978, 63 more antelope were moved from Wyoming to Kansas' Clark County and 37 to Chase County. In 1979, 98 newcomers from Wyoming's burgeoning herds were released in Chase County, 75 in Ellsworth, 74 in Clark, 37 in Morton, and 68 in Gove County. The thinking behind these transplants seems to have been that the discrete populations would grow to the point where they would intermingle, thus increasing the pitifully small gene pool and giving the species a better chance of continuing to exist in the Sunflower State. As elsewhere, the pronghorn has suffered from human settlement of his pre-Columbian range, by conversion of rangeland to cropland, and by unrestricted shooting in pioneer days.

There is still a degree of migration across state boundaries that causes the Kansas pronghorn count to fluctuate, but it is no longer the one thing that keeps Kansas in the pronghorn picture. Kansas pronghorns have profited by the development of an ecological conscience that has sparked landowner protection of the pronghorn herds, by careful management of the herds, and above all, by the transplants from Colorado, Wyoming, Montana, and Nebraska.

Hunting has been used as a management tool in Kansas ever since the herds built up to the point where they could support hunting of males only (see accompanying table).

Kansas Hunter Success Rates

Year	No. Killed	% Hunter Success
Rifle Seasons		
1974	70	97.2
1975	76	97.4
1976	72	93.5
1977	91	95.0
1978	90	93.0
1979	91	97.0
1980	142	95.9
1981	169	93.9
1982	171	94.5
1983	321	88.7
Archery Seasons		
1976	7	17.0
1977	4	8.0
1978	4	8.0
1979	2	3.0
1980	10	19.6
1981	12	13.9
1982	11	15.9
1983	18	14.2

Why Transplant Pronghorns?

No species of game animal has ever profited so much from transplanting as has the pronghorn antelope.

If we study the history of these restocking projects, we will notice situations where pronghorns went from State A to State B. A few years later, or many years later, pronghorns went from State B to

Headed for a new home, this young pronghorn exits the truck. *New Mexico Game and Fish Department photo.*

State A! Why?

Texas has received pronghorns from New Mexico, from Colorado, from Wyoming, and from Montana, if my memory serves me correctly. Yet Texas has trapped hundreds of its pronghorns and sent them to other states. Why?

Many states have allowed their stocks to be trapped and sent to other states, even before their own range has saturated its pronghorn carrying capacity. They have chosen to supply new stock to other states ahead of the obvious objective of providing maximum hunting opportunity to their own hunters. Why?

Why this generosity on the part of the "have" states toward the "have-not" states?

The answers are complex, but also easy to understand.

First of all, remember that no state game and fish department has enough money to do the work it is asked to do. This was especially true in the years before World War II. There is no limit to what might be done, if money were unlimited. Sorrowfully, we must face the facts that money is very hard to come by for even the most well-funded state department. Now, with cash money in short supply, all states are anxious to build up their "barter" business. Pronghorns made excellent trading stock for cash-poor state departments.

Trading might go like this: Manitoba provides walleye eggs to North Dakota. North Dakota quickly develops its own walleye fishery, and adds good walleye hatchery facilities. North Dakota then provides walleye eggs, or fingerlings, to Wyoming, in return for sage grouse, which are released in North Dakota. The two states are happy, and the province of Manitoba has established a "brownie point" with North Dakota which it may call in that year, or decades later. This particular brownie point was cashed years later when North Dakota sent largemouth bass to Manitoba for a special stocking project.

Usually these trades are not formalized agreements with contracts and such. Usually, they are simply a word of understanding among fellow workers. It works.

Colorado has received stocks of pronghorns from several states and has also sent its own pronghorns to four or five states.

Okay, so there is available a source of trading stock. When pronghorn reproduction and fawn survival conditions are right, pronghorns can put on quite a population explosion. Once the upswing started in many states, they were immediately willing to share their largesse with other states—which is particularly true of Montana, Wyoming and Colorado.

Why does a state want to receive new

As crew moves the mesh wing wall, pronghorns in the trap are slowly and quietly squeezed down into a smaller area for handling. *New Mexico Game and Fish Department photo.*

When released at night, pronghorns sometimes are reluctant to move into unknown territory. *New Mexico Game and Fish Department photo.*

pronghorn stocks if its own are doing well? For the same reason that cattle breeders regularly bring in new bulls, from outside their own known bloodlines, to breed the cows in their fine herds. To instill new vigor!

It is my personal opinion, not backed by scientific research results, that the vigorous rebound of the pronghorn populations was due in part to the introduction of new family genes, of different bloodlines, to mix with those already at hand.

With the re-introduction of any species into a territory other than the habitat in which it grew up, there is always a danger of unwanted diseases or parasites. However, the pronghorn has shown itself to be remarkably free from diseases. The pronghorn is surprisingly free from external parasites, and the parasites it carries internally do not seem to hurt the health and vigor of the host animal. This hardiness in the face of disease and parasitism makes the pronghorn an admirable candidate for restocking.

Introduction of pronghorn genes from other states had a twofold purpose: To speed up the resurgence of native pronghorn populations, and to promote vigor (I'd like to call it "hybrid vigor," but that

Manhandling pronghorns into captivity for restocking. They usually stop struggling when all feet are off the ground. *New Mexico Game and Fish Department photo.*

wouldn't set well with the semanticists). After all, it is my contention that there is only one pronghorn family on the North American continent, so there could not be any possibility of "hybridization" between differing stocks of pronghorns. There *are* no differing stocks of pronghorns.

Another salient effect of the transplanting that has been done so many times is the erasing of differences between populations that were once (mistakenly, I think) used to rationalize the separation of *Antilocapridae* into subspecies. If there was a difference between *Antilocapra americana mexicana* and *Antilocapra americana sonorensis* when biologists first studied these splendid animals, there surely is no difference now.

My theory is that transplanting has effectively homogenized the entire pronghorn population in North America. The few discrete populations which have escaped this mixing and stirring of the gene pool are those in Chihuahua (there was a release of New Mexico pronghorns into Chihuahua areas, but it was too small to do any good, and the herd was in a perilous situation, prior to the release) and in Baja California. As I have stated elsewhere in this work, it would be a good idea to acclimate some healthy bucks from Texas or New Mexico's southern parts and release them with the remnant herds found near Scammon's Lagoon on the Baja Peninsula in Old Mexico and in the country near the city of Chihuahua—unless it is already too late to rescue those too-small herds with an infusion of new blood.

Transplanting has been very important in the resurgence of the pronghorn from a low of 14,000 animals in 1924 to its present place as America's number two big-game animal.

The airplane put this fine bunch of pronghorns into the trap at one time. *New Mexico Game and Fish Department photo.*

Pronghorns being allowed to calm down in holding pen before handling. *New Mexico Game and Fish Department photo.*

Transplanting should still play a part in the management of discrete herds. Given the enlightened leadership of the game departments in the pronghorn states, I am sure that transplanting will continue to be recognized as an invaluable tool of pronghorn management.

5

The Impossible Dream

Sportsmen from the East, upon seeing their first herds of antelope, are often tempted to ask, "Why can't we have antelope back where I come from?"

The answer is obvious: The antelope that evolved on the western plains is superbly suited to the western plains. He does not do well on forested lands—and did not occur in the forested one-half of our nation when the first Europeans came to settle. The pronghorn does well in the wide-open spaces, where he can see for miles, where he can anticipate danger, and where he has room to outrun his enemies. But the temptation to stock antelope into habitats not suited to antelope is always with us, and there have been a few unsuitable habitats stocked during the renascence of the herds in the years from 1935 to 1975.

Hawaii, Florida, and Washington state all undertook transplants of antelope.

Washington would seem to have optimum habitat in some parts of its southeast, but the Columbia River had always been the northern limit of the western part of the pronghorns' range, and the animals have not done well north of the Columbia. Washington's pronghorn herd has not prospered.

Hawaii stocked pronghorns, but the results were not exactly spectacular. It all began when qualified wildlife biologists noted that there was an unoccupied big-game animal niche on the island of Lanai. The Hawaiian Pineapple Company owned almost all of the 141-square-mile island. Only 14,000 acres were in pineapple pro-

Restocked antelope being released after a long trip. New Mexico Game and Fish Department photo.

duction, and the company had dedicated almost all of the rest of the island to wildlife. In so doing, the company had turned over the wildlife management of the entire island to the State of Hawaii.

Much of Lanai rises to 3000 feet above sea level, and that habitat was occupied by feral goats, gone very wild and hunted as game animals on a regular basis.

The lower elevations, from 500 feet down to sea level, contained a healthy herd of Axis deer, carefully managed for hunting, and producing a lot of sport.

Still another niche, from 500 feet up to about 1200 feet above sea level, was kept for mouflon sheep — in all the lower elevations that did not seem to be suited to Axis deer.

That left about 35 square miles of the upper slopes, not forested enough for the Axis deer, which did not seem to be suited to goats, Axis deer, or mouflon. Although vegetation was lush and abundant, including many species that seemed to be ideal for pronghorn antelope, no big-game animal had found its way to this 35-square-

The Impossible Dream

mile habitat.

Resident wildlife biologist Lyman Nichols, sent to Lanai in 1957, started thinking about the unoccupied niche of wildlife habitat—and concluded that it seemed to present an ideal situation for pronghorned antelope. He began the investigations which led to the State's decision to go ahead with the experimental transplanting of pronghorns onto Lanai.

Jim McLucas and company trapped 56 pronghorns in Montana, and Jim accompanied the shipment to Hawaii. This is the same Jim McLucas who showed us North Dakotans how to handle the trapped antelope that went to North Dakota in 1954. Jim was probably the most experienced pronghorn trapper in the world by that time.

The shipment was made in 4 x 4 x 8-foot plywood crates, each holding five or six animals. After thorough checking for disease, they were trucked from Montana to Seattle and then by ocean freighter to Honolulu. They were delivered in Honolulu on December 9, 1959. Twelve failed to survive the trip, with the deaths enroute blamed on pneumonia due to cold and rainy weather. The remaining 44 were disposed of in this manner: four were given to the Honolulu Zoo, and 40 were flown from Hickam Air Force Base to Lanai for release. Two more died between Honolulu and Lanai.

Now comes the sad, but comical, part. The 38 animals were released into a small holding pen at the 1700-foot elevation. When they were all grouped together, the gate was opened and they were eased into freedom. Because there were no natural waterholes on Lanai, artificial water units had been established for the pronghorns. But the pronghorns took one look at the huge lake—the Pacific Ocean—and decided to run down there and get themselves a drink. They bypassed the water units and went all the way down to the ocean, forcing their way through thorny algaroba trees enroute. They took one taste of the salt water and were dumbfounded. Clean blue water wasn't supposed to taste that way, certainly not to a pronghorn raised on the plains of Montana.

Attempts were made to drive the animals back up to the freshwater units provided for them. To escape the drive, some of the pronghorns took to the sea and tried to swim out over the reef. The famous Hawaiian surf discouraged them and they were quickly back on the sand. No animals were lost to the sea, although it is feared that two died later as a result of drinking salt water. The "release" fiasco was seemingly over. Most of the pronghorns found the freshwater units atop the preferred level and seemed to settle down into their new habitat. Inexplicably, only 18 remained from the original 56 trapped half a world away.

The lush vegetation and heavy dew seemed to conspire against the pronghorns, and many developed a bad case of the scours. As a result of careful observation of the entire transplanting operation, it was learned that adults were able to withstand the trauma of the transplant much better than the juveniles. It was suggested that future transplanted pronghorns should be tranquilized so that they would go slowly—giving them a better chance of finding the water units. It was also suggested that future releases—if any—should be made where the pronghorns could not see the ocean and make that fatal saltwater mistake. It was hoped that tranquilizers would avoid the losses caused by panicky animals running into the thorny algaroba and into thickly forested areas.

As of 1961, it seemed as if the transplant was an unqualified success. The herd grew phenomenally to a high of 216 animals in 1965. In 1966, the only hunt was held, and 27 bucks and six does were harvested. But then the impossible dream turned sour. The herd declined to the present. In answer to my question in mid-1985, game wildlife biologist Timothy W. Sutterfield estimated the Lanai population of pronghorns at a pitiful five animals. Stating that the exact causes of the decline cannot be pinpointed, he pointed to a possible mineral deficiency, poaching in the very limited habitat, or rapid succession of plants on the pronghorn's range.

Perhaps the most significant factor was the simple fact that only 35 square miles of suitable habitat were present. That is simply not enough room to give the noble experiment a real try. To all intents and

Pronghorns being loaded into truck after capture. Restocking release will be made on the same day, if possible. *New Mexico Game and Fish Department photo.*

purposes, the pronghorned antelope is not present in Hawaii as of today.

A fascinating sidelight of the Hawaiian transplant is that the pronghorns on Hawaii became different animals insofar as breeding habits were concerned. Under the romantic influence of the perfumed islands, the pronghorns changed from once-a-year breeding animals to animals that bred throughout the year. In his thought-provoking book, *The Social Contract*, Robert Ardrey points out that the ability to offer sex the year around, thus greatly strengthening the pair bond, is perhaps the greatest evolutionary achievement of the human female. It is too bad that the Hawaiian experiment was too limited in scope; it might have meant a revolution in pronghorn reproduction.

Florida stocked pronghorns on January 23, 1966, when 38 Colorado pronghorns were released on Maxcy's Ranch in Okeechobee County. This Kissimmee Valley was selected as a release site because it is flat prairie and possesses some similarity to the optimum antelope range found in the West.

All of the antelope had disappeared by September 4, 1966. At least, none were found in the weekly search by plane and helicopter. The reporting biologist said that he had last seen a live pronghorn on June 10, when he counted eight within one-half mile of the release site.

The report by Florida Game and Fresh Water Fish Commission biologist Carlton Chappell does not hazard a guess as to why the transplant failed so dramatically and so quickly. One local wildlife officer reported that he had heard rumors of five being taken illegally, but could not confirm that rumor.

Major Kenneth L. Stivers, director of Florida's Office of Informational Services, in a personal letter to me, stated that the "animals, unfortunately, were unable to adapt to the habitat conditions in the Florida Everglades, so the experiment failed." Why they failed to adapt is, of course, the question. It is too bad that the reasons for the Florida failure are not known.

If we remember that cattle prosper on most antelope ranges and that cattle are very numerous in Florida, ranking in the top three or four states in numbers, then we are puzzled as to why the pronghorns couldn't make a go of it. Remember these adaptable animals survive in the furnace heat of the Baja Peninsula and the cold blizzards of the Dakotas and Saskatchewan. But the impossible dream failed in Florida.

According to some accounts, South Carolina and Louisiana also tried to stock pronghorns. But reports have not been verifiable.

Louisiana's information officer, Bob Dennie, put it this way: "In reference to the pronghorn. I have discussed this project with all the grey beards here and no one can ever recall these critters being in Louisiana, nor any reference to them. I have searched the archives and other reference material to no avail."

Somewhere in the distant past, some researcher printed the story that the pronghorned antelope had been released into the wilds of South Carolina as a transplant. This story has been repeated for many years, in other research reports.

I wondered about this, for the State of South Carolina is a lovely place, and it is a grand wildlife state, but it is not a home for pronghorned antelope. The humid forestlands of South Carolina, the swampy lands, the festoons of Spanish moss—lovely, but not for antelope that require barren pastures, gravelly soils, and rocky outcroppings as the centerpieces of their scenery. In an effort to track down this report, I wrote to the South Carolina Department of Wildlife and Marine Resources, and received a reply from Mr. Derrell Shipes, deer project leader: "I can find no record and have no information concerning the release of pronghorn in South Carolina. The animal was not native to the state and does not presently occur within the state."

Mr. Shipes went on to postulate a reasonable explanation for this error in print. He noted that South Carolina comes next to South Dakota (an excellent pronghorn state) in any alphabetical listing and that, somehow or another, some researcher may have read from the wrong line. Could be. One thing is certain: If the pronghorn was stocked into South Carolina, I will now hear about it. But, as of today, there are no pronghorns in the wild in South Carolina.

6

From Montana with Love

My first experience in trapping and transplanting pronghorned antelope came in 1954, when I was working for the North Dakota Game and Fish Department. With biologists Bill McKean, Art Brazda, and Jim Sjordahl, I went to Townsend, Montana, to "pick up" approximately 130 antelope for transfer to North Dakota. The plan was to release them in the Prophet's Mountain-Dogden Butte area, east of the Missouri River. This would be the first-ever release east of the Missouri, which had seemed to be a natural eastern limit to pronghorns for several decades.

"Picking up" the pronghorns proved to be more than we had bargained for.

The capture method was this: Veteran flier Cliff McBratney would pilot a small aircraft and locate the antelope, then herd them into a run for the trap. The trap was a series of heavy rope mesh walls that narrowed to a funnel-like opening into a high walled catch pen. There was a small holding pen connected to the side of the big catch pen. More about that later.

McBratney, who had more than 7500 hours in small planes, knew his job and did it well. He found a herd of 65 and brought them on the run. His technique seemed to be to get the antelope running on a course that would bring them past the open mouth of the wing walls leading to the trap. At the precise instant that they were in perfect position, he would roar in, wheels almost clipping the ground, and scare the antelope into a 90-degree turn that put them into the trap before they had time to realize that they were going between walls. His technique worked well, as he corralled 65 the first day and 81 the second day.

McBratney, who was perhaps in his 70s,

had tried many different ways of herding antelope from fixed-wing aircraft. At times he had used a syrup pail with stones in it, dangling at the end of a rope. He used to bounce it on the ground at the appropriate time, and said that it was effective. But the inevitable happened: He caught his pail on a sagebrush and nearly pulled his arm off. End of that tactic. He also carried along an 83-year-old friend who popped away indiscriminately with a 22 automatic pistol. It is doubtful if the antelope ever heard the tiny report of the run above the roar of the engine, but the reason Cliff stopped the shooting was that his passenger—although he enjoyed the acrobatics in flight—was seldom able to point to the ground with certainty. Some of the bullets went flying off into the air, destination unknown. So Cliff eliminated the shooting, calling it unnecessary. He refined his tactics, and eventually became one of the foremost authorities on the subject of antelope reactions when being chased by an airplane.

But it was after the pronghorns were penned that our troubles started. The Montana men who were experienced in this type of thing didn't come out to help us that first morning. We had to catch each antelope, take a blood sample, put an identifying colored tag in its ear, then load the animals into the semi-trailer stock truck that would take them to their new home.

It seemed simple enough: We would simply start the frightened animals circling around the round catch pen, open the side door, and let one antelope at a time into the holding pen. Then we would manhandle the beast, subdue it, take blood samples, and attach an ear tag.

Art Brazda, who went on to a distinguished career as pilot-biologist with the U.S. Fish and Wildlife Service, was a big, rugged man in the prime of life. A former

Wildlife managers crowd captured pronghorns by moving the solid wall forward. *South Dakota Game, Fish and Parks photo.*

Penned pronghorns await their fate. *South Dakota Game, Fish and Parks photo.*

high-school football player, Art was ready for anything. Stripping off his jacket, Art put on his work gloves and got into the "holding pen." We circled the antelope and opened the door to let just one animal into the holding pen. But we didn't take into account how fast these animals could move. There was a blur of tan and white, a cloud of dust, and Art was suddenly jammed flat against the far end of the holding pen by the press of 22 frightened antelope. That didn't work too well. We thought it over and tried other ways of putting just one or two in the pen at a time. Finally, we fooled one young buck. He jumped into the holding pen and we slammed the door shut before he could reverse his course. Art moved in for the catch.

There was a huge cloud of dust, a blurred whirling of man and pronghorn, and then Art loomed up out of the cloud of dust. He had the antelope in a bear hug, clutched around the middle, just behind the front legs, and he held the 100-pound animal off the ground. Blood streamed from Art's forehead. "I believe the bastard drew blood!" Art yelled. We moved in and got the necessary blood sample and ear-tagged the buck, then lugged him to the waiting semi-trailer.

The second antelope ripped Art's blue jeans all the way down one side. The third one caused more damage. Art was a tough man, but obviously he had little chance of enduring the capture of all 134 antelope. Putting two men into the holding pen helped a little, but only a little. When we had 13 antelope processed, Art's blue jeans were a series of rags hanging from

Young antelope in capture pen. Adults withstand trauma of capture and handling better than the youngest do. *South Dakota Game, Fish and Parks photo.*

Wild melee develops in the catch pen as frantic pronghorns leap over prostrate biologists who are each wrestling one animal. *South Dakota Game, Fish and Parks photo.*

his belt and his long johns were beginning to show the wear.

About that time our Montana friends arrived on the scene. Jim McLucas, trapping foreman for the Montana department, had handled more than 4000 antelope in their transplanting efforts. He was experienced. He taught us how it should be done. Getting into the holding pen, McLucas showed us how to reach over the animal's back, grab the near foreleg, and lift the antelope on a bent knee. He did it all so smoothly, and the antelope, finding all four feet off the ground and its weight supported against McLucas' leg, didn't even struggle.

With McLucas' help, the 134 animals were all loaded by noon, and the two big trucks drove straight through—about 850 miles from Townsend, Montana, to the release site east of the Big Muddy. We were told that the antelope would not lie down inside the truck, but would remain on their feet for the entire journey. Before the trucks even pulled out, all of the animals were lying down, and most of them stayed down for the entire trip. They were bedded on hay, and some even chewed on the hay during the long trip.

When we released the antelope, before a small group of active wildlifers, I got ready with camera to record the historic moment. I used a big 4 × 5 Speed Graphic in those days. I signaled that I was ready, and one of the men opened the big door. I hadn't counted on the antelopes' quick-

The late Wendell Bever, one of wildlife management's immortals, bulldogs a penned pronghorn in western South Dakota. *South Dakota Game, Fish and Parks photo.*

When human movements are slow and quiet, pronghorns can be maneuvered easily, but let them get excited and it is like trying to saddle a bumblebee with boxing gloves on. *New Mexico Game and Fish Department photo.*

ness. The first animal out was a big buck—they tell me! I missed him and recorded the next three as they jumped out, all three on one shot.

This transplant would seem to have been nearly perfect. The source of supply was easy; Montana had more antelope than antelope hunters in those days, and they wanted to cut back the herd size before it overgrazed its range. That took care of supply. Demand was ensured by the careful work done by Bill McKean and Art Brazda in preparing the public for the restocking. They enlisted the help of wildlife clubs in Garrison, McClusky, Velva, and Turtle Lake to publicize the idea. Mass meetings were held, at which the two biologists answered landowner questions about the probable results of adding antelope to the farmlands of McLean County. In addition, a letter was sent to all landowners in the area, asking for their reaction to the proposal. A high percentage of respondents favored the transplant. The few who didn't were (understandably) worried about antelope damage to standing crops, especially to flax.

Despite the good planning and the cooperation of landowners, this transplant wasn't a permanent success. At first the herd prospered. In 1961, the State Game and Fish Department was able to open a limited-permit hunting season in the area. During the next 17 years, 13 hunts were held. The seasons were very well regulated, with a total of only 1200 permits being issued in the years from 1961 to 1977. Roughly 1000 pronghorns were taken in these hunts. Then winter changed things, as it so often changes things in North Dakota. A sleet storm in early December covered this area with ice as much as one inch thick. Forced to move or starve, the herd began to drift southward along the east side of the Missouri River. A couple of hundred pronghorns actually came right into the state capital city of Bismarck. In their weakened condition, many of the antelope died—because of harassment by both dogs and humans.

The herd split, with half going right through Bismarck and the other half crossing the frozen Missouri to the Mandan side. The group that tried to run the gauntlet of Bismarck was wiped out! According to biologist Jim McKenzie, the deaths were directly attributable to dog kills, road kills, disease, starvation, direct freezing, and smothering. Indirectly, however, all of the deaths were attributable to the sheet of ice that blanketed the antelopes' winter food supply.

The group that crossed the river to the Mandan side was pushed onto lands owned by the Amoco Refinery, and there some 40 of them lived through the winter of 1977–1978. Permitted to leave the refinery grounds early the next spring, these 40 head rejoined the "west river" herds in North Dakota.

In all fairness to the antelope herd from Dogden Butte-Prophet Mountain, it should be pointed out that their home range had been converted from grasslands to agricultural lands during the 23 years from 1954 to 1977. Again, man had crowded out an antelope population. It was during that period that circle irrigation became popular in North Dakota — the kind of irrigation system where a long section of pipe topped with sprinklers travels around a center point — and thousands of acres were diverted from range into what was then a new cash crop for Dakota — sunflowers.

However, transplanting continued in North Dakota as well as most other states within the historic occupied range of the pronghorn. It worked. The antelope increased and multiplied — one of the greatest success stories in the history of wildlife management.

7

Pronghorn Habits

Migration from summer to winter pastures, and vice versa, seems to be an inherited trait of pronghorns, one that does not serve them well in today's world. It is possible that there was a compelling reason for migrations in eons past, but it is hard to find those reasons today.

In 1929, Grinnell wrote: "The habits of antelope which greatly contributed to its destruction were its seasonal migration from a summer to a winter range, and its gathering on the winter range in great herds from which large numbers were slaughtered by meat hunters. . . . the migration routes over which the antelope shifted from summer to winter range, were as well determined as were the migration routes of the elk or of the mule deer, and were well known to local hunters."

Weather conditions, or at least weather changes, trigger the movements of pronghorn herds. The distance is seldom great, but rather involves a movement from exposed flat plains to slightly more protected areas, or to areas where winter forage is more readily accessible. Some herds seem to have an ingrained migration pattern, which is triggered by the coming of the first snows. The logic of their migration is seldom apparent, though. In other words, the winter range differs so slightly from the summer range that it might have been better to forego the annual movement. This migration could serve to spare the forage from overgrazing, although the browsing or foraging patterns of individual pronghorns are such that overgrazing is hardly to be feared. The pronghorn seldom eats a plant to the destructive stage, but rather takes a nip here and a bite there, thus sparing the forage.

Drought conditions will trigger rather

Aerial view of pronghorn herd running. Picture is unusual in that a prime buck is leading. More often an adult doe leads the herd. *BLM photo.*

remarkable migrations at times, with the herds making long journeys to areas where water is available, or where range conditions are better. However, this is not an annual happening, but is rather a reaction to abnormal conditions. The provision of auxiliary watering places will prevent such migrations, and can be a management technique—if food is not also extremely scarce as a result of drought.

Some researchers speak of migrations to areas that are inaccessible to hunting. To my eyes, this is silly—for the mobile, modern hunter is capable of reaching any area that pronghorns can reach.

Respected authority Einarsen stated that pronghorns should not be classed as migratory animals. They may change feeding areas several times a year, but do not exhibit an annual rhythm to their movements. Kansas research shows that pronghorn herds do move to take advantage of seasonally-available forbs and even of newly available domestic crops.

There is a very definite possibility that the pronghorn is much less migratory in habits than he was before man put so many obstacles in his path. Seton and Audubon wrote of regular seasonal migrations that involved tens of thousands of animals and which were definitely repeated every spring and fall. These movements were observed before fences, of

During summer, the larger bucks are usually found off by themselves. These four bucks were photographed on the Fort Wingate Ordnance Depot in western New Mexico, during July.

course. In the reality of the 1980s, migration is a tough act considering the fences that have sprung up across every single mile of most migration routes. Pronghorns do not handle fences well, as discussed elsewhere in this volume. Way back in 1877, Caton wrote about the pronghorn's jumping ability: "The inability to leap over high objects may no doubt be attributable to the fact that they live upon the plains, where they rarely meet with such obstructions, and so they and their ancestors for untold generations have had no occasion to overleap high obstructions, and thus from disuse they do not know how to do so, and never attempt it when they meet them."

Einarsen, who stated that pronghorns should not be classed as "migratory," has written of observing pronghorns crossing large rivers during seasonal movements. Pronghorns enter the water readily when a river or lake is in their way. They swim well, seemingly buoyed up by that coat of hollow hairs which traps a lot of air to assist in flotation.

A Texas report by Tommy L. Hailey, a competent observer, states that: "Perhaps at one time during distant history, the pronghorn antelope herds were migratory somewhat like the buffalo; however, it is doubtful that their migrations ever approached the magnitude of the buffalo. Although some herds in the northwestern states annually migrate between winter and summer ranges, covering distances exceeding 100 miles, in Texas antelope may never have migrated great distances on a time-period basis. In Wyoming, according to Rouse (1954) antelope movements were apparently more affected by storms, forage supplies and availability of water than by any fixed migration pattern or seasonal movement. In Texas, Buechner (1950) noted that movements of as much as 5 to 10 miles within pastures or between pastures fenced with barbed wire are related to weather, fawning seasons and grazing conditions."

To sum up the migration question: Pronghorns are much less migratory now than in past centuries, simply because there are so many barriers placed (by man) in their way. Obviously, this situation will become more limiting, rather than easing, so we can expect that the pronghorn will completely lose its tendency to migrate over distances. Short seasonal movements to take advantage of forage changes, or to reach more sheltered wintering areas, will undoubtedly continue.

The Buck and His Harem

It has been written many times that the pronghorn buck is one of the most lustful creatures in all the animal kingdom. Personally, I find this a bit much to swallow. True, the polygamous pronghorn wants as many mates as he can gather—and keep—together. He is quite capable of impregnating as many as 30 does, if they are available to him, although the conditions of open range make this unlikely.

In normal conditions, the buck begins trying to gather a harem in late August. At this time, the mature bucks seem to take a great interest in bedding areas used by the does and routinely approach these areas and sniff them. Obviously, the sense of smell tells the buck that estrus is near. At this time of the year, the buck usually will approach every doe he sees lying down. When he gets near, the doe will hurriedly get up and move away. The buck then sniffs the bedding area and goes on about his business.

During this late-August to mid-September period, the bucks show great interest

Typical summertime grouping of Wyoming antelope.

A pronghorn buck keeps watch over four of his harem in early September, Wyoming.

in any area where does or fawns have urinated or defecated. He usually will go to these areas and sniff them. Then he will usually urinate on the same spot. At the same time, he will often paw the ground with his forefeet, even to the extent of actually scooping out a trough in the dirt.

As September wears along, the bucks gather the mature does together in harems. Each buck's ambitions are bigger than his ability, for he tries to gather all of the does in sight. This provides him with enough exercise to last the full year. He must chase each doe individually and herd her back toward the harem center. As soon as he gets her back into the harem, another will set out on a trot, and he must go after her.

There is no resting period in this game. If the buck does not chase the doe and bring her back into the harem, one of two things will happen. Most often, the doe, with her feelings hurt by his obvious lack of desire for her charms, will circle around and come back close enough to entice the buck again—and this will force him to again chase her and add her to the harem. On rare occasions, however, the doe will go on to join another harem. Seemingly, the does enjoy this game, for they will slow up and let the buck catch them if he seems to lag behind.

Harems as large as 35 does have been reported, but this occurs only when overhunting has reduced the number of dominant bucks available to handle the breed-

Pronghorn Habits

ing chores in fall. Normal conditions lead to harems of as few as five does and as many as 18.

Breeding takes place in late September and early October over most of the pronghorns' range. Although the dominant male often allows smaller and weaker bucks to join the harem herd, these smaller bucks do not attempt to breed the does when this occurs. In other words, the dominant buck does all of the breeding in the harem. Exceptions to this occur when sub-dominant males sneak in from their position on the perimeter of the harem and find a receptive doe while the master is attending to other chores. This does happen, but it is still true that the dominant males does about 90 percent of the actual breeding. Biologists believe that most copulation takes place at night, and that the displaying, posturing, fighting over does, and other signs of the rut take up most of the daylight hours. At night, the harem is less apt to move around, and the dominant buck claims each receptive doe when his sense of smell tells him that she is ready to accept his advances.

Unlike white-tailed and mule deer bucks, which can be very rough in their lovemaking—actually using their antlers to punish the doe when she is not receptive—the pronghorn buck is patient and waits until the doe shows signs of being receptive. Then he approaches her, swinging his head from side to side as a signal. He will hold his head over her withers, or sometimes over her back. If the doe wants a little bit more time, she keeps on walking. If she is ready, she stops walking and the buck will mount her almost immediately. As with all ungulates, coitus takes only seconds. Here we must make a distinction between the two acts of "mounting" and "coitus." Does often allow younger bucks to mount them, to get into position for breeding, but not actually

Early in the courtship period, young buck follows the doe. When the breeding period actually starts, the harem boss will run this young buck away from the does.

At the onset of the breeding season, a young buck attempts to mount a doe. She refuses his favors by simply continuing to walk. *South Dakota Game and Fish Photo.*

penetrate. This is mounting. But when the dominant buck mounts the doe, he almost never fails to penetrate and complete the act of coition.

About 60 percent of all coition takes place after the sun drops to the horizon, the twilight period being the onset of mating, which reaches a peak during the darkness hours and slows down and almost stops at sunrise.

Researchers are almost unanimous in believing that every mature doe is bred every year, regardless of the number of bucks available to handle the chores. In other words, if there are only five bucks per 100 does, all does will be bred. If there are 50 bucks per 100 does, again all does will be bred. Because the pronghorn is a gregarious "herd" animal, every doe that comes in heat is found by the vigilant buck, and copulation takes place. In more solitary ungulates, it is possible—although not probable—that a receptive female will not be found by a mature male during the period when she is in estrus.

Although some yearling does have been bred in their first rutting season, the norm is for does to breed for the first time in their second season. The period of gestation is approximately 240 days. However, captive females, watched closely from copulation to parturition, had gestation periods of as much as 252 days. Another competent study in California put the gestation period at between 217 to 220 days. We still stick with the 240-day estimate. Obviously, there are exceptions, just as there are in human pregnancies.

Although the actual timetable varies with the latitude (but only slightly), most fawns are dropped into the world during the month of June. Their mothers are very nervous and fidgety during the last two weeks or so of their pregnancy, and will often take flight and "spook" away from things that usually would not bother them at all. Their graceful silhouettes have filled out with the growth of the fawn(s), and they are much less agile than before.

The doe goes off by herself, if possible, and carefully picks her fawning area. This choice is one of the most important ever made by any pronghorn, for the survival of the fawn is definitely affected by the kind of cover chosen. If the cover is sufficiently lush to do a good job of hiding the fawn(s), they stand a good chance of not being found by coyotes, bobcats, or other predators during the first three days of their lives. After that, they are able to outrun any but the most determined coyote pair, and their chances of living to a ripe old age (and Texas has recorded lifespans in the wild of as much as 12 years) are very good. This is why the elimination of sagebrush over much of the western range has been such a catastrophe for the pronghorn. Waist-high sage has been the best fawning cover for this species since time immemorial. Without it, the doe drops her fawns in sparse cover, the predator finds them, and that is the end of that year's crop from that doe.

When time for birth approaches, the doe—now off by herself, in good fawning habitat—will become very restless. She will get up and lie down again all the time, and will often turn round and around,

Sexually mature buck attempts to copulate with a doe. *South Dakota Game and Fish photo.*

Although sagebrush is preferred fawning habitat, this young fawn is holding tight in sparse vegetation. Note how light and shadow help his camouflage. *BLM photo.*

making a motion similar to the one a dog uses when it's about to lie down in tall grass. When the birthing process is underway and the fawn is partially extruded, the doe will get up and turn about, almost whirl about, as if anxious to rid herself of the burden. This turning and whirling motion may actually aid the birthing process — sort of helping to move the fawn through the birth canal by centrifugal force.

The fawn is dropped, and I do mean *dropped*. Perhaps the impact of hitting the ground starts the newborn fawn to breathing? The doe will immediately begin licking the newborn fawn, which is already struggling to stand up, and may begin eating the birth membranes. As there is almost always a second fawn waiting to be born, the process is quickly repeated. The second fawn usually makes its way into the world more easily than the first born, for reasons that I do not understand. Does conceiving for the first time usually have but one fawn. After that, twins are an almost unvarying rule. In 1962, Tileston reported that: "though the percentage is high in antelope, twinning is not the result of a single egg splitting in the early stages of development, but the result of double ovulation and fertilization. Examination of the published records show that both male and female embryos frequently occur in the same uterus. Thus, if it were a case of identical twinning (both embryos rising from a single egg) the sexes would always be the same, i.e. both female or both male."

Pronghorn Habits

In less than one hour, the doe is teaching the newborn fawns to follow her, urging them to come with her by making a bluff at leaving them, then waiting for them to catch up. This first hour or two is very important to the newborn, for it is during this time that he is imprinted on his mother and vice versa. She now knows the scent of her own offspring and can unerringly pick them out of a herd.

Within this first hour, the doe is also allowing the newborn to take their first meal. She will stand with her back bent in a concave arc to make the udder more easily accessible to the teetering, wobbly fawn. Once he learns how to find the teat, he feeds eagerly and roughly. The fawn quickly gets his tiny stomach filled with the rich milk, with nursing lasting less than a full minute in most cases of newborn feedings. When the doe feels that her fawn has had enough to eat, she shuts off the faucet by simply walking away. In some cases she may knock the newborn fawn off his feet as she moves away. Later on, when the fawns are larger, they may have to get down on bended knees to put their muzzles in the proper position to nurse from the doe's udders.

During their first three days, the fawns remain hidden, except when they stand up to nurse. The doe leaves them and feeds at a distance, not wanting to attract attention to the hidden fawns by her presence. So

A day-old fawn assumes the hiding position. Fawns remain motionless even when closely approached, during the first few days of their lives. *South Dakota Game, Fish and Parks photo.*

Innately curious, young pronghorns approach the photo blind in northeastern Wyoming.

well trained are they to lie perfectly still, "feigning death" in the words of one researcher, that they will usually hold their position even when the doe approaches quite near to their hiding place. Once she stops walking, however, they jump up and run quickly to nurse.

The antelope fawn is remarkably precocious, and can usually outrun a man when it is only 36 hours old. Researchers attempting to tag or attach radio-telemetry transmitters to the young antelope face a difficult decision. If they touch and handle very young pronghorns, it is possible (but not probable) that the doe will abandon them, as she has not yet completed the process of "imprinting" on and with her own young. On the other hand, if they wait until the imprinting is completed, the biologists find themselves faced with the problem of trying to catch a 3-day-old youngster. Even armed with a long-handled net, the biologist is at a distinct disadvantage, for the pronghorn's middle name is "fast," even when only days old. However, if the handling is accomplished quickly, and the humans leave the vicinity quickly, the doe in most cases will return to her young and quickly grow accustomed to the strange odor of men on her own fawns. Her usual reaction then is to move the fawns to a different hiding place, but not to abandon them.

By the fourth day, the fawn is able to keep up with his mother on quarter-mile runs. It is rare for the pronghorn to run more than a quarter of a mile at a stretch, except when alarmed by man or man's machines. At 2 weeks of age he can often outstrip his parent.

A curious thing about pronghorn running is that they—old and young, male and female—commonly run with the mouth wide open and the tongue hanging out. This makes them look as if they are completely exhausted, but this is not the case. It seems to me that the tongue is simply put out of the way, so as to allow the maximum air flow into the windpipe. Pronghorns possess oversized windpipes, oversized lungs, and a very big heart for the size of the body. This equipment explains their ability to run fast for long distances. However, it is not unheard of for a pronghorn to fall dead from exhaustion when forced to run long distances.

At 5 months old, this young pronghorn can easily outrun any man.

Curiosity killed more than the cat. This young pronghorn knows that something is there, but what and where? *Photo by Judd Cooney.*

Chewing the Cud

Like most grazing and browsing animals, the pronghorn has a complicated digestive system that enables him to bring up previously swallowed food, and chew it again, before returning it to the stomach again. This is called rumination, and animals that "chew the cud" are known as ruminants.

Why?

Much of the forage of the pronghorn is very rough and woody in character. It obviously needs to be chewed very thoroughly before the digestive juices can convert it to usable proteins and carbohydrates. But the pronghorn evolved over millennia when large predators were watching, eager to dine on them. Because of this, animals which fed avidly, taking but a short time to fill the paunch, had an evolutionary advantage over those which fed slowly. Minimizing the period of time during which they are exposed to the eyes of predatory animals was undoubtedly a trait to be desired. Those that fed quickly, then went back into safer habitats to finish the job of chewing, were more apt to live long enough to pass on their habits.

We call the wad of partially chewed food a *bolus*. When the pronghorn thinks it is safe, and in a relaxed mood, the bolus is regurgitated into the mouth and chewed again, with the food ground into a pulpy mass that the stomach is better able to handle than before the second chewing. If the animal is startled while ruminating, it will immediately swallow the bolus—no matter what the stage of chewing is—and be ready to handle the emergency without having its mouth full of food. One time, in Wyoming, I saw a mature pronghorn buck shot while standing quietly, chewing its cud. The bolus filled the entire mouth cavity of the pronghorn when we went up to examine the instantaneous kill. Perhaps it is my imagination, but it has seemed to me that the pronghorn is more apt to go to water after ruminating than before. The significance of this bit of trivia escapes me.

Drinking

Some strange words have been published concerning the question of whether or not the pronghorn needs to have free water to drink. I have read that they were able to accustom themselves to drinking sea water—which is not true. I have read that they invariably go to water every single day of the summer—which also is not true.

As usual, the correct answer lies somewhere in-between. The pronghorn is remarkably well adapted to arid lands, and his lean, elegant body can make do with remarkably little water. But he must drink free water once in a while to live. It is true that some desert vegetation, the cacti and succulents, sometimes, but not always, contain large amounts of water, and that the pronghorn can exist without free-standing water when he has a plentiful supply of such water-bearing plants. But this condition is a rare one, and it is my belief, after searching all the literature I could find on the subject, and after half a century of watching pronghorns, that the animal does require free-standing water, at some time or another, every week. I think that he requires it every 24 hours, but some evidence that the pronghorn stays away from water for periods longer than 24 hours makes me wary.

Let's see what others have to say about this matter. Henry Wicher is quoted by a Colorado Game and Fish Department publication as saying that pronghorns

Twin fawns are the pronghorn rule rather than the oddity. These two were hiding in very short cover, probably all that was available to the doe. *South Dakota Game, Fish and Parks photo.*

Pronghorns seem to realize that they are vulnerable when drinking. They often take a long time to approach, then drink quickly and move away at once. This buck is taking one last look before lowering his muzzle to the water. *Photo by Judd Cooney.*

generally drink every three days, and usually the biggest groups of animals drink near midday.

The same publication quotes Kautz as saying that females drank once daily while males seemed to frequent the watering areas a great deal less. Warren suggested that pronghorns drink once daily, but when water is scarce they will take considerable amounts of cacti which (usually) contain large quantities of water.

In 1924 Skinner reported that "antelope can flourish in deserts so waterless, so forbidding, that neither deer, goats, sheep, elk nor bison could exist for a week." I'll go along with that, but I insist that even in that "waterless" place, the antelope found water to drink. Antelope, coyotes, and desert bighorns once inhabited Tiburon Island, a seemingly waterless place in the Gulf of California, down Mexico way. I've been there in summer, and I defy any land mammal to exist there without standing water to drink. Its furnace-like temperatures will surely bring out the "water-seeking" qualities in any mammal. After long searching, I found several places where the coyotes water today—and I am sure that antelope and bighorns found those same places and many others, during the cen-

Suspicious and wary, this buck stares at photographer's blind before approaching waterhole in Colorado. *Photo by Judd Cooney.*

Water and mud are flying as this pronghorn buck explodes into action, startled by click of the camera. *Photo by Judd Cooney.*

Going to the waterhole is a social function, as well as a necessity. *Photo by Judd Cooney.*

turies that pronghorns existed on those Midriff Islands.

One of the foremost authorities on the pronghorn, Einarsen, stated that pronghorns have no preference for freshwater springs over stagnant water. Pronghorns are pragmatists: It is the water they need, not the cool, clear water that the sons of the pioneers made famous.

In Texas research, Davis stated that the pronghorn evidently has the ability to conserve body water and to produce metabolic water. There is much evidence to support this belief, but I still feel that the pronghorn finds free water to drink, and that he finds it every single day of his life, in normal situations. When forced to do so, the pronghorn can go up to five days without free-standing water to drink, *if* (and this is a big if) water-bearing plants are available to him.

During the heat of summer, pronghorn watchers on the hot, dry plains of northeastern Wyoming have reported that the young and female pronghorns came to water as many as three times per day. Trophy bucks came only once a day. This squares with my observations in North

Pronghorns come to water daily when it is available, and they seem to show no preference for clean water over stagnant, muddy ponds. *Photo by Judd Cooney.*

Dakota, Wyoming, and New Mexico. I believe that the visit to the waterhole may be as much a social function as a necessity for life. I have watched young bucks in the rutting season, watched them approach the water as many as five times in a day, but fail to take on any water at any one of the visits. The does and fawns all drank on each trip.

Obviously, snow is an acceptable substitute for free water during winter. If it were not, the northern two-thirds of the pronghorn range would be uninhabited today. Pronghorns eat snow easily and casually, taking a drink now and then as they browse along. When there is snow upon the ground, antelope will seldom go far to free water. However, when liquid water is readily available to them, they will usually go to it at least once a day (again, in my experience), which may indicate that they find more satisfaction in liquid water than they do in nipping a mouthful of snow.

Obviously, conditions change with changed habitat. Water is of more concern to a sun-baked pronghorn on the scorched flats near Scammons Lagoon on the Baja Peninsula than it is to a pronghorn lolling in the lush green vegetation of a stream valley in central Montana. The availability of minerals may have an important bearing on the question of water need, too. Some researchers have reported that free-ranging pronghorns showed no interest in salt/mineral blocks; other researchers have found that scattering salt/mineral blocks had a good influence on spreading the pronghorn herds out across the available range.

Perhaps both researchers are correct. Perhaps the forage of one pasture contains everything the pronghorn needs, while another pasture leaves him with a driving need to find salt, or some other mineral, because it is not present in his natural diet.

Let's leave it at that. The pronghorn *does* need free water in summer, but he is perfectly adapted to survive on very little such water. If you want to improve conditions for your pronghorns, provide them with more water.

8

Pronghorns and Predators

No facet of wildlife management has been so hotly debated over the years as the subject of predators and their effect upon game animal populations. Let's start our discussion with a few facts:

1. Coyotes do kill newborn antelope, and have been shown to be *the* limiting factor on some antelope herds.
2. Predators have preyed on pronghorns for millennia, and they were not a limiting factor in the centuries prior to man's usurpation of pronghorn range for his own purposes.
3. Upon rare occasions, coyotes have been known to kill healthy adult pronghorns. The number of times this happens is statistically insignificant, according to most authorities.
4. Factors that reduce the pronghorn's mobility increase the damaging effects of predation; for example, woven-wire fences may increase the pronghorn's vulnerability to mortality caused by coyotes.
5. Pronghorn numbers showed a significant increase after the introduction of Compound 1080, the most effective coyote-killing agent ever developed. Some may argue that this is a case of "Post hoc, ergo propter hoc" reasoning, but the timing can hardly be coincidental, and the results are inarguably evident.

Before we go further into the subject of Compound 1080, let's dispel a few myths about this efficient predacide. First of all, its chemical name is sodium monofluoroacetate, and it got its short name of Compound 1080 because it was the 1080th compound investigated by U.S. Government scientists looking for lethal agents to be used in wartime against a human enemy. When its chemical properties became well known, it was turned over to the U.S. Fish and Wildlife Service for further study and possible use against coyotes.

It is a fine-grained white powder, amazingly soluble in water, or even humid air. When a tiny bit of 1080 is dissolved in water and the resulting diluted solution injected into large chunks of meat with a brine gun, the entire piece of meat becomes a deadly invitation to the banquet to canids and felines. There is no known antidote!

Compound 1080 is remarkably specific, in that it takes a tiny amount to kill a dog, wolf, coyote, or bobcat, yet it takes a ridiculously big amount of the treated meat to kill an opossum or badger, while a golden eagle or vulture is almost immune to the poison. I have personally observed a situation where a badger took up residence under a 200-pound piece of treated horse meat—in southwestern South Dakota—and lived there for four months, dining on the frozen meat all the while. When the meat became warm enough in the spring, the badger ingested huge quantities of the poisoned meat, and was very healthy when last observed. In fact, he objected vigorously when federal coyote killers removed the well-rotted remains of the bait in the springtime.

Actual testing, under caged-animal conditions, has resulted in development of LD 50 figures for most species. By LD 50, we mean the amount of properly prepared bait that will cause death in 50 percent of the individuals in a particular species (see accompanying table).

These figures are significant for they show that only a bite or two will kill any canine or feline, but that a vulture—the scavenger of the plains—couldn't possibly ingest enough of the properly treated bait to cause him to even have a bellyache.

The statement that secondary poisoning is a danger when 1080 is used is simply not borne out by field experience. According to the theory advanced by those who oppose the use of 1080, one animal dies and is fed upon by other animals that also die in a sort of "chain letter" series of mortalities that never ends. In actual field work, and I spent seven years of my life with Compound 1080, I have never observed any chain reaction. In fact, I know only

LD 50 Results

Species	LD 50 mg/kg	Average Weight	Amount of Bait Needed to Reach LD 50
Coyote	.1	30	1.4 oz.
Cat (domestic)	.2	3	.3 oz.
Fox	.3	12	1.6 oz.
Bobcat	.66	22	6.6 oz.
Bear	.15	300	68.0 oz.
Mink	1.00	3	1.4 oz.
Marten	1.00	3	1.4 oz.
Magpie	0.6–1.3	.5	0.1–0.3 oz.
Badger	1.0–1.5	19	8.0–13.0 oz.
Golden Eagle	1.25–5.0	7	4.0–15.9 oz.
Turkey Vulture	20.0	6	54.0 oz.

one case in which the second animal was killed by a meal of 1080. This was graphically illustrated by tracks in new snow in the Texas Panhandle when 1080 was first introduced there in the early 1960s. A coyote took a bite or two from a horse bait that had been treated with Compound 1080. He walked for half a mile, then exhibited the characteristic "motor nerves running wild, without a governor" effect of 1080, fell and died. In his death throes—and Compound 1080 does not produce a quick nor humane death—he vomited up the meat. A second coyote came to investigate the body of his dead kinfolk. Coyotes eating dead coyotes would be nothing new, of course. The second coyote ate the vomitus. I followed his tracks for several miles, then found him, still alive, but moribund. He would have died in a few more minutes. Upon killing him and opening the stomach, we found still recognizable horse meat. This was a rare occurrence, however. It is rare because of the high solubility of the chemical, which causes it to be quickly absorbed in the body with a great degree of dilution, thus making it no longer lethal to the next diner.

Compound 1080 is odorless and, supposedly, tasteless. It is readily accepted by almost any wildlife species, without suspicions being aroused. Yet there exists a "warning factor" of some kind, according to my observations. Because of this warning factor—I think the coyote simply gets a message that something is not quite right here—most carnivores ingest only a small amount of meat treated with Compound 1080. There are exceptions, of course. In the vicinity of Laredo, Texas, one coyote swallowed about 10 pounds of properly prepared 1080 horse meat. It simply wasn't his day, for he then ran into a snare placed in an opening in the fence and strangled himself before the poison could start its work. There were many coyotes in that area—enough to clean up a 1200-pound horse in one night!—and this may have accounted for the coyote's gluttony. He was simply trying to eat it all before his relatives arrived to compete for the windfall banquet presented by the poisoned bait.

Here are some items from around the pronghorn range in the western part of North America. Each item may be considered significant and, taken together, they all constitute evidence bearing on the question, "Do predators limit pronghorn populations?"

Item: From a Texas report in 1982: "Coyote depredation is a significant factor concerning fawning success, especially during recent years in the Panhandle where the number of fawns per 100 does has not exceeded 22 during each of the past four years. Coyote predation is a severe limiting factor in the Trans-Pecos also, but it is thought to have a net beneficial effect as it has removed sheep ranching from large areas of antelope habitat. Intensive grazing competition from domestic sheep is considered to be more detrimental to antelope survival than the lesser evil of coyote depredation."

That interesting sidelight was presented by Herbert G. Kothmann of the Texas Parks and Wildlife Department. My comment is that it would surely be nice if we could eliminate both coyote depredation upon antelope and competition between sheep and antelope. Here the trained Texas observer says that given a choice, he'll take coyotes over sheep any day.

Item: Antelope biologist James D. Yoakum of the Bureau of Land Management sums it up tersely in the book, *Big*

Game of North America, as follows: "Factors affecting the survival of pronghorns have been studied extensively for the past three decades. Of these, predation has been researched most. Coyotes and bobcats are recorded as the most consistent predators, especially on newborn fawns. Raptor predation is recorded as nominal."

Item: Robert E. Autenreith of the Idaho Department of Fish and Game reported on results of a pronghorn fawn mortality study as follows: "Mortalities began almost immediately after birth and continued for 15 to 20 days. Predator kills accounted for a 50% loss of transmittered fawns in 1978, 44% in 1979 and 29% in 1980. . . . Golden eagles were the most important predator, accounting for 8 kills. Coyotes took 7 fawns and bobcats accounted for 3. Six fawns were killed by unidentified predators."

Autenreith goes on to point out that the year-round use of this antelope range by feral horses had caused significant range deterioration. Would the antelope mortality have been less if the habitat provided concealment for the fawns?

Autenreith continues: "Total canopy coverage increased 60% in 1980 due to May precipitation 53% greater than normal. The resulting response, particularly in lupine, was dramatic and created an understory not seen in 1978 or 1979. This additional cover appeared to have importance in reducing the ability of predators to locate fawns. Neff and Woolsey (1979) indicated poor cover was a factor in the probability of coyotes locating bedded fawns in Arizona as did McNay (1980) in Nevada. Barrett (1981) determined that Alberta sagebrush lands contributed to the highest survival of antelope fawns."

Item: The Anderson Mesa (Arizona) study of coyote predation upon pronghorns is one of the classic cases. A recent magazine item asked, "Is the use of helicopters to shoot coyotes justified? Officials of the Arizona Game and Fish Department believe it is on the Anderson Mesa. In 1979, researchers working in Unit 5B on the mesa counted only 11 pronghorn antelope fawns for every 100 does. The biologists blamed coyotes. Each spring since then, U.S. Fish and Wildlife Service personnel, working from choppers, have shot coyotes on the mesa. The result? The count went up to 98 fawns for every 100 does."

Let's look a little more closely at this research project, shall we?

Anderson Mesa is a 7000-foot elevation plateau south of Flagstaff. It is summer range for a pronghorn herd that numbered as many as 3000 in the 1930s, dropped to 1500 in the 1950 aerial census, was decimated by a severe winter of 1967–1968, and then remained stable at 250 to 400 animals.

Arizona researchers state that "there is abundant evidence of coyote predation on neonatal fawns, confirming earlier research in coyote control in this area which has a 30-year history." The research team of Don C. Neff and Norman G. Woolsey of the Arizona Game and Fish Department concluded that coyote predation on neonatal fawns is the most important single factor and is largely responsible for the decline in numbers of the Anderson Mesa herd.

At the onset of their study, the Arizona researchers determined the rate of fetal pregnancies for the does in this herd. They did this by necropsies of winter killed does, and found the fawns per 100 does to be:

1974   130

1975	139
1976	164
1977	149
1978	132
1979	131

Obviously the pronghorn bucks had done their work. The Anderson Mesa does were pregnant at, or near, the normal rate. This enabled the researchers to determine that fawn mortality was postnatal. If the fawns died after birth, we have the problem of determining what killed them.

This was tackled by observations from Pine Hill Tower, which enabled the observers to record two actual instances of coyotes killing pronghorn fawns, and to see does that exhibited an agitated behavior indicative of the loss of fawns. They supplemented the data from these observations by using hounds trained to lead the observers to the remains of dead antelope.

In this manner, they were able to document the obvious, that coyotes were killing a high percentage of the antelope fawns produced on Anderson Mesa. In true scientific manner, Neff and Woolsey commented that they were "unable to rule out mortality factors such as malnutrition, disease, parasites, injuries or abandonment." However, they added that, of 865 antelope fawn observations, they had not seen one instance where any of these mortality factors was evident.

Now that they knew what was limiting recruitment of new individuals into the Anderson Mesa herd, what could be done about it? To quote from the Neff-Woolsey Report: "Steel trapping alone from January to June 1946 north of Canyon Diablo produced a July aerial survey ratio of 50 fawns per 100 does, while a similar but untrapped area south of Diablo produced only 17 fawns per 100 does."

Evidently, history showed that reducing the number of coyotes increased the survival of pronghorn fawns.

On the spring fawning grounds of Anderson Mesa, researchers found that 63 percent of the coyote scats contained pronghorn remains. The coyote was *the* limiting factor on herd increase. Need more proof?

Arizona records show the following picture, relating fawns per 100 does to the question of whether or not coyote control measures had been used in the Anderson Mesa locality. The results are shown in the accompanying table.

It doesn't take a genius to interpret these data. In years wherein coyote numbers were reduced by control methods, pronghorn does did not lose their fawns to coyotes at the same disastrous rate they did in years when coyote numbers were not controlled. Take a good look at 1969, when there were 93 fawns per 100 does still alive and well in the midsummer aerial census, as a result of coyote-reduction programs featuring Compound 1080 poison baits. 1080 was in use from 1948 to 1970.

To my mind, this Anderson Mesa study is the most convincing piece of evidence that we can — within limits — increase pronghorn populations by reducing coyote populations.

The Oregon Department of Fish and Wildlife came up with an interesting report in 1983, which summed up findings of their investigation into causes of pronghorn fawn mortality on two study areas, Bear Valley and Jackass Creek. In this research, the biologists captured 1- or 2-day-old fawns by simply watching the doe give birth from afar with a spotting

Anderson Mesa Coyote Control

Control Work During Preceding Winter		1 Yr. Since Control Work		2 or More Yrs. Since Control Work	
1946	62 fawns	1947	66	1944	30
1948	74	1951	62	1945	39
1949	79	1953	57	1956	62
1950	90	1955	66	1957	32
1952	81	1960	48	1958	34
1954	71	1971	55	1961	28
1959	80			1962	22
1966	69			1963	48
1967	67			1964	48
1969	93			1965	23
1970	74			1972	46
				1974	44
				1975	30
				1976	21
				1977	28
				1978	28
				1979	14

scope, then focussing the spotting scope on the spot where the doe hid her offspring when she went off to feed. Leaving the fawn for several hours or overnight allowed her time to clean it up and for the maternal bond to develop — as insurance against the doe abandoning the fawn after it had been handled by humans.

Capture was accomplished by encircling and then running down the fawn. In some cases, a large "salmon-landing" net was used to good effect because antelope fawns are remarkably nimble and speedy, even at the tender age of 2 days. Captured, the fawn was equipped with a special radio-telemetry collar that signaled its whereabouts to the watching biologists at all times.

When the radio transmitter remained in one place for long periods, the investigators hastened to the spot and determined the cause of death. To quote from page 42 of this excellent report: "Predation was the leading cause of fawn loss, accounting for 83 (91%) of the 91 mortalities occurring during this study. Most fawns that died were killed by coyotes — a finding corroborated by several observations of coyotes hunting and attacking fawns before neonates (newly born fawns: author) could be captured for instrumentation. Known and probable coyote kills comprised 55 (60%) of the 91 recorded fawn mortalities. Rates of fawn mortality resulting from coyote and probable coyote kills were 66 and 65%, at Jackass Creek in 1981 and 1982 respectively, and 31 and 17% at Bear Valley during 1981 and 1982 respectively. Although nearly all fawns perished at Jackass Creek each summer, losses occurred more rapidly in 1982."

The Oregon investigators found bobcats to be the cause of 8 percent of the mortality; golden eagles were blamed for 9 percent; and two fawns, 5 and 8 days of age, were killed by badgers. They also reported that, "Losses of fawns to causes other than predation were minimal."

This Oregon investigation shows clearly that coyotes are an important negative factor in pronghorn production. The study also pointed up that losses were worst where bedding cover was short, with fawn survival best where bedding cover was higher. However, pronghorn does in some parts of the study area showed a perverse preference for the shorter cover.

Oregon investigators did a very scientific job of correlating other factors that might have influenced their figures. The high population of coyotes at Jackass Creek and the very low population of coyotes at Bear Valley during part of the study period were quantified accurately and taken into account in assessment of the different mortality rates on the two study areas. They also kept records of the abundance of other natural coyote foods, such as jackrabbits and other rodents, on both study areas. By keeping close records of the physical condition of the does preparturition and by weighing and measuring the neonatal fawns, the researchers ruled out any chance that the very low survival rates could be attributed to a general poor condition of the breeding stock. Predation was the culprit: That is the message of this landmark study conducted in Oregon in 1981 and 1982. However, let's read a bit farther and note this from page 86 of the report: "Results of this study, as well as the analysis of 1946–1982 data, indicate that predation by coyotes is currently an important factor limiting pronghorn populations below the carrying capacity of the range in the Harney Wildlife District, including the Jackass Creek Area. Pronghorn populations at Bear Valley have recently been limited by hunter harvest and removals for transplanting. Emigration from Bear Valley may also be a factor keeping population growth from reaching potential. At present, neither predation nor nutrition appear to be limiting this population."

The report quoted so extensively is *Oregon State Game Commission's Wildlife Research Report Number 12*, and it is enthusiastically recommended to the serious student of this subject. The men responsible for this research work are Charles E. Trainer, Mitchell J. Willis, George P. Keister, Jr., and Dennis P. Sheehy.

Item: Howard Martley wrote a *History of Organized Cooperative Predator Control in Wyoming*, when he was an employee of the Bureau of Sport Fisheries and Wildlife. As Mr. Martley was engaged in coyote control work, his writing must be assessed as having a bias favoring this work. However, the logic of his summation merits its inclusion here:

"Since it is the firm belief of this writer that predator control played an important part in the almost phenomenal increase in some species of big game animals (in Wyoming) it is believed that this history will be enhanced by a few observations in this connection. The big game harvest was recorded by the (Wyoming) Game and Fish Commission as follows:

	1942 Seasons	*1952 Seasons*
Elk	9046	7816
Deer	11,980	40,433
Moose	121	437
Big Horn sheep	22	59
Antelope	6050	41,020

"Noting the increase in the pronghorn kill from 6000 to 41,000 between 1942 and 1952, we need only add the obvious fact that Compound 1080 was introduced to the coyotes of Wyoming in 1946, and that it had become the principal control agent by 1947."

I spent four interesting years in Texas, working with the Fish and Wildlife Service's program for controlling coyote numbers. It is my personal opinion that Texas had more coyotes than all the rest of the United States put together in the period 1959 through 1962. At least that's the way it seemed. It is interesting to note, also, that the individual trapper records for most coyotes killed in one month and most coyotes killed in a year were both set in Texas during that period.

A Texas Game and Fish Commission Report, dated 1979, has this to say:

"In Texas, predation has been considered a major factor in antelope population for a number of years. There have been many instances recorded throughout the years by field personnel of the Department which indicate that the coyote is a formidable foe of the antelope. Some of the typical happenings are as follows:

"In May of 1972, while conducting an aerial survey of a ranch near Valentine, Texas, the author (Tommy L. Hailey) observed two coyotes chasing a doe and two fawns. Subsequently each coyote selected a fawn and pressed their chase with vigor. The aircraft was used to distract one of the coyotes long enough for the fawn it was pursuing to escape. The coyote then went immediately to help its companion. With both coyotes working as a team, the second fawn was soon dragged down and killed despite repeated buzzings with the aircraft and persistent attacks by the mother antelope. The fawn, which appeared to be 3 to 4 weeks of age, was torn apart and most of it consumed within a short interval.

"While making an aerial survey in the Panhandle during July of 1969, two coyotes were seen stalking a fully grown buck antelope. From his actions, the buck was a normal healthy animal. The observers watched as the coyotes, working as a team, caught the animal after a chase of approximately one mile. Repeated low level buzzing with the aircraft drove the coyotes away and the buck escaped. However, it is evident that two or more coyotes can and do catch adult antelope as well as fawns.

"During May, June and July of 1969, 13 coyotes were collected from antelope fawning sites within the Trans-Pecos Area and an analysis made of their stomach contents. Five of the animals checked had nothing in their stomachs. Of the remaining eight coyotes, six analyses showed all or the majority of their diet to be composed of the remains of antelope fawns as determined from meat, hair and bones. Based on the data derived from the eight samples, their stomach contents consisted of 75 percent antelope, and 25 percent rabbits, small rodents, insects and grass.

"During the late fall and early winter months of 1971 and 1972, the U.S. Fish and Wildlife Service, in cooperation with landowners, placed sodium monofluoracetate (Compound 1080) within a 214,000 acre study area located north of Valentine, Texas, for the purpose of controlling coyotes. Horse meat was treated with the poison and distributed at the rate of two stations per township. The stations were baited in November 1970 and remained active until April 1971 when all bait was removed. During the winter of 1971–1972, the stations were baited in November, but had to be deactivated during the month of January 1972 as a result of an executive order of the President of the United States

(Nixon, in case your history memory is poor) declaring a moratorium on the use of certain poisons for predator control. During this same period a study was initiated by Texas Parks and Wildlife personnel to monitor the effects of the coyote control on antelope fawn production within the 214,000 acre study area. For several years prior to the Compound 1080 treatment, Department personnel had been receiving reports from landowners located within the area concerning antelope fawn losses attributed to predation by coyotes. Also records from the annual Trans-Pecos antelope census indicated that during the previous 5 year period (1966 through 1970) fawn production in this particular area was from 13 to 57 percent below the average for the Trans-Pecos Region (see accompanying table).

Antelope Fawn Production North of Valentine, Texas

Fawn Year	Study Area Percent Fawn Crop	Total Trans-Pecos Percent Fawn Crop
1966	30.66%	43.15%
1967	60.92%	70.01%
1968	32.28%	47.77%
1969	26.79%	62.25%
1970	28.89%	53.92%
1971	79.34%	63.66%
1972	64.65%	59.43%

"Results concerning fawn production on the study site following treatment with the 1080 compound were immediate and rather decisive. Fawn production on the area increased from only 29 percent during the summer of 1970 to a high of 79 percent during the summer of 1971. This was an increase of 25 percent over the average production for the rest of the Trans-Pecos area. In 1972, with only the short term treatment of the area with Compound 1080 (because of the stations having to be removed in January instead of in April), the fawn production was still 9 percent above the average for the rest of the Trans-Pecos region and at a production rate of 65 percent as compared to the 29% recorded during 1970 when no treatment for control of coyotes was used."

We have known that coyote predation limits pronghorn populations, and we have known it for many years. One of the most respected names in all of wildlife management, Ira Gabrielson, reported a happening way back in 1920. Listen to what he had to say: "An outstanding example of the effect of predator control occurred with the upswing of the antelope herd in the territory adjoining the common boundary of Nevada, Oregon and California. In that region a small herd remained in 1920 and 1921, when the species had reached its lowest ebb there. The antelope were protected by state laws, and there is little evidence that any considerable number were killed illegally. After their low point in 1920, when the animals had decreased noticeably from disease and possibly other causes, predator control operations were undertaken by the Biological Survey, and between January 1, 1921, and June 30, 1934, a total of 7595 coyotes and bobcats were removed. While this reduction of the predator population was being carried on the antelope herds, which had for several years been stationary, with comparatively little success in rearing fawns, gradually increased from about 500 animals to their present population of 7000 to 8000. Now the antelope are numerous enough for the same or even greater predator pressure to be of less importance than formerly, and other factors affecting the herd may become more serious."

In another part of the same report, the Texans sum up the situation tersely as follows: "Control of the coyote population of the Trans-Pecos Area will have to be practiced if the full potential of the antelope as a game animal is to be realized."

The opportunity is ours. If we wish to increase neonatal fawn survival, thus increasing the population of adult pronghorns available to the sport hunter, we must reduce the numbers of coyotes. For some reason, many state conservation agencies refuse to admit that obvious fact, even when their own research proves it to be true.

Golden Eagle Predation

The golden eagle has often been blamed for the loss of pronghorn fawns. Studies in Wyoming, Idaho, and Oregon indicate that the golden eagle does cause some mortality among neonatal fawns. The only study we know of, aimed directly at quantifying these losses to golden eagles, was conducted by Texas. We quote from their report of that study:

"Nineteen golden eagle nests were found in an area covering approximately 500 square miles of native antelope range in Hartley and Oldham Counties. Of these nests, 5 had been used during the 1948 nesting season. Seven nests were in cottonwood trees while the other 12 were in crevices on the faces of sheer bluffs.

"A quantity of debris was collected from 4 of the freshly used nests for food habits study. A cursory examination of this material revealed the bulk of the food consumed by the nesting eagles and young consisted of rabbits, prairie dogs, rats, an owl, one or two hawks, cattle carrion and one nest contained the remains of 14 long-billed curlews.

"A series of 21 eagle pellets and a group of bones collected from the same general vicinity during the winter of 1947–1948 from beneath windmill towers and trees where eagles customarily roosted was examined and added to the information collected during the study. These contained remains of striped skunk, green-winged teal, cottontail rabbits, jackrabbits, a red racer snake, prairie dogs, a hawk and a coyote. One group of bones taken from a nest in Gray County were found to be from a lesser prairie chicken."

While the study itself was quite meager in its scope and accomplishments, it does tend to indicate that the golden eagle, if for no other reason than its presence in small numbers (five pairs of nesting eagles on 500 square miles of range) during the antelope fawning season, is probably not as limiting a factor as many persons have believed.

9

Pronghorn Management

Although the pronghorn has shown itself capable of remarkable recuperative powers, and demonstrated the ability to increase and multiply when the situation is right, management of pronghorn populations is never simple. There are so many things to be taken into account when discussing the right measures and the wrong measures to be taken to perpetuate or increase the herd.

Basic questions to be answered are these:

1. Is the herd stable in numbers now? Is that what we want?

2. Do we want to increase the total numbers of the herd?

3. Do we want to maximize the population of all ages and sexes? Or do we want to maximize the production of trophy heads?

4. Are there limiting physical factors that endanger the herd, such as "uncrossable" fences, dangerous open ditches, or moats that may cause drownings?

5. Is forage production on the available range equal to, less than, or more than the amount needed to sustain the present population over a period of years?

6. Is the present water supply adequate in all 12 months of the year? Can it be improved? Would use of the pasture be more uniform if there were more waterings? If so, where should they be placed?

7. Is there an illegal harvest of pronghorns? Can that be stopped? If so, how?

8. What is the attitude of landowners? Do they welcome pronghorns in their pastures? Do they fear pronghorns feeding upon their agricultural crops? Do they benefit financially from hunter harvest of pronghorns? If not, can some arrange-

ment be devised to let them enter into the equation, to the benefit of all parties concerned?

9. Do we have available data from past studies of this herd, on this ground, in this state, which will help us answer some of the questions that are bound to come up?

10. What is the attitude of the public land administering agency toward pronghorns, if there are public lands involved? Is this attitude, and this management, permanent, or will it change?

After we have decided which of the 10 questions listed can be answered, we are ready to consider steps that might help us gain our ends. Before we do that, let's get a copy of the Bureau of Land Management's publication (Technical Note #347), titled *Habitat Management Guides for the American Pronghorn Antelope*, which is the outstanding work of its kind in this field. It is written by Jim Yoakum, BLM wildlife biologist, Reno, Nevada.

For our purposes in this book, we will not attempt to discuss management, which is a lifelong study, a professional pursuit. We will content ourselves with describing some of the techniques that are used, and which may be of interest to those who wish to know more about the pronghorn.

Trapping a Few Antelope at One Time

The commonly used method of trapping pronghorns involves the use of an airplane to drive them within wing walls, which guide them into the trap. However, there is concern that capture myopathy develops among pronghorns handled in this manner. Panicky animals are severely stressed by the long run into the trap, and by the traumatic experience of being handled by humans immediately after the long run.

Archie F. Reeve, of the Department of Zoology of the University of Wyoming, developed a second method when he needed to capture a few pronghorns in connection with studies aimed at determining the effect upon pronghorns of the Wind Energy Project near Medicine Bow, Wyoming. It was his plan to capture and tag a small number of antelope, place radio telemetry equipment on the pronghorns, and monitor their movements in and near the operations of the Wind Energy Project. Because the heart rate telemetry required surgical implantation of the sensing devices, he wanted to get his pronghorns in as stress-free a condition as possible.

Setting up light but strong nylon netting around three-fourths of the perimeter of a waterhole—used as the lure to get pronghorns inside the trap—Reeves rigged a method whereby the final one-fourth of the perimeter could be closed almost instantly. This was done by furling the nylon net on the ground, and allowing the animals to become accustomed to it. Then, the trap was fired electrically by a control placed in an observation blind. Closing the switch allowed counterbalance weights to fall, snapping the nylon net into the upright position and thus closing the circle.

Reeves found that the pronghorns thus encircled usually remained motionless, looking for a way out of the circle, until the researchers approached. Then the pronghorns panicked and dashed headlong into the nylon net. When hit by a pronghorn, the nylon net broke away from its fastenings at top and bottom and entangled the animal. Two men then held the animal, while the third quickly attached the telemetry sensors and ear tag to the animal.

It worked. Pronghorns were easily captured using this method, and stress was minimized. In 1981, the trap was used seven times, capturing a total of 17 animals. No trap-related mortality nor post-capture mortality occurred with any of the telemetered animals.

Obviously, this method has application in many specific situations where there is no need to capture large numbers of antelope. It is very cost effective, per animal captured, when compared with the usual aircraft/drive trap method. It is also important to note that it is better than using succinyl chloride capture methods, if the captured animal is to be anesthetized, as was the case in this study. It is thought that the combined effects of succinyl chloride and surgical anesthesia might be too much for the captured animal to withstand.

It should also be pointed out that blindfolding captured animals greatly reduces their struggles, thus reducing capture stress. When I had the privilege of handling antelope with Jim McLucas, the Montana expert on trapping and transporting pronghorns, he emphasized putting the captured animals into a darkened truck as rapidly as possible after capture. He believed that the darkened interior had a calming effect upon the animals, somewhat similar to the effect of the blindfold.

Censusing Techniques

Because pronghorns are mainly herd animals, it is usually possible to get an accurate count of their numbers by flying aerial transects. Each pilot-observer team must develop its own methods of working, but it is essential that the runs be flown in exactly the same manner, at exactly the same height, at the same time of day, each year, in order for the results to be statistically comparable. Texas experiments in the early days of aerial censusing showed that the 200-foot level worked best with the slow-flying aircraft in use at that time. They found that pronghorn herds, lying down, would seldom even bother to stand up when a plane flew over at the 500-foot elevation. This was especially true in areas where the animals had become accustomed to aircraft and had little fear of them. Getting down below the 200-foot level caused error by reason of missing pronghorns, because the relative visibility time was reduced so greatly. In addition, they found that eye fatigue was greater at the lower elevations. To reduce duplication in counts, the experienced teams flew toward the herd from the side which would cause the pronghorns to run to areas already covered in that day's counting activity. The shadow of the plane served to move pronghorns away from the line of flight.

When using light planes (85 horsepower or less), it became dangerous, as well as difficult, to census pronghorns when wind velocities were stronger than 20 m.p.h. To increase the safety margin, census crews moved up to higher elevations when winds were above 20 m.p.h., but the ride was distinctly unpleasant. Speaking as one who battled air sickness in an Aeronca on census flights, I can agree that calm air is a requisite for census work.

After aerial census work is completed in late May or early June, it is then necessary to fly a second count one month or six weeks later, to establish the doe:fawn ratio for the year. The longer this count is delayed, the more accurate it will be. Neona-

If not pushed too hard, antelope are easily counted from fixed-wing aircraft. A helicopter is even better, but much more expensive to operate. *South Dakota Game and Fish photo.*

tal fawns, well hidden by their mothers, are not usually counted in the aerial doe:fawn ratio flights. As they become more capable of running with the adults, however, they are more readily seen and counted. Many states follow up the gross aerial count method of determining doe:fawn ratios with an intensive doe:fawn count on the ground.

How Many Bucks Can We Harvest?

Most landowners wish to take the maximum number of bucks allowable, in order to return the greatest economic gain from the sale of their hunting privileges. We call it by other names, such as "landowners' stubs," or "trespass rights," but the fact remains that the landowner controls the right of access; he provides the forage for the pronghorn crop; and he reaps the economic gain. I see nothing wrong with that arrangement.

How many bucks can we take? There are really two factors worth consideration here: One, we must leave enough bucks to guarantee that all does that come in season will be bred; and two, we must not kill adult bucks as fast as they become adults. We must make sure that a few bucks survive into their third and fourth years, in order to grow the trophy horns that hunters prize.

Most state game departments managing pronghorns now seem to achieve a buck harvest in the nature of 35 to 45 percent of the available bucks. This is obviously conservative management. There is no case known to me where a buck harvest of 50 percent of the available bucks has hurt the pronghorn population in any way. Such a heavy harvest will not reduce the fawn crop the next year, but it surely will reduce the opportunities to harvest the real trophy bucks that are usually 5 years old or better. Under a heavy harvest regulation, bucks simply do not live long enough to grow 16-inch trophies.

When Do We Kill Does?

We can safely harvest does when the population is at or near the carrying capacity of the land area, when drought

In typical tightly bunched formation, a herd of pronghorns flees from the airplane. Note the spread of horns on that buck in the front rank, and note that the last animal is stretched out in a long, lateral leap, clearing a bit of brush in his way. *New Mexico Game and Fish photo.*

conditions warn that the carrying capacity of the land is about to decrease, or when we want to reduce an individual population for some other management reason. It is one of the givens of hunter psychology, however, that hunters will not take a doe until they have seemingly exhausted their chances to take a buck. Even a very small buck seems to be preferable to taking a doe in the minds of most hunters. This is borne out by the fact that most does taken are taken on the last day of an open season. It is worth mentioning that a doe harvest may be necessary when the management goal is the production of larger "trophy" bucks. Removal of does reduces the total overall population and this brings the herd back within the limits of the carrying capacity of the land. This in turn allows the bucks to grow and to stay healthy. And that is the formula for growing big-horned antelope: Let them live well for more than 4 years. Nature will take care of the horn growth.

If trophy bucks every year is the management goal, it is certainly better to carry a smaller herd, with ample feed, than to carry a bigger herd with marginal forage. In this situation, it is wise to carry only enough does to replace the trophy buck mortality each year.

For normal healthy reproduction, a buck:doe ratio of one to four is recommended. But remember, special management aims—such as herd increase or decrease, or the production of large trophies—can change that sex ratio. It is not carved in stone.

When Should We Hunt Pronghorns?

The hunting season should open after the rut is complete. It should close before the bucks begin to shed their antlers. Within those two limiting factors, there is plenty of time to allow for a generous hunting season, so there is really no reason to ever overlap the rut, or to continue into the "baldheaded" bucks time of year.

Carrying Capacity of the Range

It is extremely difficult to determine the correct answer to the question of exactly how many pronghorns a certain range will support. This is due in part to the fact that antelope may choose completely different ranges for wintering and for summering. It is necessary first of all to know the terrain over which a particular population will range in a year. If that pasture is enclosed within a pronghorn-tight fence, the job is much simpler. But this is seldom the case in this enlightened day and age. Once the range is known, the carrying capacity is determined by: winter conditions as to temperatures and snowfall; ice conditions that may cover the forage; available water in the form of standing water and in the form of succulents and water-carrying cacti; availability of fawning cover, especially sagebrush; and the availability of sagebrush itself, the *sine qua non* of antelope survival. In the Texas Trans-Pecos area, the single determining factor of greatest importance is the amount of rainfall received in the three months starting September 1. Texas has been able to document resorption of embryos in does encountering drought conditions. This is an adaptation meant for herd survival. If it is not possible to feed a neonatal fawn, then Nature dictates that the doe simply will not produce that fawn. In North Dakota, the greatest determinant is the nature of the winter months, especially February and March, after the pronghorns are weakened by a long winter.

Water as a Management Tool

It is possible to spread pronghorn pasturage by spreading available water spots. If a range contains only one watering area, it is certain that the forage areas farthest from that water will not be utilized to the extent that nearer pastures are utilized. If a windmill will produce a watering in a remote part of the range, it will soon be a lure for pronghorns and will allow for more uniform (hence more efficient) use of available forage. The fact that waterings have been historically important to pronghorns is shown by pioneer place names, where Antelope Springs in Texas and Antelope Wells in New Mexico and Arizona show that water allowed the pronghorn to exist in these desert-like surroundings.

Supplemental Feeding?

I cannot imagine a situation wherein artificial feeding will be beneficial to a large pronghorn population. In the case of a very small population, it may be economically possible to feed enough individual pronghorns to nurse them through the stress condition (be it winter or drought conditions), but this is extremely unlikely. Pronghorns do not like hay, although they will accept alfalfa in winter conditions. They do not seem to recognize cake or feed pellets as being food. If it is going to be necessary to start supplemental feeding, it would be wise to start it early in the season, allowing plenty of time for the pronghorns to find out that the pellets are good, and that they are nourishing.

To feed a large herd of pronghorns would, obviously, be economically impractical.

Landowner Involvement

It is obviously good business to involve the landowner in the process of managing the pronghorns that live on his land. Pragmatically, this means providing some measure of economic repayment to the landowner. I favor the set percentage of the license fee going to the landowner, as being the most fair and most practical method of repaying the landowner for AUM rental of his land for our pronghorns. (By AUM, I mean the animal unit month, which is the unit used to compute grazing fees for other livestock in national forests and other federal lands.)

In New Mexico, this repayment to the landowner takes the form of providing landowner permits directly to the landowner, who may then sell them for whatever the traffic will bear.

Why involve the landowner, other than the consideration of fairness? Because a concerned landowner will prevent poaching. He will provide guide services to hunters, thus greatly reducing crippling losses during open season. He will help the hunter get within easy shooting range of the pronghorns, thus increasing the "clean kill" part of the harvest and reducing the "shot but not retrieved" part of the harvest.

An involved landowner will monitor the needs of the herd, will remove fences that bar pronghorn movements, will break ice on pronghorn waterings when necessary— will be an ally to the game manager in producing a good and healthy herd.

What Time of Year to Transplant?

The preferred time of year to trap and transplant pronghorns is, obviously, the time of year during which the mortality due to handling will be less. Most technicians agree that this is best accomplished between the end of hunting season, (usually about October 20) and December 10. This time period of about 50 days gives an opportunity—after the rut, when all does are successfully bred, and before the time when the does become heavy with young. It also occurs at a time of year when, in most latitudes, weather conditions are good—not too hot and not too cold. Experience has shown that harassing pronghorns during periods of extreme heat can result in a surprisingly high mortality due to overheating. The same overheating can be a cause of mortality in extremely cold weather, if the animals are forced to run for great distances, becoming over-hot and then cooled rapidly by being stopped in an enclosure. When a plane is used in corralling the animals, an experienced pilot will use gentle procedures, sort of easing the animals into the corral, rather than panicking them into it.

If it should happen that any animals are injured during the penning procedures, they should not be taken along to the release site, but should be released on their familiar grounds where they have a better chance of recovering.

It is important to provide plenty of fresh air ventilation, even in winter, for pronghorns during transport. These animals are accustomed to outside temperatures; they've lived their lives without seeking shelter. If the pronghorns being transported feel that they are over-crowded or do not have enough ventilation, they may panic and struggle violently to get loose, thus causing unnecessary mortality and injury.

10

What Pronghorns Eat

According to one California farmer I spoke with, pronghorns eat nothing but alfalfa.

From an inspection of the Desierto de Vizcaino on the scorched Baja California peninsula, I had previously concluded that pronghorns had to exist on stunted, sun-dried cactus; for across great expanses of that country, there seemed to be nothing else that was edible.

The answer lies somewhere between. We must assume that pronghorn foods have changed greatly since settlement of the western part of our nation. In pre-settlement days, most antelope were found on grasslands. Now most antelope are found on sagebrush habitat. Pronghorns do eat grass, but it is not the major part of their diet. Perhaps it was at one time, but those grasslands are now in cultivation, and the adaptable pronghorn has learned to love sagebrush and other rougher feeds.

They are partial to forbs, to perennial plants other than grasses, and they do include a lot of cactus in their diet whenever it is available. They will not choose a tall grass prairie, but will choose a sagebrush habitat. In fact, if there is any *sine qua non* to the antelope's choice of food plants, it would have to be the sagebrush that covers so much of its preferred range. This is especially true in winter.

Vegetation types that have not yet reached the climax stage (where the species composition of the plants will remain fairly constant) seem to be very attractive to pronghorns. Where prairie fires have blazed across a big area, and the new vegetation has sprung up, the pronghorn finds delicious dining. As is discussed elsewhere in this book, the grazing animals that were sympatric with pronghorns (especially bison and, to a lesser degree, elk) actually helped the pronghorn by their preference for grass.

Pronghorns seldom choose homogeneous stands of vegetation, of any kind. They seem to prefer mixed stands of grasses, shrubs, and forbs, and typically feed while moving—a nip here, a bite there. This gives them the chance to vary their diet to include all of the preferred plant forms available.

In Arizona, Cindy L. Edwards and Robert D. Ohmart, of Arizona State University, studied the food habits of the Sonoran pronghorn. They noted that the literature showed that Sonoran pronghorns ate the dried and withered remains of annual and biennial plants, including forbs. This had been reported by Gale Monson on the Fish and Wildlife Services Cabeza Prieta Game Range, which is a desert environment. Monson also noted that these pronghorns browsed on paloverde, honey mesquite, and ironwood, and relished the pendant fruits of the cholla cactus.

The Arizona researchers studied fecal samples collected on the Cabeza Prieta Game Range. They found that the pronghorn diet consisted of 69 percent forbs, 22 percent shrubs, 7 percent cactus, and less than 1 percent grasses.

In 1950 Beuchner performed a food study in the Trans-Pecos area of Texas. He found that the pronghorn diet was 66.6 percent forbs, 29.7 percent browse (which included both shrubs and cacti), and 3.7 percent grass.

The Arizona study listed the following foods for Sonoran pronghorns: chain cholla and jumping cholla, brittlebrush, bladder-stem, little leaf palo verde, honey

An average pronghorn buck in typical plant community of northeastern Wyoming.

mesquite, plantain, white ratany, deer vetch, indigo bush, mistletoe, spurge, ocotillo, white bur sage, stick leaf, Spanish needles, desert marigold, wire lettuce, and ironwood.

Remember that this was a study of a desert area. The pronghorns utilized so many different plants that it is almost true to say that they ate everything—everything that was available to them. Opportunists as always, they dined heavily on the fruits of the various cacti when such fruits were available. It is also apparent that the juicy cactus fruits helped supply some of the moisture that they needed in their diet. In general, however, it should be noted that the percentages of forbs, shrubs, and grasses eaten in Arizona and Sonora did not vary much from that observed in other, more temperate climes.

Quoting from a Nebraska publication on pronghorns: "Studies have indicated that antelope-livestock competition is nearly negligible, and in some cases is beneficial to the range in general. Because their food habits do not overlap significantly, it would take about 105 pronghorns to utilize as much cattle forage as 1 cow. Pronghorns consume many poisonous and injurious plants, including larkspur, loco weeds, rubber weed, rayless goldenrod, cockleburs, needle and thread grass and yucca. Other undesirable range plants consumed by antelope are snakeweed, rabbitbrush, fringed sage, Russian thistle and saltbush. Wise range managers encourage pronghorns to use their rangeland to discourage the increase of undesirable species of plants."

Kansas researchers Mark L. Sexson, Jerry R. Choate, and Robert A. Nicholson tackled a very different study. Pronghorns had been reintroduced, after complete extirpation from the state, into lands that were farmed rather intensively. Large areas of winter wheat and cattle pastures were included in their study area. In fact, the study area itself contained 44,220 acres of native shortgrass prairie and cultivated cropland. Shortgrass rangeland totalled 31,244 acres, hard winter wheat 11,880 acres, feed grain and forage 766 acres, and alfalfa 310 acres. Dining on this smorgasbord of riches were approximately 100 pronghorns. Fecal samples were obtained by watching the pronghorns, making them nervous and then moving in to pick up the fresh fecal samples. The discussion at the end of this report is worth reading. It says:

"Forbs constituted an important component of the diet of pronghorn in late spring, summer and fall. On the study area, forbs made up only 5.2% of the species composition of the short grass prairie ecosystem, but accounted for more than 90% of the diet of pronghorn during certain months of the year. During May through September, an average of 95% of the diet of pronghorn consisted of plants other than grasses. Forbs also were important, but to a lesser degree, in April, October and November. Similar results have been obtained in other studies of pronghorn on the High Plains of Kansas; Hlavachick (1968) reported that the diet of pronghorn in Kansas consisted of 78% non-grass species, of which prickly pear made up 40% and Kansas sage made up 16%. Two of the forbs (scarlet globemallow and prickly pear) utilized extensively by pronghorn in this study were common on the research area. Sand sagebrush on the other hand, was an important forage plant during April, May and June even though it was found growing only in the lower drainages. Pronghorns seldom were seen in those areas except during those months. Barrington (1975) explained that, in southeastern Colorado, 'Areas where sand sage was moderately dense and the understory vegetation was vigorous and diverse, seemed to be more heavily utilized by pronghorn does for fawning.' Autenreith (1976) also suggested that fawning often is associated with woody habitats. Most forbs, other than prickly pear, scarlet globemallow, and sand sagebrush, were not plentiful in the vegetation samples but were conspicuous because of their size and showy appearance.

"Winter wheat made up a substantial part of the diet of pronghorn during late autumn, winter and early spring (October through March) and alfalfa was consumed more in April and November than in other months. These observations suggest that pronghorn in western Kansas utilize wheat as a substitute for green forbs during months when green forbs are not available. In spring, when alfalfa emerges, but rangeland forbs are not yet abundant, pronghorn use alfalfa to supplement their diet of native dicots. Cultivated crops are an insignificant component of the diet during summer, but increase in importance when green forbs become scarce in autumn. Damage to winter wheat by pronghorn is unlikely. Grazing of wheat by livestock in this region is not common, however, the period (mid-October to mid-April) during which pronghorn consume wheat coincides with the time when wheat might possibly be used for grazing."

John Newman, writing about southeastern Wyoming antelope, had this to say: "During late winter and early spring, antelope prefer the first plants that green up. Forbs and native grasses make up a significant portion of the antelope's diet during this period. Alfalfa and winter wheat are also taken by antelope when available. During summer, when antelope can afford to be more selective, most of the forbs available on the range at that time will be eaten. The small fringe sage is a favored food of antelope and they take it at all times of year when it is available. Big sagebrush, being an evergreen species, provides carbohydrates and proteins in the leaves and stems during the entire year and antelope will turn more to this standby as grasses and forbs cure. Analyses of stomach contents show that sagebrush will provide a large portion of the animals diet for the rest of the winter.

"The importance of sagebrush to the diet of antelope in Wyoming cannot be overemphasized. . . . Antelope can and do digest sagebrush satisfactorily and will exist on it over extended periods of time."

Big-game biologist Fred Priewert, who later became director of the Iowa State Conservation Department, wrote the following about South Dakota pronghorns in 1959: "During periods of low rainfall, and as the native ranges become dry, pronghorns move into cultivated areas where farming practices or irrigation provide green oases. Crops in these areas are damaged by the pronghorns in two ways, by losses through feeding and by matting from herds bedding down.

"While the effects of pronghorn movement into areas of cultivation are noticeable, the migration of herds into ranchland is far less discernible.

"The pronghorn furnishes little, if any, competition to the cow herd, just as he was compatible with the bison. A forb eater, the pronghorn does compete, to a small degree, with the sheep, though the average density of three pronghorn per section in the major antelope range has little effect even on sheep range, where sheep are carried at much higher densities."

In 1951, Wendell Bever found that sagebrush made up 83 percent of the winter diet of South Dakota pronghorns.

Other researchers found differing results in different habitats, proving only that the pronghorn is adaptable and that his dietary tastes are catholic. Forrest A. Sneva of the Department of Agriculture, Burns, Oregon, and M. Vavra, of the Agricultural Research Station, Union, Oregon, found that: "Microhistological examination of pronghorn antelope feces were conducted over a 2-year period to determine botanical composition. On this juniper-sagebrush-bunchgrass community the mean annual botanical composition was 62.2, 21.0, 13.1 and 4 percent browse, grass, forbs and unidentified, respectively. Sandbergs bluegrass *(Poa secunda)* was the principal grass taken in the spring and downy bromegrass *(Bromus tectorum)* taken following green-up in the fall. Bitterbrush *(Purshia tridentata)* was more important in the summer than in the winter while sagebrush was a component year around. Juniper was an important constituent during one winter. Forbs, primarily blue mustard *(Streptanthus cordatus)* was selected during the spring and summer months."

To continue picking out pertinent quotes from the Sneva-Vavra report: "Seasonal means of dietary composition observed in this study and results reported by Yoakum (1958) are shown in [the accompanying table]. Browse composition is alike except for the spring period during which we found less browse in the feces.

The decrease in browse was compensated mainly by an increase of the grass component. Grass composition was least important during the summer period, whereas forb composition during the winter months was extremely low, less than 2 percent. In [the accompanying table] Y2 indicates results according to Yoakum, while SV3 indicates results from Sneva-Vavra research."

Another quote from the Sneva-Vavra report indicates:

"Sagebrush was the major browse contributor in our study but use of it by antelope varied throughout the season. Diet composition of sagebrush was greatest in the winter periods; however, in 1976 from 39 to 67 per cent of the diet was comprised of this species in late August to late September. Yet, in 1975 sagebrush in the late summer-fall period was less than 20 per cent of the diet.

"Bitterbrush was more important in the summer period than in the winter period. In the summer of 1975 bitterbrush in the diet ranged from 71 to 89 percent and in late June 1976, composition was 54 percent bitterbrush. Bitterbrush in the remaining seasons constituted less than ten percent of the total diet. This selectivity of bitterbrush by antelope in the summer season compares well with that reported by Mason in 1952.

"Surprisingly, juniper was a substantial contributor to the winter diet of antelope during the winter of 1975-76. From October 1 to mid-January this tree furnished

Seasonal Dietary Composition of the Pronghorn

	Winter		Spring		Summer		Fall	
	Y2	SV3	Y2	SV3	Y2	SV3	Y2	SV3
Grass	5.7	11.8	9.2	36.0	Trace	6.6	13.2	29.6
Forb	7.2	1.8	23.3	21.0	32.4	21.5	21.0	8.2
Browse	85.3	83.9	65.6	37.1	64.9	68.4	59.1	59.6

37 percent or more to the antelope diet. In the winter of 1976-77 juniper in the diet did not exceed 20 percent. . . ."

Another quote from Sneva-Vavra: "The high proportion of juniper and sagebrush browse intake during the fall and winter is of some concern. Nagy and Tengerdy (1967) suggested that essential oils in deer diets containing more than 50 percent sagebrush may depress bacterial action in the rumen. However, Smith et al (1965) did not indicate any visible nutritional impacts on antelope sustained on a diet of 75 percent sagebrush and 21 percent juniper. They suggested that antelope may have different digestive attributes than deer. Perhaps the essential oil components in sagebrush or those in juniper are not all inhibitory; some may stimulate digestion, as has been shown by Oh et al (1967) for essential oils in Douglas fir *Pseudotsuga menziesii)* needles."

Roebuck, Simpson, and Dahl of Texas Tech University in Lubbock, Texas, reported on pronghorn diets in three different areas of the Texas pronghorn range. Their findings were that on the High Plains Area of northwest Oldham County, pronghorns consumed 80 percent forbs, 14 percent cactus and shrubs, 1 percent grasses and grasslike plants, plus unidentifiable materials and traces of others.

The pronghorn diet in the Sandhills area, in Cochran and Yoakum counties, 13 miles northeast of Plains, Texas, consisted of 68 percent forbs, 22 percent shrubs and cacti, 6 percent unknown, and 4 percent grasses and grasslike plants.

On the Rolling Plains study area, Borden County, Texas, the percentage of forbs in the diet rose to 90 percent, 4 percent shrubs and cacti, 3 percent grasses and grasslike plants, and 3 percent unknown. The authors' conclusions were stated thusly: "From the shrub dominated Sandhills to the grassland savanna of the Rollling Plains to the open prairie of the High Plains, forbs were the major and most preferred foods of pronghorn. . . .

"Apparently availability of succulent forbs is one of the most important factors in determining pronghorn success in the Panhandle (of Texas). In proportion of grasses, forbs and shrubs eaten, flexibility in pronghorn diets was not seen. . . . From the areas of worst pronghorn habitat (Sandhills) to the best habitat (High Plains), forbs were consistently sought out and shrubs were used only as emergency or supplemental forage. Important forb species were trailing ratany and scarlet globemallow, which were the only species preferred on all areas."

Texas biologists have reported that walkingstick cholla and prickly pear (tunas and pads) both receive heavy use in late winter and spring. In fact, observations of this use show that the plant itself may be entirely consumed, and Texas biologists believe that the availability of these two plants make the difference between death and survival for the pronghorns using them.

One thing to be remembered about the food of the pronghorn is that grass is the least important part of its diet — which rules out worry about competition with domestic livestock for grass forage. On a year-round basis, grass makes up less than 6 percent of the pronghorn diet nationwide. Only when other plants are not available does the pronghorn turn to grass forage.

Pronghorns and Cattle Relationships

Again we quote from Tommy L. Hailey's report of food habits of pronghorns in Texas:

"The degree of competition between antelope and cattle is light since those plants preferred by antelope are not usually taken in any large quantity by cattle. Cattle are primarily grass consumers with occasional use of browse and forbs. Antelope, however, prefer forbs and browse with extremely light utilization of grass species. On a yearly basis, it has been shown that antelope take an average of only 6.5% grass in their diet.

"Buechner (1950) states that overgrazing by cattle appears to have little effect upon the pronghorn. With the improved management techniques and stocking rates utilized by today's ranchers, antelope and cattle can be managed together with little conflict.

"Jones (1949) states that 'as far as cattle are concerned, they evidently regard antelope as a natural element in their surroundings and pay them no attention whatsoever.' In another part of the same Texas report, Jones writes: 'All observations made during the course of the study indicate there is no friction between antelope and cattle or horses. As a matter of fact, it often appeared that antelope preferred to feed and water near herds of cattle and that they attempted to remain in pastures where cattle were present. In this connection, in 1947 a group of antelope was released in a pasture with a herd of cows and calves. Several weeks later the cattle were moved to an adjoining pasture and the antelope promptly crossed the fence and moved into the same pasture. . . . It was frequently noted that if a group of cattle was watering at a pond or windmill tank, a band of antelope might wait until the cattle were finished before going to water. However, this was not true in every case and on several occasions antelope and cattle were seen watering from windmill tanks at the same time.'"

From my own experience, I once watched a pronghorn doe and a Black Angus bull drinking from opposite sides of a 12-foot-diameter windmill tank in northeastern Wyoming. This was in the fall of 1984.

On many occasions, I have observed cattle and antelope feeding together with the presence of either animal apparently not bothering the other.

Pronghorns Versus Sheep

Again, let's listen to Tommy Hailey:

"The competition between antelope and sheep in the Trans-Pecos Area is severe and usually results in the loss of antelope where they are found ranging together. Buechner (1950) stated that when trapped and confined to heavily grazed sheep ranges by the construction of sheep-proof fences, antelope are literally enclosed in a death trap, and populations are reduced to mere remnants or are completely eliminated within a few years. Jones (1949) stated that 'since sheep are usually present in far superior numbers, and often are maintained by supplemental feeding, they frequently cause the antelope to leave the area or starve.' The overlapping feeding habits of sheep and antelope eliminate forbs that are necessary for antelope survival.

"Forbs, which comprise up to 76.8 of the antelopes diet during periods of the year, are also highly preferred by sheep. Antelope die-offs on sheep ranches have occurred on numerous occasions. Buechner (1950) reported that the pattern of slow starvation for a year or two followed by a large loss at the most critical season of the year when food is scarcest is typical of what has occurred on many sheep ranches in the Trans-Pecos."

And again from the same source: "The

fact that sheep and antelope compete directly for the same foods has been well documented on several occasions over the past several years. One example recorded in the Lower Plains involved a 264 section ranch located in the southern portion of the area. There were 160 sections of the ranch occupied by antelope herds numbering 1,000 head during the summer of 1965. This same range was stocked with sheep at the rate of approximately 65 sheep per section and cattle at 20 head per section. This stocking rate of domestic livestock prevailed until October of 1969 when all sheep were removed. During this period, the adult antelope populations were 1,084 in 1967, 1,381 in 1968, and 1,156 in 1969. Also during this period fawn crops were 67 percent in 1967 and 35 percent in 1969 (no fawn counts were conducted in 1968). It should be noted that during the years sheep were on the range, the adult antelope populations remained at almost the same level even with high fawn crops. This indicated that the antelope had reached the carrying capacity of the range and that the potential increment was lost each year. For the next two years, the population remained relatively static at 1,155 in 1970 and 1,217 in 1971. This indicated that the effects of the competition from the sheep were still affecting the total population during the spring of 1971. However, there was an 84 percent fawn crop recorded during the summer of 1971, which resulted in a 50 percent increase in the adult population observed during the counts conducted in the spring of 1972.

"It will never be known if the 1972 population was the highest attainable in this habitat type without competition from sheep because during the month of November in 1972 and 1973, over 1,100 antelope were removed by the Texas Parks and Wildlife Department for restocking purposes. Although the population on the ranch was lower after the trapping operation was completed, by 1977 it had increased to 887 adults and expected fawn production would have placed the 1978 population at approximately 900. However, severe drought in the winter and spring of 1978 and a lack of browse as a result of chemical spraying in the mid-1970's resulted in a major die-off, leaving a 1978 adult population of only 461 antelope. Consequently the benefits to antelope that may have resulted from the removal of sheep in 1969 were more than offset by the elimination of a critical forage class in an effort to improve the range for cattle."

For our purposes, the situation as regards competition for forage between pronghorns and domestic livestock can be summed up thusly: "Cattle and pronghorns, no problem at all. Sheep and pronghorns, one of them has got to go."

One of the most interesting statistics that has emerged from the food habits study of the pronghorn is this:

Pronghorns are today consuming less than 1 percent of the forage available on public lands.

11

A Strange and Wondrous Animal

Running Speed

The question of how fast an antelope can run will never be settled to anyone's satisfaction, I'm afraid. How fast can a human run? Do you mean how fast did Jesse Owens run, or how fast can the over-age, deskbound athlete run? Obviously, the answer would be different for every individual. Suffice it to say that the pronghorn can run faster for long distances than any other mammal on the North American continent. I once had the privilege of seeing some big Irish wolfhounds—coursing hounds—turned loose on a young pronghorn buck that was standing stock-still 150 yards away. The hounds hit the dirt running and the pronghorn "left out of there." Hounds and pronghorn disappeared over a rise. We drove up to see what had happened. The dogs were standing half a mile down the slope, their tongues hanging out. The young pronghorn buck stood in plain sight on the next ridge, looking back and wondering why the hounds did not follow. It is obviously illegal to course pronghorns with hounds, but it is also no danger to the pronghorn population.

I will never tire of watching the pronghorn run, for the performance is a display of beautiful athletic ability. In 1948, Einarsen defined the performance thusly: "a synchronization of motion so that forward progress is marked by the gain that each foot makes, and in direct proportion to the speed with which it is made. Deer lope or bound, making slow progress as compared to antelope. In the antelope, running is an accomplishment that has reached near perfection."

Well said, Mr. Einarsen, well said!

I like to watch pronghorns run for the

same reasons that I like to hear Tony Bennett sing, or Horowitz play the piano. They are very good at what they do. What the pronghorn does is run, and he does it better than any other animal on the continent.

Ernest Thompson Seton wrote eloquently of the differing results obtained by differing methods of running in the deer family. He noted that the "pogo stick bounding" of the mule deer seemed very inefficient when compared to the bounding, slashing run of the whitetail. He also noted that when the terrain was rough and uneven, the mule's gait suddenly seemed efficient, and that the mule was using the best locomotion suited to his particular terrain. In other words, each deer species had evolved a locomotion that fit his environment.

The same thing can be said of the pronghorn. Adapted to the nearly flat, wide-open western plains, pronghorn locomotion is beautiful to watch, but more important, it gets him from here to there faster than any other possible method of locomotion.

But the pronghorn has many gaits, and they have even been named by Einarsen and other researchers. Einarsen recognized the Sedate Walk; the Leisurely Trot; the Sudden Bound; the Pompous, Alarmed Walk; the Elegant Trot; and the Lope. To these six, I would like to add my own favorite: the Flat-Out, Vest-Pocket Scooping-Up-Gravel, Faster'n Belief Run. That makes seven different gears. Let's take a look into these seven.

1. The Sedate Walk. This is the most commonly used locomotion, and the lowest gear used by these speedsters. The erectile rump hairs are flattened, and two feet are in contact with the ground at all times. Pronghorns travel great distances using this gait, and it is seen every day in routine travel, such as going to the waterhole to drink.

2. The Leisurely Trot, shifts gears up one notch. Only one foot is in contact with the ground at all times. Speed is about twice that of the sedate walk. No alarm here, so erectile rump hairs are not in use.

3. The Sudden Bounding Leap. Startle a pronghorn while it is drinking and you'll see this mode of movement at its best. The erectile hairs of the rump flash snow-white in the sunlight, the entire body crouches and launches itself upward and forward all in one motion. In fact, it was not until I took slow-motion movies that I noticed the crouch that precedes the sudden bounding leap upward and forward. Your attention is directed to the photograph of an antelope using the Sudden Bounding Leap, in this chapter. Note the water thrown off the muzzle as the animal's head is swung around with startling speed? This bound may be all the motion there is. The forward motion may stop instantly, as it began, if the pronghorn notices that the danger is not real.

If the danger is perceived to be real, the next motion may be the Flat-Out Run.

4. If the animal is not certain of the situation, if he is slightly scared, but not enough to send him into precipitate flight, he may use the Pompous, Alarmed Walk. The gait is only slightly faster than the leisurely trot—may even be slower—but the hairs of the heliograph rump are erected, the animal's head is held higher than normal, and his rump seems to bounce as he walks. His every motion and attitude seem to telegraph the message that he is worried, but not quite ready to admit that he has to run. Here it should be

A Strange and Wondrous Animal

mentioned that this locomotion method is exhibited by both sexes. A buck normally runs with his head held out in front of the body, not as erect as the doe's. He seems to be saying that those lordly horns are heavy. In the Pompous Alarmed Walk, either sex will hold the head higher than normal, which brings the buck's head position up nearly to where the doe normally holds her head. In this gait, it always seems to me that the pronghorn seems embarrassed, but not ready to flee.

5. Next gear shifts the pronghorn into the Elegant Trot. Head erect more than usual, erectile rump flashing, the animal goes into a bouncing trot, with only one foot touching the ground most of the time. This is a precautionary movement, not a flight, for the pronghorn is still using less than one-half of his speed potential. If you stop your car to put the binoculars on a pronghorn within 300 yards (and it isn't hunting season), and the animal decides to put some more precautionary space between he and thee, he is apt to use the Elegant Trot. He seems to be

Note the water thrown from the muzzles of these two, startled by the click of camera. *Photo by Judd Cooney.*

Startled into a fast getaway, this buck shows typical gait, with hind legs reaching forward to get a new purchase, then drive the hurtling body even faster. *Photo by Judd Cooney.*

saying, "I am not afraid, but I think I'll move disdainfully away from you, you slow thing, you."

6. The pronghorn's usual running gait for putting distance behind—but not in all-out flight—is the Lope. Here, the speed indicator goes up to about three-quarters of potential, or maybe only half of potential, but there is evident a "rocking chair" motion that is quite beautiful to watch. His erectile rump hairs are usually in full view, and the length of his stride has noticeably increased. Now it is apparent that the hind legs furnish a lot of the forward motion, for they seem to stream out behind his fast-moving body at times. Now for the first time in this "going through the gears" you will notice that the tongue is placed to the side, seemingly hanging out, to allow for better ingress of air into the oversized windpipe.

7. Those six locomotion gaits are those recognized by Einarsen et al. I want to describe the seventh, the "passing gear" gait of the truly "moving out" pronghorn. Head and neck are carried lower in both species, with bucks seeming to hold the neck below the horizontal at times. Tongues are protruding, out of the way, in both old and young, both feeble and hale and hearty individuals. Erectile rump hairs are flashed at first, but as the flight continues, these white rump hairs may be allowed to flatten down again, so that the fright message is not being sent. After all, it is no longer needed, for surely the entire band is in headlong flight by this time.

In this gait, there is no hint of any rocking up and down motion. This is the efficient movement, and the only direction is

A Strange and Wondrous Animal

forward. Hind legs reach farther forward than they did in the lope, and seem to spread apart slightly, as if not to hit the front legs. Seen from directly behind, the hind legs seem to move stiffly, almost clumsily, but the results are splendid. From the side, the spectacle is one of perfectly level bodies, with the legs just a blur beneath the body, and the transmission is definitely in passing gear, for the animal is giving it all he's got. This is a poor time to toss a bullet at his speeding body. Ninety times out of 91, you'll miss. There is also a very good chance that you will have underestimated the lead so badly that you will hit — probably in the paunch — an animal running well behind the one you were hoping to hit.

No matter what gait he is in, the pronghorn is a beautiful thing to watch, pure poetry in motion.

Group dynamics affect pronghorn running patterns, of course. If the group is tightly bunched when they start to run, they will move out in a tight bunch. However, when they have been running for some distance, they have a tendency to string out and run in single file. Many observers have tried to learn which individual is the leader of a particular band, and the results have never been conclusive. The one generalization that can be made is that the leader is usually a female. The

Running pronghorns often have the tongue protruding to allow air to enter more easily. *Photo by Judd Cooney.*

Running parallel to a fence, this buck is really getting into high gear. Photo by Judd Cooney.

dominant bucks are usually found in the rear. One postulate is that the buck follows behind to prod laggards and keep the group together. That's a romantic notion, but it smacks of anthropomorphism, attributing to the buck some altruistic motive, something for the good of the herd. I think it is more a case of survival: The buck knows that the leaders often get into trouble, so the safest place is hiding behind all the others. When pronghorn herds are galvanized into the All-Out Run, they certainly do not wait until the leader starts out and then follow. Rather they get into high gear almost instantly and the animal on the perimeter of the group nearest to the desired direction of flight becomes the leader. That individual may be passed up by a faster one, a more frightened one, or by a wiser one, I'm not sure. However, the eventual direction of the sustained flight is almost always set by an older female. The decision to stop running and take a check of the situation is almost always made by an older female, too. The buck may disappear at that time, hiding his desirable carcass from the hunter by getting into the middle of the group. As a general rule, which has exceptions, the herd will usually prefer to run uphill rather than down. I attribute this to the desire to get the better observation elevation, where they can look back and see if pursuit is coming.

That Heliograph Rump

When startled, or when discovering danger to be present, the pronghorn has the ability to erect white hairs on the rump patch. This makes the rump patch shine remarkably bright, so that it has a mirror effect, reflecting the bright sunshine of the western plains to a startling degree. When this heliograph operation is performed simultaneously by an entire herd, the end result is a startling flash of white, visible for several miles under the right conditions.

Einarsen, one of our best wildlife observers, reported in 1948 that the pronghorn heliograph is not as bright, nor is it used as often in winter as it is doing the other three seasons. He postulated that the body oils did not make the heliograph shiny during winter due to lower temperatures. He also suggested that the "herd alerting" device was not as necessary in winter, when the usual practice was for the entire herd to be together in one place, rather than scattered across miles of plains. It is a good subject for thought to try to understand just how this ability to erect the rump hairs, and the development of white rump hairs, was evolved over the millennia. What purpose did it serve? Obviously, it was a part of the survival of the herd, as a unit, but not a part of the survival of the individual.

This young pronghorn has just flashed his heliograph rump, denoting alarm.

Carefully watching the photographer, these young does show no sign of alarm. Note that the rump patch is not erected.

Way back in 1925 Seton reported that: "When one of the animals escapes by running, after erecting its rump patch, it alerts the others in the group, even if they are widely scattered. Such a 'worrying' device greatly increases the security of the herd."

Glands and Scents

Pronghorn antelope have 11 cutaneous glands and the scientist describes their locations as follows: one postmandibular (paired), one ishial (paired), one hock (paired), interdigital (four), and one median on the lower back above the rump patch.

We do not know the exact purposes of these glands, although they obviously play a part in the sexual system. The postmandibular glands, near the cheek patch of the male, are rubbed against bushes, against other pronghorns, during the excitement of the rutting season. There are suggestions that this helps to mark the territory claimed by the buck. However, this does not jibe with the fact that the buck's territory is not a stationary or permanent thing, but varies with the size of the harem, and with the vigor with which the buck gathers and protects a harem.

"The glandular system of the pronghorn closely resembles that of the domestic sheep. However, there are no scent-producing glands in the rump patch. The only glands found there are similar to the sebaceous glands found in the human hand, and they produce only a thin oil." This is a quotation from Dr. M. P. Chapman of the veterinary staff of Oregon State University, and is in direct contradiction to the statements made by Mace and Skinner in their separate descriptions of the pronghorn. Both describe a pair of musk-producing glands located on the ventral area of the rump patch.

Personal observation is that there must be a musk-producing gland located somewhere on the body of the pronghorn, for the pronghorn has an easily detected odor, similar to musk, at all times of the year. After spending 10 hours handling pronghorns, as we did when transplanting, we went to the local restaurant to eat. Two different waitresses wrinkled their noses and said, "You guys smell like goats. Whatcha been doing?" We had picked up the "goat-like" smell from the pronghorns, obviously.

Bones

A recent report published in a sporting magazine stated that the antelope leg bones can resist a breaking torque 10 times greater than the same sized bone in a cow. This undoubtedly is true, for pronghorns almost never break their leg bones, despite the speed with which they flash over the uneven ground, and despite the sudden turns they make.

Horns

Both male and female pronghorns grow horns, although the horns of the females are much smaller than those of the males. These unique horns are composed of a hairlike outer sheath over a bony structure. The horn grows over the bony structure, covering it like a sheath covers a knife blade. The outer covering is shed every year; the bony structure is a permanent part of the skeleton.

The male animal grows a forward-pointing prong on the horn, as shown in the accompanying photo. This prong is usually absent in the female. The horns of both sexes curve backward, forming a hook, although this curve is much more pronounced in the male. In fact, younger females may grow only the erect part of the horn, lacking both the prong and the rearward curve.

Both sexes grow the horns to maturity by July, and keep them until late September or early October. The trophy bucks shed their horns a bit earlier than the young bucks and does do. This may be due to the battering the horns receive during the harem-gathering fights of early fall. Late July and early August, before the rutting begins, are when the trophy horns are at their best, for they have yet to be damaged by any fall fighting. It is not unusual for the horny sheath to be lost during fighting, for it is loosely attached. That attachment is accomplished by means of hair filaments which seemingly tie the sheath to the bony core. The horn cores are smooth and well protected during most of the year by the sheath. The tip of that bony core is very specialized and

Short yearlings, these does exhibit "very small" horns of the female at this stage of development.

very important. It is made up of material much softer and unlike the bony core itself. After the horns are shed, this tip develops and grows much larger—forming the tip of the newly sprouting horn. This tip then grows downward! Material for its formation is evidently brought by the pronghorn's circulatory system. In addition to the horn tip of denser material, the horn core is covered with a membrane that grows downward to contact the coarse hairs which surround the base of the core. Gradually this membrane and the "hair material" tip grow together, and gradually the completed horn takes shape. We say "gradually," for the process is smoothly accomplished. Actually, however, the horn growth takes place in a remarkably short time. On adult bucks, the prong may be visible shortly after the first of the year in most latitudes.

In 1961, Morrison published some findings about pronghorn horn growth. To quote:

"The horn sheath is composed principally of compressed cornified epithelial cells. As was previously believed, hairs do not constitute a major portion of the antelope horn sheath. Hairs within the horn sheath probably serve for some structural support and anchorage to the tissue layer beneath. Hairs are rare or absent in the upper portions of the horn sheath.

"Hormonal relationships are probably the main factors causing the annual growth and shedding of the horn sheath. Horn growth apparently begins during the early fall when the male sex hormone is at its height. Growth of new horn tissue beneath the old horn sheath is responsible for the shedding of the horn of the previous year. The horn sheaths are shed in

A Strange and Wondrous Animal

November or December. Growth of the new horn apparently ceases in the late spring or early summer.

"The new horn sheath, immediately after the shedding of the sheath of the previous year, is well developed, particularly at the apex. Hairs are abundant upon the surface of the new horn sheath, particularly at the base. Horn development proceeds both upward and downward from the level of the apex of the horn core. The hairs within the lower portions of the horn are incorporated into the mass of cornified epithelial cells which form the main body of the horn."

For the serious student of pronghorn horn development, we refer to the article printed in the *Journal of Mammalogy*, November 1975, co-authored by Dr. Bart W. O'Gara and Gary Matson. We will try to give the gist of the abstract here, in our own words, rather than in the precise scientific terms.

Pronghorn males' horn growth stopped in August, because the layer feeding the horn growth process became inactive under the completed sheaths. The horns remained the same until October, after the completion of the rut. At that time, new growth began underneath the existing horn. Hard keratin tips formed atop the bony foundation for the horn. This swelling aided in loosening the outer horn by pushing it away from the bony support. The old horns, thus loosened, were dropped in November. The new horns grew rapidly in December, forming the curved horn tips and frontal prongs that give this animal its name. By February, horn growth was materially completed.

That's a nice buck between those does, but there is no safe shot in this picture. *Photo by Judd Cooney.*

Do the horns appear to be twice as long as the ears? If so, you might have yourself a trophy. *Photo by Judd Cooney.*

ment for taking the pronghorn out of its special listing as the only member of the family *Antilocapridae*, on the basis of its distinction of being the only animal that casts off true horns every year. O'Gara admits that the claim is true, but points out that many members of the *Bovidae* exfoliate at least part of their horns, or all of their horns, several times during their lives. The pronghorn is still the only species that annually sheds true horns. I like to think that the pronghorn is a one-of-a-kind animal, but I am also one who resists the tendency to split off new families, taxonomically, on the basis of slight evidence

Wide, branching horns of this buck make him a desirable trophy. *Photo by Judd Cooney.*

From March through July, hard keratin formed around the cores while skin around the bases of the cores thickened and sent out horny material to lengthen the horns. At this time, some hairs were incorporated into the horny sheaths, but there is no basis for calling these "hair horns."

In this same *Journal of Mammalogy* article, Dr. O'Gara makes a good argu-

of difference. I'm a lumper, not a splitter, and thus I find much to recommend Dr. O'Gara's suggestion that *Antilocapridae* should be reclassified as the *Antilocaprinae*, merely the sixth subfamily of *Bovidae*.

No matter how you look at it, the horn formation process of the pronghorn is a strange one, but it has worked well for millennia, so why should he change it?

The resulting crowning glory of the male pronghorn is a much-sought-after trophy, unique in the big-game world of North America. It serves the buck well in the annual combats that settle possession of the harem questions. Although it is rare, pronghorn bucks do occasionally become locked together, horn to horn, and do perish. My brother, Ken, once found a pair of bucks locked together while bow-

A typical pronghorn buck in summer coat. Note length of ears as compared to height of horns. *Photo by Judd Cooney.*

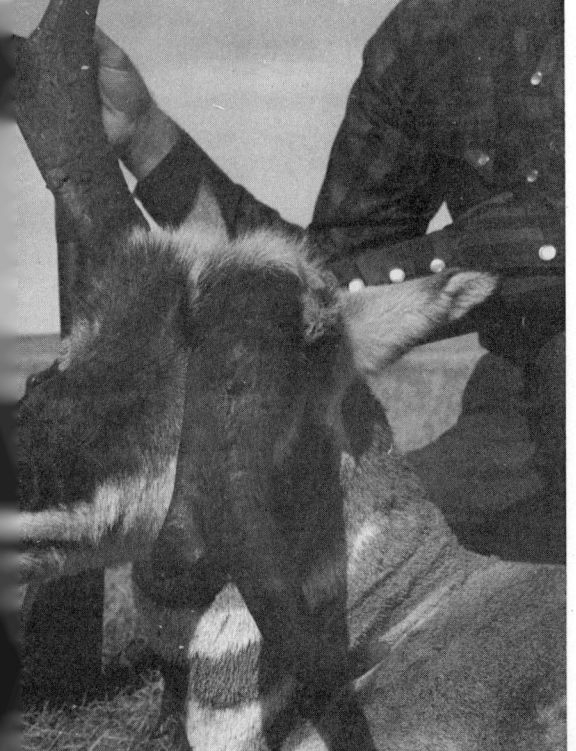

This buck sports a freak set of antlers, one growing up, one down. This is probably the result of an accident that deformed the bony core prior to horn development. *South Dakota Game and Fish photo.*

hunting for pronghorns in Harding County, South Dakota. The back curved tip of each animal's horns had gone under the jawbone of the other animal, effectively locking them together. One animal was dead; the other in very bad shape. I later photographed the two heads in the locked-together position.

Battles between bucks can become very violent and do more than just knock chunks out of the other animal's horns. The back-curved horns would seem to be a poor choice to do much damage, but they do draw blood, and in extremely rare cases, have been known to cause death. Most mating-season fights, however, are

Here's a problem for the trophy hunter: Which one of these fine bucks would you shoot?

settled by strict adherence to the pecking order, with all of the males concerned seemingly aware of which animal is dominant over which other animal. Subordinate bucks do succeed in accomplishing some of the breeding, simply because the dominant buck is busy elsewhere, either repelling a challenge or herding a doe back into the harem. Usually, it is enough for the dominant male to start a short "bluffing" charge toward an overly amorous young buck. The young buck retreats in haste and that settles that. Some observers have reported that they've never seen actual contact between rival males; the bluff is usually enough to establish dominance. However, there *are* authentic records of one buck killing a rival during these fights.

Yes, the pronghorn is a strange and wondrous animal, the only North American mammal that annually sheds its horns, the only member of its order, the sole representative of an ancient group which has prospered since the early Pliocene. He's not a goat, and not a true antelope. He's the pronghorn!

12

Mortality Factors

The pronghorn antelope has a tremendous potential for reproduction, with annual production of fawns in the neighborhood of 180 fawns per 100 does. Habitat conditions can alter this ratio upward or downward, but the fact remains: We would be up to our ears in pronghorns if nothing killed them.

Delicately built (or so it seems to the casual observer), nervous, flighty, high strung, unpredictable — yet the pronghorn has proved itself to be remarkably capable of increasing its kind under ordinary conditions, capable of perpetuating itself under the most severe conditions.

At the present time, when pronghorns are riding a high wave of population increases, and management must limit the populations to keep them within the carrying capacity of the land, hunting is undoubtedly the largest mortality factor. In 1983, hunters in Wyoming alone harvested almost 100,000 pronghorns, five times as many as existed in the entire world in 1923. Hunting is the prime cause of mortality, but hunting can be strictly regulated. Hunting is regulated to the point where it is a tool of management and is not a danger to pronghorn perpetuation of the species. Illegal hunting is still a serious loss in some states, but is not statistically significant over the pronghorn's continental range. Crippling losses during hunting season can run quite high, for the fast-running pronghorn is a very elusive target. A hunter whose desire far exceeds his ability to place a bullet may shoot at the running herd, without aiming at the vital spot of a particular animal. This tactic may result in hitting an animal in a non-vital spot. The animal escapes and then dies a lingering death, usually unseen and uncounted. Biologists, however, do factor this crippling loss into their computations when setting the hunting seasons and regulations.

The second most important cause of pronghorn mortality is the loss to predation in the first few days of life. The results of research on Anderson Mesa in Arizona, described in detail in Chapter 8, show conclusively that a large percentage of the new fawn crop can be lost to predators, especially coyotes. Two comments are germane here. One, the coyote and the pronghorn did exist together, without serious permanent harm to each other, for millennia—and should be expected to continue to live together in the same manner. Two, man has so altered the habitat for both animals that the balance has swung greatly in favor of the coyote. When the pronghorn doe had the entire North American continent in which to hide her newborn fawn, the coyote had a hard time finding the fawn during the critical first week after birth, before the fawn could outrun the coyote. But when man's fences limited access to fawning grounds, and when man's programs of sagebrush eradication removed most of the prime fawning habitat, we made the job much easier for the coyote seeking a hidden fawn. *We* caused the change that favored the coyote. *We* have the ability to change that balance back again, by severely limiting coyote numbers. Emotion bordering on hysteria surrounds this question in some areas, and the only logical solution is to leave the matter strictly up to professional game managers, who have access to all the information and can make sane, unemotional, decisions.

In the pioneer days on the Great Plains, there was a saying about people that "Old folks don't winter well." This bit of folklore had a basis in fact, for it was wintertime when life came to an end for many of the older generation. This is a biological fact, for wintertime is a stressful time, and this added stress often proves to be the straw that breaks the camel's back, the final push which ends a life that had neared its end.

To a far greater extent, winter is a time of stress for pronghorns, and old pronghorns do not winter well. In Chapter 6 we told the story of the harrowing winter that eliminated a prospering pronghorn herd in North Dakota. The animals found their food supply covered by crusted ice and snow, so they made a heroic migration southward in search of food. Their stamina and stored energy ran out before they found accessible food. Surely this microcosm was repeated thousands of times across the winter range of the pronghorn; surely winter has been a limiting factor in pronghorn populations.

But winter, per se, is not the cause of mortality. Winter serves to accentuate the seriousness of other mortality factors. Predation on adult pronghorns is not a problem over 11½ months of the year. But one severe snowstorm can so reduce the mobility of the pronghorn that predators find easy prey—are able to run down and kill antelope that would have easily outdistanced that same predator on dry ground.

Pronghorns are host to parasites which weaken them. Some of these parasites are carried for a normal lifetime, without evident harm. But allow the body to become weakened under the stress of winter and the damage done by the parasite becomes a mortality factor. In the words of a disease research scientist, "If winter foraging conditions become severe and persist for several weeks, the nutritional stress on the

Mortality Factors

Pronghorns seem to handle normal winters easily. This young doe seems to be floundering in soft snow. *South Dakota Game and Fish photo.*

pronghorn may predispose them to nutritional and infectious disease."

Pronghorns introduced into the habitat of the Wichita Mountains Wildlife Refuge in Oklahoma were found to be heavily infested with brown winter ticks, *Dermacentor nigrolineatus*. Buechner reported that as many as 500 ticks would attach themselves to a single animal, causing the pronghorn severe stress to which it was not accustomed. How much this contributed to the mortality of the pronghorns is impossible to assess.

Pronghorns have been found to carry Actinomycosis, an inflammatory disease caused by parasites, and often referred to as "lumpy jaw." This is seldom a contributing factor to mortality, and poses no danger to humans.

Wyoming researchers stated that the two age classes most often killed during winter's hardships were the less than

1-year-olds and the "overly-mature" animals. But they sagely questioned whether those "overly-mature" animals died of winter stress or simply died of old age. After all, we all come to the end of our lives sometime—and most often, it happens in winter.

Drought conditions are a significant cause of mortality. In Oregon, Deming reported that "during the past decade our lowest reproduction and survival of kids has been during the drought years and our highest has been during the wet years." It is easy to rationalize that forage is short during drought years, that travel to available water may impose another stress factor—simply to state the obvious, that "times are tough during the drought."

However, the timing of the rains is also important. In 1952, Wyoming researcher Baker found that especially wet weather could cause kid losses. As in most other

Group of pronghorns in South Dakota winter concentration. Note absence of bucks. Pronghorns typically paw through this depth of snow to feed on forbs beneath. *South Dakota Game and Fish Department photo.*

questions, the optimum is somewhere in the middle. The wet, cold rains that fall during the fawning period are definitely a limiting factor in fawn survival. But if it doesn't rain at all, that's just as bad. It is simply better to be in the middle.

Livestock Diseases

Because pronghorns occupy the same habitat as domestic sheep, goats, cattle, and horses, and because they eat many of the same forage plants, it might be assumed that they would share some of the diseases of domestic animals. Let's take a look:

Brucellosis, also called Bang's Disease or Undulant Fever, is one of the most feared diseases of meat-producing animals, especially cattle. But despite tens of thousands of serological tests, there is no case in the literature where *brucellae* have been isolated from pronghorns.

Leptospirosis is a bacteria-caused disease of domestic animals, wildlife, and man. It causes fever, loss of appetite, blood in the urine, and pneumonia. It also causes abortions in cattle. Although it has been claimed that pronghorns carry the disease and might transmit it to cattle, we hasten to point out there is no evidence of this. In fact, *Leptospira* has not been isolated from seropositive individual pronghorns. The most damaging indictment of pronghorns along this line was produced in Texas, where the serologically positive reactions ranged as high as 37 percent in hunter-killed pronghorns. These were taken from areas with very low fawn reproduction, signaling the presence of some unexplained mortality factor. Although no attempt was made to isolate *Leptospira* from these blood samples, leptospirosis was a problem in domestic cattle herds in that region at that time. Evidence is mainly circumstantial and serological tests are not thought to be reliable in the case of pronghorns, simply because no one has isolated *Leptospira* from any pronghorn blood sample.

Believe it or not, there has been a confirmed case of rabies in pronghorns. This was a 10-week-old fawn in South Dakota that died 35 days after being bitten by a rabid skunk. The diagnosis was confirmed by all the modern tests. It was rabies. This is the only case on record, to the best of my knowledge. There is no indication that rabies is carried by pronghorns; this is simply a case where the pronghorn was the victim of rabies in a skunk population.

Parasites

Pronghorns are remarkably free of external parasites. A careful examination of 97 pronghorns in North Dakota, for example, did not turn up external parasites. In New Mexico, some studies have found the pronghorn free of parasites, while other examinations have found low-level infestations of spinose ear ticks. The same spinose ear tick was found in Texas studies, along with a heavy infestation of brown winter ticks *(Dermacenter albipictus)*.

Many different internal parasites have been identified in pronghorn populations, and it can be said that the average pronghorn harbors several different kinds of intestinal parasites. In a North Dakota study, 97 percent of the animals examined were found to harbor helminths, with *Haemonchus*, *Ostertagia*, *Nematodirus*, and *Menatodirella* being the most commonly found genera. All of these animals were in good physical condition, indicating that the parasites were not causing severe bodily harm.

Wyoming studies found *Marshallagia marshallii* to be the most common, with 47 percent of the pronghorns studied harboring this parasite. Interestingly, investigators did not find heavy infestations in any one specimen.

Abomasal parasites reported from pronghorns included *Haemonchus contortus* and *Pseudostertagia bullosa* as fairly common occurrences, and the various *Cooperia* as being rare. Occasional occurrences included *Osterlagia trifurcata*, *Osterlagia circumcentia*, and *Marshallagia marshalli*.

Lungworms

The lungworm *Orthostrongylus spp.* is so prevalent in free-ranging pronghorns that infestation percentages of 97 percent were found in Wyoming and Montana. This lungworm, a common parasite of almost all big-game species in the West, does not cause any pathological changes worthy of mention. It is undoubtedly a nuisance to the pronghorn, but has very little, if any, harmful effect. It is not a danger to a man who uses the pronghorn for meat.

There have been clinical reports of at least 15 other internal parasites isolated from the intestinal tract of pronghorns. Not one of these has been determined to have a harmful effect upon the host.

Poisonous Plants

The commonly repeated story of locoweed killing pronghorns cannot be substantiated. There is only one visual report, attributing the death to locoweed, and that was not confirmed by clinical or postmortem investigation, unfortunately.

There is confirmed evidence that pronghorns have poisoned themselves by eating the leaves of the common chokecherry, which is a known producer of clinical hydrocyanide poisoning.

Tommy Hailey, a good observer of Texas pronghorns, west of Pecos, documented a serious decline in pronghorn populations due to being starved into eating tarbush. Range improvement ended that mortality factor.

Pronghorns are tough animals, well adapted to life on the plains of the West. They seem to be remarkably resistant to the effects of plants that might be poisonous to other ungulates. A Colorado publication postulates that four things might be happening: (1) pronghorns avoid poisonous plants; (2) they only ingest subtoxic amounts of these poisonous plants; (3) they ingest toxic amounts, but withstand them (that seems to be contradictory), or; (4) they die of poisonous plants but are not noticed, or are misdiagnosed as to cause of death. That publication comes to the conclusion that poisonous plants have very little, if any, effect upon free-ranging populations of pronghorns.

For further information about diseases and parasites of pronghorns, I refer you to Special Report Number 57 of the Colorado Division of Wildlife, dated June 1984. It was the source of much of the foregoing information and is an excellent short review of the subject.

Fences

It bears repeating many times: Pronghorns do not handle fences well. Listen to Texas pronghorn expert, Tommy L. Hailey, in a 1979 report on pronghorn management:

One reason why pronghorns do not like to jump over fences is shown here. Caught on the barbed wire, this pronghorn struggled and died. *Photo by Judd Cooney.*

"Net wire fences present a serious problem to the free movement of antelope. Buechner noted that antelope in the Trans-Pecos Area of Texas are unaware of their ability to jump and often die of starvation rather than jump a net wire fence to reach suitable ranges. In the Marfa Flats Area that joins the Del Norte Mountains along the Brewster-Presidio County line, restrictive fencing caused a severe die-off during the winter of 1964-65. Antelope losses ranged up to 90 percent in pastures located in the flats which were enclosed by net wire fences. Denied access to winter-spring range which would have provided essential forage and cover, the antelope succumbed to starvation and exposure to the harsh weather. In the adjoining pastures encompassing foothills of the Del Norte Mountains with excellent browse species for winter-spring ranges, no antelope losses occurred. The animals

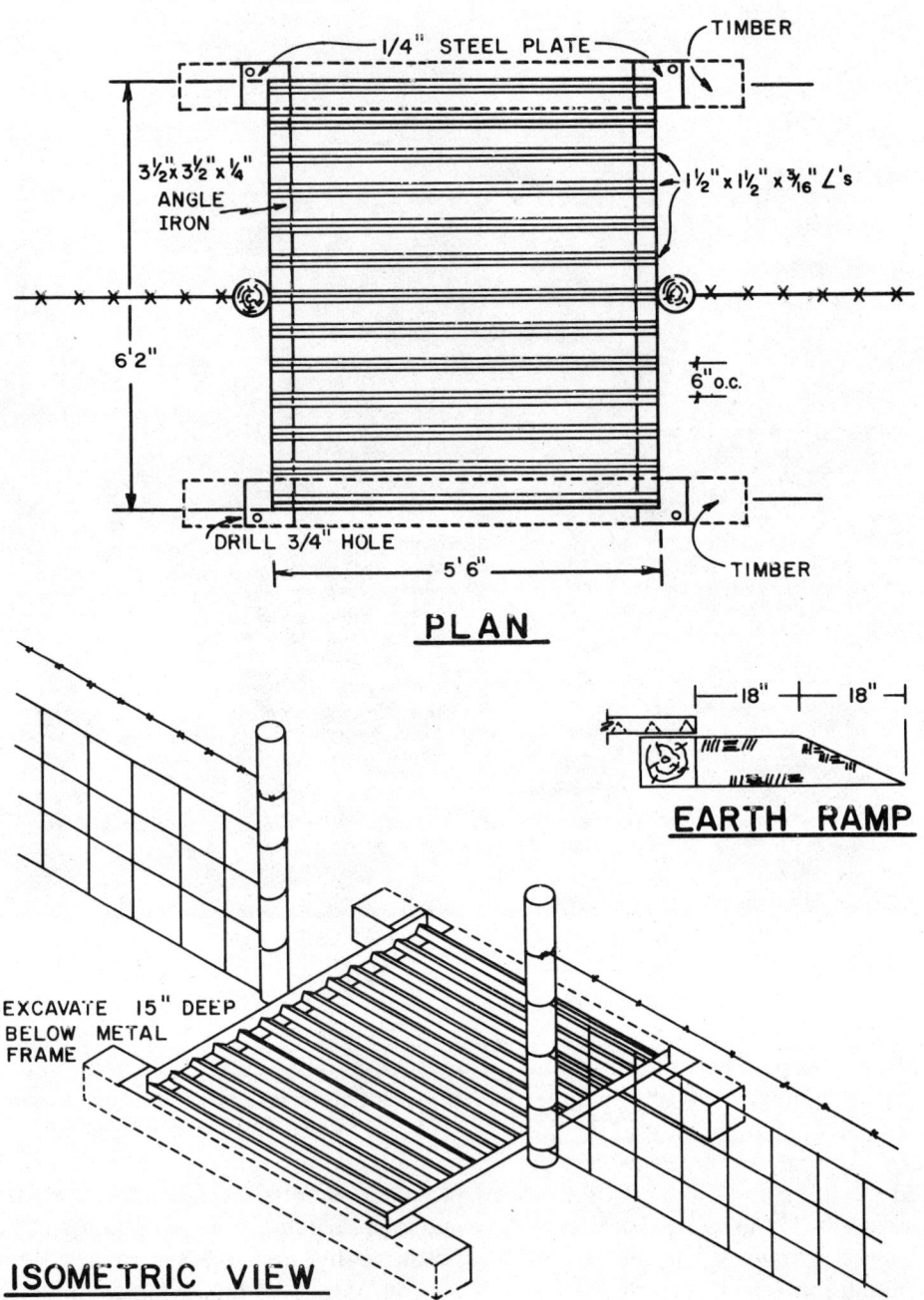

This structure allows the free passage of pronghorns through a fence, yet stops cattle and sheep quite effectively. For best results, it should be put in place well before winter's arrival, so that the animals become accustomed to using it before they need to use it. *BLM illustration.*

Mortality Factors

in these pastures were able to move unrestricted from summer-fall range in the flats to the winter-spring range in the foothills.

"The unrestricted movement of antelope between pastures and ranches is essential to prevent die-offs."

And once again, from the same report:

"Jones established the fact that in the Texas Panhandle four or five strand barbed wire fences do not usually deter the movement of antelope from one pasture to another.

"However, well-constructed, closely-spaced wire with the bottom wire less than 16 inches above ground level will prevent free movement. Net wire fences present a severe problem. With the changing of livestock operations from sheep to cattle, the repair of net wire fences is not as demanding. Normal deterioration of the net wire fence will allow some passage of antelope, but additional steps can be taken to increase antelope movement and at the same time retain the purpose of the fence for containing cattle.

"One of the quickest methods for allowing movement of antelope through net wire fences is to fold the bottom of the net wire fence up and leave a space of approximately 16 to 18 inches between the fence and ground level. Sections of the net can be raised up for 100-yard distances at one-half mile intervals along the fence line. This only requires pulling staples from the bottom, folding the wire up and restapling the wire to the post."

We can't even count on the pronghorn's ability to remember how to get on the other side of the fence, even if that animal has already done it once! An early report from Texas stated: ". . . an old doe was seen to cross a fence several times one morning. Later in the day, when she

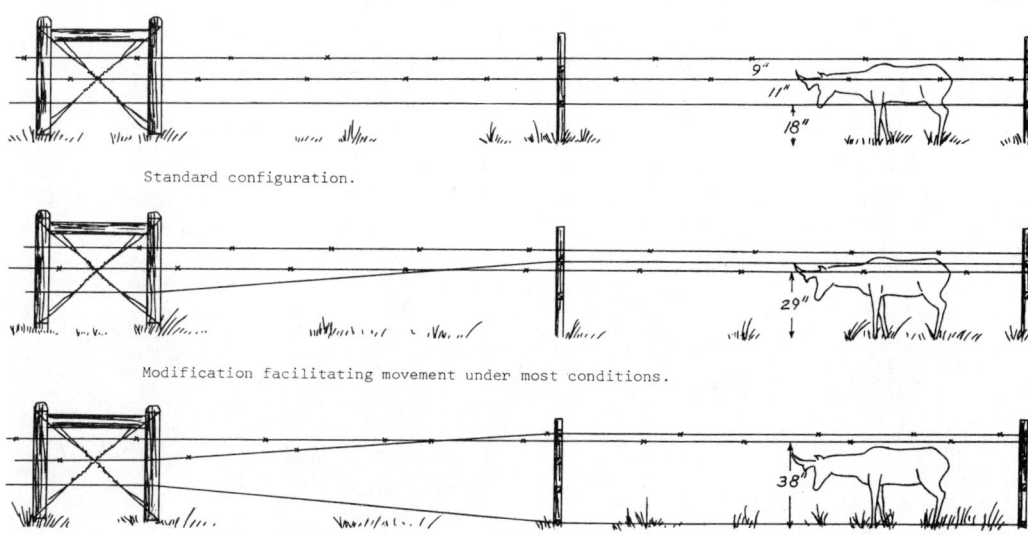

Standard configuration.

Modification facilitating movement under most conditions.

Adjustment allowing almost total freedom of movement.

This diagram shows ways in which a three-strand barbed-wire fence can be modified to allow free passage of pronghorns. *Courtesy of BLM.*

Pronghorn passing through gate with BLM-developed pass structure. *BLM photo.*

Fawns develop very quickly. When they are a month old, they are able to jump across the pass structure. *BLM photo.*

The jump starts with a rearing movement, followed by a strong push with the hind legs. *BLM photo.*

started to cross again, she appeared to have forgotten the procedure. For six days she paced up and down the fence in her efforts to get through. Eventually, it was necessary to take down about 24 feet of the fence to permit her to re-enter the pasture."

Our comment is that this doe might have been senile.

How to solve this problem? Cattleguards (also called cattle passes) will allow pronghorns to jump over them, if not too wide. In some cases, pronghorns have been observed carefully walking across cattleguards. But this measure alone is usually not sufficient to solve the problem to the satisfaction of the pronghorn. A fence that is really "sheep tight" will also be pronghorn tight, for all intents and purposes. When coyotes drove many Trans-Peco Texas ranchers out of the sheep business and into the cattle business (after President Nixon stopped the use of Compound 1080, the only effective method of keeping coyote numbers low), they allowed woven wire fences to deteriorate, and pronghorns quickly found "water gaps" and other spots where they could slide under the fence. As woven wire fence rusted out, it was replaced by much less expensive barbed wire. Leaving the bottom strand 16 or more inches above ground level did nothing to impair the fences' ability to hold cattle, but it made life much easier for the pronghorn.

Fences cause trouble all year-round, of course, as they restrict movement of does to optimum fawning grounds, restrict movement to better pastures, and restrict access to water. But it is in winter that the fence really causes mortality among pronghorns. When the blizzard comes, the pronghorn herd (commonly bunched in winter) usually drifts ahead of the storm, and may travel great distances to reach better wintering cover — such as a protected valley, or a series of breaks in the plains — and if that drifting with the wind maneuver is stopped by a fence, the bunched herd often stands with its tail to the wind and waits for death, which may not be long in coming. Strangely enough, we usually think of winter storms as killing the old and the very young, and this is true. But when winter storms combine with fences to prevent the herd from reaching forage, it may well be the mature bucks that suffer the most. This is true when the storm comes shortly after the completion of the rut. In this situation, the bucks are in their weakest condition of the year, and are ill-equipped to withstand

Power, agility and coordination are combined in one easy motion as the pronghorn jumps the pass structure. Obviously, antelope *could* **leap the usual wire fence, but they don't seem to know that.** *BLM photo.*

the added stress of being stopped by a fence, and held there—away from life-giving forage.

Yes, pronghorns can starve to death when fenced away from food. This is passing strange, for the ability of antelope to jump six-foot-high fences has been amply demonstrated. They can jump six-foot fences; they do not jump six-foot fences. No one knows why except the pronghorns, and they are not telling.

During a penning operation in Presidio County, Texas, 10 pronghorns easily cleared a five-foot mesh fence with ease. The wildlife technicians consequently raised the mesh fence eight inches and trapped the pronghorns again. The pronghorns jumped it again! That was a case of badly frightened, panicky pronghorns. Usually, they *will not* jump fences.

13

Go Underground for Pronghorns

If you are more than 34 inches around the middle, you haven't got a chance to sneak up on a pronghorned antelope! Despite this, lots of us middle-aged hunters, big around the middle, still like to hunt antelope.

No hunter can outrun a pronghorn, for they've been clocked at more than 50 m.p.h. for short stretches, and can do 30 m.p.h. all afternoon.

To bag an antelope, you must see it, aim, and shoot before he sees you. Now that is a difficult task, because the antelope has vision equal to ours aided by 8X binoculars. The old saying is "by the time you've spotted the pronghorn, he has already read the writing on the Bull Durham tag hanging out of your shirt pocket." There's no Bull Durham sack tag hanging out of my shirt pocket anymore, but you get the idea. In addition to having sharp eyesight, the antelope is incredibly well attuned to his surroundings, and anything that changes in his sight is noticed. If there is a new bump on the horizon, he sees it and his paranoid nature comes into play; he is instantly alert and watching that bump. If that bump turns out to be the rump of a man more than 34 inches around the middle, he knows it. He stares in fascination at the wriggling buttocks of a man slightly more than 34 inches around the middle. He has good enough eyesight to read the markings on the rifle barrel, too. When he reads 270 or even 243 or larger, he knows how far to stay away from that jiggling *gluteus maxima* on his horizon.

So the belly-crawl stalk is out for 90 percent of us.

If you can't outrun them, and if you can't sneak up on them, how do you get a good shot at a trophy pronghorned antelope? Some 40,000 are killed in the state of Wyoming alone each year, and goodly numbers are bagged in the two Dakotas, Nebraska, Colorado, New Mexico, Arizona, Utah, Montana, and Oregon. Now, how come?

First of all, most of those bagged are youngsters, stupid, or naive. They are not trophy bucks. For every 1000 antelope with headgear measuring 16 inches, there is probably only one that measures to a lofty 17 inches. And there are only about a dozen in the world's record books that measure 18 or over. Most of the antelope taken today are nice specimens, but hardly trophy antelope.

Of about 10,000 trophy antelope bucks taken each year, at least half (I'm guessing, of course) are taken by excellent riflemen who can hit a running antelope at 400 or 500 yards. Frankly, I don't bet on my ability — or yours, for that matter — to hit a running pronghorn at those ranges. In fact, I've never shot at a running antelope and I don't plan to shoot at a running antelope in the near future. I'm a hunter, not a shooter. If you are sure of your ability to hit the prairie speedster in full flight, you can skip the rest of this chapter. The more honest readers will follow along with me.

Another 1000 or so trophy-sized antelope are killed by a combination of good luck and clean living. I've seen the time when we were driving to the hunt area, saw a trophy buck, got out, and killed him before he realized that the season was open. But that doesn't happen often enough to count on it.

I'm in the second half of my 60s, measure slightly more than 34 inches around the middle, and am allergic to crawling on my belly in cactus country, which is where the pronghorn lives. I've learned that I don't dare show any part of my body above the ground level; if I do, the pronghorn will see it. My rear end is no longer hidden by six-inch sagebrush. The only time I tried to outrun an antelope the contest was between me and a day-old antelope kid. The antelope won. But I've never failed to bring home an antelope when I went after one. And I've never shot at a moving antelope. The secret is found below ground level.

It's really quite simple. I go underground for pronghorns.

Pete Anastasi and I were slated to hunt on the Chris Slagle ranch, near Upton, in the heart of Wyoming's excellent antelope country. The ranch manager, Ira Willis, tipped us off to the fact that there was a pit blind, already dug, near a windmill watering place, a couple of miles south of the headquarters buildings. He also told us that there were 19 large bulls in the pasture, and suggested that it might be wise to keep an eye on two of the Black Angus, and that it would be unwise to park our pickup in the bull pasture because the bulls might scratch their itching hides on the pickup and do some damage. Friend rancher also volunteered to take us to the windmill in the pre-dawn blackness.

As we got out of his pickup the next morning, he left us with the parting shot, "The bulls usually come to water about 10 o'clock, and they won't bother you if you leave them alone. And stay well away from those two black ones."

Pete and I found the pit blind, carefully built by a successful bowhunter who had had his choice of 24 good bucks in one day of bowhunting. He had made the blind big enough to be comfortable in, yet it was still well concealed. A lot of work had gone into its construction. First he

Cadieux stands up in pit blind to show depth to which it must be dug. Blind should be in place well before season opener, in order to allow animals to get accustomed to it.

had chopped off the sage at ground level, and kept the sage as movable upper parts of the blind. Then he had dug down far enough to allow a big man to sit comfortably on the bench (carved out of the hard clay) at the back of the circular pit. He had scattered the dry clay over the area around the blind, and strewn the debris so artfully that it was almost invisible from 20 feet. With both of us in the blind, we just barely had room for standing our rifles in front of us, separated by the sack containing apples, sandwiches, thermos of coffee, two pairs of binoculars, and extra shells.

There were no bulls in sight as it slowly grew pink in the east, nor antelope, for that matter. In whispers we discussed the fact that there was drinking water available for game almost anywhere, as there had been lots of rain, and we wondered why the antelope would come to this particular spa to slake their thirst.

I knew that antelope go to water three or four times per day, when there is no reason not to. I know that these incredibly mobile creatures don't mind traveling two or three miles to have a sociable drink with their friends and neighbors. When it is really hot, the pronghorn will often go to water five or six times a day.

Our blind was facing slightly downslope toward the windmill, the stock watering tank, and the small earthen dam that held the spillover from the metal tank. Our rifles were placed with their muzzles toward the watering spot, only 35 yards away. It was obvious that the bowman had planned that the target buck would come to the water's edge, allowing the archer to draw and release while the animal had his head down, drinking. It was a perfect spot for a bowhunter, a good spot for a rifleman.

The brightening eastern horizon now allowed us to see six antelope about a mile toward the expected sunrise. They seemed to be feeding slowly from north to south,

When hunter is seated in pit blind, his head is concealed by native brush left around perimeter of pit.

Pit blind must be deep enough to allow concealment, but not too deep—which would make for awkward shooting.

and weren't planning on approaching our hideout, at least not soon.

Six mallards swung to the water, splashed in, and dabbled not 30 feet in front of us. A big flock of sage grouse flew to the hillside on the other side of the water tank and walked slowly and sedately to water.

Pete is a Virginian, and he was whispering that they were bigger than a lot of wild turkeys, when we jumped to the sound of an explosive snort from behind us. We hadn't been seen, because we were underground, but the oncoming antelope had noticed something—probably heard us, as the gentle breeze would not have betrayed

Go Underground for Pronghorns

our scent. We swiveled our necks and guns around to see behind us—50 feet away, six antelope were staring intently at the spot in the sage where we hid. There was one small buck and the rest were does. "Let them come in for decoys," I whispered to Pete, and we both ducked lower in the blind. The sage grouse, thirst satisfied, were walking slowly up the hill, going back the way they had come.

I got my camera into position and began clicking away. Each time the shutter clicked, the buck winced, as if stuck with a pin. But he held his ground. One of the smaller does stamped her feet and snorted again, a sound like a high-pitched *cheeeeaow*, almost explosive in nature.

One of the smaller does came trotting daintily past our blind, no more than 15 feet to the north, and went unhesitatingly down to drink. Three others followed her lead, but the young buck, already showing the prudence that would stand him in good stead if he intended to live to see his second summer, took a long detour around to the north. He approached the windmill with much skittish moving in, then darting away, and finally took off running like the wind, without having a drink.

When the next group of pronghorns came in, they also came from the higher ground to the west, and it was apparent that this was the usual procedure. Evidently every single animal circled to get to the high ground to the west, then walked down that ridge—the one we were dug in on—to the water. Two good bucks were among the visitors, but both grew cautious when they were close to our blind, and did not come in.

"If I was in that windmill, sitting right between the legs, I could see that ridge and get a good shot," Pete opined.

"Remember the bulls," I told him, as he climbed out of the blind and trudged to the windmill. He moved a couple of loose planks that were leaning against the metal legs and soon had a good blind right in the mill itself. Once immobile, the only thing that gave him away was his blaze-orange hat. I am fairly well convinced that antelope don't worry about blaze orange, so I ducked lower in the pit blind and opened the coffee thermos.

As I enjoyed the first sip of black coffee, I saw Pete's camouflaged arm move, ever so slowly, to level his rifle across the windmill support. In ultra-slow motion, his head inclined to the gun, which was aimed to the north of my position, near where the other antelope had come. I found myself holding my breath, until Pete's 30-06 bellowed. Coming to my feet, I saw three antelope racing off to the west, but I also heard Pete say calmly, "I got him!"

We both ran to where two legs were waving slowly over the tops of the short sage. The 150-grain slug had smashed the buck's spinal column at 200 yards. I congratulated Pete on a nice neck shot and we went to work gutting the animal. That done, Pete started the long walk to get our pickup camper and come back for his buck. Like most Wyoming ranchers, our host takes a mighty dim view of hunters driving off the roads—unless they have an animal down. Wheels are hard on pastures in a land where the rains don't always come when the pastures need rain.

Before Pete was a city block away, I had taken his place in the windmill blind. I could see much farther than I could from the pit blind, and in the right direction. There was only one thing wrong. The bulls came to water early. At 9:30 a.m. there were six of the placid Herefords licking

Pete Anastasi traveled from Virginia to Wyoming to bag this nice buck with one shot from his .30–06.

the salt blocks, but one Black Angus was very annoyed by my presence. If I had seen him coming, I would have vacated the premises and given him a wide berth. We had washed our bloody hands in the tank, and the smell of blood did things to his emotions, I guess. He snorted, pawed the ground, threw dirt all over himself, and approached as close as he could to me. He didn't seem to have any way to get at me, inside the flimsy metal framework of the windmill, but I remembered what Ira had said, "Watch that black devil, he knocked a man down here last week, and it might be permanent."

It was the bellowing that bothered me. Have you ever looked down the throat of a Black Angus bull at a distance of three feet? It can destroy your desire to hunt, I can tell you that. After a nervous 10 minutes, he trudged over to have his morning fix of the salt block, and I vacated the other side of the mill and walked—trying to appear nonchalant—back to the pit blind. The bull never even glanced my way, so I felt better as I slid into the blind. He couldn't get at me there, I reasoned, without falling in on top of me and that would be a disaster for both of us. Me most of all.

Within 10 minutes, more antelope came down the ridge in back of the blind. Carefully raising one eyebrow to ground level, I checked out a herd of seven does and two small bucks. The two males were intent on showing off to each other, so they were minus their usual caution. The does went unconcernedly down to drink, without even a snort at passing my hidey-hole. After drinking, several of them even lay down for a few minutes, then the young bucks prodded them to their feet and the whole gang went off to the west.

On their way west they passed another group coming in, and this group held a good buck. I put the binoculars on him as he showed over the near horizon. The horns were tall, symmetrical, the bases seemed husky enough, and the tips were turned in at just the right angle.

"You'll do just fine," I muttered soundlessly, and eased the 7mm into position in front of me. Because the seat was now on the wrong side, I was half crouched in the blind, one knee on the floor, my elbows braced against the rim of the blind.

One of the does suddenly dashed off to the north and the buck took off after her. Like a good quarter horse, he cut her off, turned her back to the group, and herded his harem into a compact group. Many times, I've seen this "chasing" behavior prior to breeding season. The does seem to enjoy the game more than the bucks, and if he turns back and doesn't follow the departing doe, she will invariably turn, look sorrowfully back at him, then come trotting back close enough to get him interested again.

Six does moved by my blind, but the buck hung back, looking worried. I could see only his head and the top half of his neck now, for that's all that stuck up over the roll in the terrain behind me. He trotted nervously back and forth, slowly coming closer with each sideways move. The does were all drinking, with some of them starting to come back my way.

I couldn't make myself believe that he would forego his morning drink of water, so I kept the scope on the slowly moving neck. Those horns looked plenty good to me right now. I had made up my mind that I would take him the minute his heart-lung area came under the crosshairs.

"One more step, you son of a gun," I was muttering quietly to myself. As if to oblige, the buck suddenly began moving straight toward me. His white chest markings came into view and my finger started to tighten on the trigger. Unbeknownst to me, though, two of the does had moved over behind me, between me and the water's edge. They were 35 feet from the blind. One of them evidently caught my scent, or perhaps a suspicious twitching of the sagebrush cover to the blind. She snorted like a blowout on an 18-wheeler. The buck stopped as if hit with a wet fish, turned, and walked away, looking back at me with suspicion written on every inch of his beautiful body.

Moving the crosshairs to the area just behind his slowly moving foreleg, I squeezed! The whole area erupted in running antelope. As I stood erect in the blind, the doe which had snorted almost jumped over me in her haste to get going. There were at least 15 antelope within close range, but the buck I had shot stood like a statue. I couldn't believe that the 7mm hadn't even knocked him down, so I

These fawns were unafraid of the photographer's blind, even though they saw him enter it. They passed within 25 feet, enroute to water.

kept the crosshairs on him and waited. In half a second, I suppose, he suddenly reared up on his hind legs and went over backwards. My hunt was over. I carefully approached the buck, rifle at the ready, for I've seen pronghorns carry off a surprising amount of lead. If the first shot hits the vitals, they come down easily. If they are wounded or scared badly enough to have the adrenaline pumping through their veins, they can be unbelievably hard to put down.

Pete came driving up, shouting congratulations. It seemed he had seen the antelope herd coming to the windmill from half a mile north and had stopped to watch the whole thing through his binoculars. "Didn't want to scare off such an easy shot!" he needled gently.

We quickly prepared the two antelope for the trip to the processing plant. My buck had taken the 150-grain Nosler boat-tail bullet just over the heart, completely pulverizing the lungs. I was pleased with the bullet performance. I had worried that the light bone structure of the antelope might not upset the bullet enough to let it expend its full energy inside the animal. I needn't have worried; it had done its job perfectly.

As we drove into town, Pete remarked, "This hunting from a blind sure makes it almost too easy!"

I agreed, but that's the way you should have it if you intend to make clean, humane kills on antelope. My record is intact; I've still never shot at a running antelope.

To score from a pit blind, you have to have many factors in your favor. First, of course, you have to put your blind where there are antelope, and where they are apt to come within range. It is far better, for the rifle hunter, to have the blind where it will allow a shot at an animal approaching the watering hole, than to have the blind right at the watering hole. If you have any proficiency with the rifle at all, a 200-yard shot is just as easy as a 50-yard shot, perhaps easier because of the telescope sight factor which makes it rough to aim properly at close range with a high magnification. When you are 200 yards away, you are much less apt to scare off a trophy buck, and you still have a good, sure shot.

Your pit blind should be on a slightly elevated part of the terrain, but not silhouetted against the skyline. If you are just under the crest of the rise—there are no real hills in most antelope country—you can see for great distances, except over the rise behind you.

Your pit blind should be dug well in advance of hunting season. Every wildlife species has a "strange object" reaction, which causes them to automatically steer well clear of something new in their world. Place the pit blind two weeks early—with the rancher's permission, of course—and let the pronghorns get used to seeing the slight change in their world.

The dirt excavated in making your blind should be carefully distributed around the blind to give it a chance to dry out and blend in with the terrain. Don't haul it away, because you will want it to fill in the hole after your hunt. Most ranchers snort fire at the idea of leaving a dangerous pit for a critter to blunder into when the snow camouflages it.

Keep the sagebrush or other vegetation that you chopped down to start your diggings. Use it to camouflage your head and rifle when you aim. Because it is movable, it permits you to arrange the top, or vegetation, part of your blind to allow a lane of fire best suited to the day's conditions, such as allowing you to accommodate a change in wind direction. Antelope will not approach a concealed hunter from downwind anymore than a deer will.

I know it is hard work to dig in that sunbaked clay, but don't skimp on your blind's size. It should allow you to sit comfortably, for you will spend many hours there. It should not be so narrow at the bottom that it forces you to keep your feet close together, for this changes your normal shooting stance. It should also have room for a rucksack full of sandwiches, thermos, binoculars, and gamebag to cover your pronghorn carcass after the kill.

Going underground for pronghorns is the surest way there is to bag an antelope if you are more than 34 inches around the middle. The two most important considerations are: proper placement of the blind to allow shots at the normal travel routes of those particular antelope, and permission from the rancher to dig up his pasture.

No, you don't need to give up antelope hunting if you find yourself allergic to crawling on your belly in the cactus. Simply go underground!

14

Where to Hunt

Where should you go to hunt pronghorns? There are easy answers to that question, and then there are sensible, correct answers. Let's try the easy answers first.

Where should you hunt pronghorns? Obviously, hunt where the most of them are. That means Wyoming. So you go hunting in Wyoming, where roughly two-thirds of all the world's pronghorns live. If you are searching for a trophy head, and you don't want to pay money for hunting access privileges, I'd suggest that you hunt in Carbon County, Wyoming. After all, about one-seventh of all the trophy pronghorns listed with Boone and Crockett came out of Carbon County. Carbon County is an 8000-square-mile chunk of red desert and rough country lying south of Rawlins and west of Laramie. As you would expect, it is sagebrush country, which is the "without which nothing" requirement for pronghorns. This country is not the easiest to hunt, so it is lightly (relatively speaking) hunted. Lightly hunted herds contain bucks that have been allowed to live past their third birthday, and it is the 5- and 6-year-olds that grow the trophy headgear.

Okay, while we are completing the easiest answer to your question, let's talk about Carbon County. There is lots of public land in the county, and you can get an ownership map from the Bureau of Land Management in Casper. For an application blank, write to Wyoming Game and Fish Department, License Division, Cheyenne, WY 82002. If you want all the odds in your favor, hire a guide. To do this, write to Wyoming Outfitters Association, Moran, WY 83013. You don't

Comparing the length of the ears to the length of the horns helps in judging a trophy. But it gets complicated when the horns cast a shadow over the ears, as in this photo. *New Mexico Game and Fish Department photo.*

really need a guide, but it will help, especially if you are serious about that *trophy buck*.

Personally, I've never hunted pronghorns in Carbon County. I've killed pronghorns in North Dakota, South Dakota, Wyoming, and New Mexico. My favorite spot is in northeastern Wyoming. Yes, I pay an access fee, and have been doing so for years. But when you consider the dollar amount invested in the hunt, with transportation, lodging, and meals, an extra $100 paid to a rancher who allows you a lot of privileges on his land, who takes a chance on some dummy shooting up a prize bull, who furnishes more information than a guide can furnish, who knows the routes used by the pronghorns like he knows the route to his own bathroom, that's the best expenditure of the trip.

One of the best-kept secrets of pronghorn hunting is the section of their range known as eastern Montana (see Norman Strung's advice to hunters in chapter 21). Here the state game department is actually trying to reduce the size of the herds. They've not had much luck the past three

It is easy to compare horns with ears in this photo. When the body of the animal is larger—or smaller—than normal, the judging of trophy horns becomes more difficult. *New Mexico Game and Fish Department photo.*

years, though, as the annual increase in the herd's size exceeds the annual hunter take. In many areas, additional animals can be taken (for a fee) on the same license. You have to put in your application in June, but that is easy to do, and allows you the rest of the summer to think about it, to practice your marksmanship, and to get your blood pressure up. It is also very easy to combine a pronghorn and mule deer hunt in this area. In fact, it may be possible to take three antelope and five mules on one license in parts of southeastern Montana. Although the ratio of public to private land is lower here than in parts of Wyoming, the chances of getting permission to hunt on private land are excellent.

Montana game managers say that it has too many pronghorns in that part of the state, and too few hunters to take the desired harvest. You might want to help them out. For further information, write to Department of Fish, Wildlife and Parks, 1420 East Sixth, Helena, MT 59620.

Which parts of this eastern Montana territory would I recommend? You might try the area around Glasgow, or the chunk of land between Harlowton and Roundup. If you are worried about access to hunting areas, put in for that part of the state in District 600, east of Fort Peck Reservoir. There's a lot of BLM land in that area, and it's open to hunting.

When planning a pronghorn hunt, easterners almost always go to Wyoming, and no one can quarrel with that. But it may come as a surprise to you to learn that South Dakota is consistently ranked third in numbers of pronghorns. Wyoming, Montana, and then South Dakota is the usual order. Sure, Wyoming is far and away the leader, but the herds of South Dakota are healthy and they do allow nonresident hunters. See Chuck Post's advice in Chapter 21.

Colorado also offers some fine pronghorn hunting, and has lately come up with some record-book heads, so they must be doing some things right. See Judd Cooney's description of taking a new world-record Pope and Young pronghorn with the bow, in Colorado. That's in Chapter 24.

New Mexico, Arizona, Utah, Nevada, Oregon, and California all offer some pronghorn hunting, but their herds are much smaller than those of the big four, and permits are harder to come by. In my home state of New Mexico, the chances of taking a truly "trophy" buck are not that good. In northeastern New Mexico, we have a lot of bucks that grow tall horns, but not massive ones. Seen from a distance, they may look like record-book material, but once you have them laid down, those horns shrink disappointingly. We crop our pronghorns closely in the Land of Enchantment, which means that the bucks do not live long enough to grow bragging-size headgear. Where and when you hunt is strictly limited in New Mexico. That's good management, but it may make planning your trip more difficult.

To sum up the question of which state to hunt, I guess we'd have to go back to the easiest answer. Wyoming is your best bet. Montana is second best. The others all offer good hunting, but if you do not possess local knowledge, go where they're thickest, and that is Wyoming and Montana.

15

Rifle Selection

Pronghorns are small, slim-boned animals. They do require a lot of killing at times, however. Those seemingly contradictory statements are easily explained. If the pronghorn doesn't know that you are within 20 miles, is completely unsuspecting, he is easily knocked down and kept down with a bullet whose placement can be either marginal or perfect. However, once his adrenaline is flowing through that oversized heart-lung area, the pronghorn is remarkably tenacious of life.

Like every gamebird or animal that man hunts, the pronghorn deserves a quick (for which read "instantaneous") and humane death. The true sportsman respects his quarry, and this respect should guarantee that the hunter never take a shot he is not sure of, that the hunter always place the bullet accurately to ensure an instantaneous death, and that the hunter not exceed his own proficiency rating by trying difficult shots.

Some hunters believe that the true sportsman should never shoot at a running antelope, because the odds against accurate bullet placement are too high. I happen to be among those who share this belief, but I have no quarrel with you if you think that you can hit the running pronghorn *in a vital area*.

Each pronghorn hunter has a responsibility to learn his weapon and to learn how to place the bullet accurately. To this end, there can be no substitute for lots of target shooting. A properly sighted rifle, chambered for an adequate cartridge, in the hands of the competent marksman who knows what his gun can do and what it cannot do, is a deadly precision instrument.

The combination should result in in-

Familiarity with the rifle and practice are both more important than the choice of caliber. *South Dakota Game, Fish and Parks photo.*

Rifle Selection

stantaneous kills on the small-bodied pronghorn all of the time. All pronghorn kills should be one-shot kills, of course. Respect for the animal hunted dictates that.

Because of the wide-open terrain favored by pronghorns, the distance from rifle to target is usually quite long. Most pronghorns are killed at ranges less than 200 yards, but many shots are fired at ranges up to 400 and even 500 yards, with the "rifleman" aiming a yard over the back of a flying pronghorn and touching it off with a prayer in his heart. The Gods of Hunting seldom answer such a prayer.

Shots at pronghorns are apt to be longer than shots at deer. Secondly, there is often a bit of wind out on the wide-open ranges of the West. This favors the larger, heavier bullet, which can retain muzzle velocity and buck wind over longer ranges than lighter projectiles can.

The school of thought which holds that the very small, very fast projectile has the best chance is not facing the realities of life on the pronghorn pastures. That incredibly "hot" projectile literally explodes upon hitting a bone, and when the range is under 200 yards, the tissue damage is too great for my tastes. It may, for example, hit a shoulder bone and explode outside of the vital area, mangling a square foot of shoulder without penetrating into the vital heart-lung boiler room. It retains its theoretical accuracy out to great ranges, but that is only theoretical when the wind is blowing.

In pioneer days, literally millions of pronghorns were killed with heavy, slow projectiles shot from big-bored rifles. They bucked the wind well, but those market hunters seldom took a shot at more than 60 yards. They didn't need to, though. Antelope had previously had experience with humans who used only bows and arrows—primitive bows, by today's standards—and they knew that a human couldn't hurt them at 100 yards. Before the pronghorn adjusted the distance at which his alarm bell sounded and he began to move away from an approaching human, millions were killed with the Sharps, the Winchester 73, and similar guns—even the 45/70, which shot a 255-grain piece of lead at the speed of a freight train.

With all of these considerations in mind, which are the better rifles for today's pronghorns?

Preferred groups of calibers are these: 250 Savage; 257 Remington Roberts and its 6mm twins by both Remington and Winchester (243 and 244); 25-06; 270; 30-06; 7mm Remington Magnum.

I am aware of the fact that many riflemen feel that the Big Seven is a bit much for pronghorn antelope, which seldom exceed 120 pounds in weight. Nevertheless, they are supremely accurate cartridges and I hunt almost all big-game species with them. They are an excellent choice for the kind of hunting I do. I never shoot at a running pronghorn, yet I feel that I can hit a standing pronghorn at ranges out to 400 yards, so long as he holds still. My last five have been instantaneous, one-shot kills, which is what they should be.

Calibers smaller than 243 should not be allowed on the antelope ranges. I am aware that this rules out the very accurate 220 Swift, but I believe that such small calibers should be ruled out by reason of being erratic in strong winds, and of causing heavy tissue destruction while still allowing some crippled animals to escape. Granted, at close range, a well-placed 22 caliber pill, hopping along at 220 Swift or even 219 Donaldson velocities, will drop a pronghorn as if he were pole-axed. But we must remember that even the 25/35 and the ancient 30/30 will work wonders at close range. So will the 22 rimfire if properly placed. After all, butchers kill bison bulls weighing three-quarters of a ton with a 22 bullet, but they place it behind the ear at close range. You seldom have that opportunity when hunting antelope.

For the average hunter, factory-loaded ammunition does an excellent job on antelope. Perhaps the best loads available from the factory are listed in the accompanying table.

Best Factory-Load Ammunition

Caliber	Bullet Weight	Muzzle Velocity
.243	100 grains	2800 fps
.250 Savage	100 grains	2700 fps
.257 Remington-Roberts	100 grains	2900 fps
.25-06 Remington	120 grains	2900 fps
.264 Win-Mag.	160 grains	2900 fps
.270	150 grains	2900 fps
.30-06	150 grains	2900 fps
7mm Rem-Mag.	154 grains	3000 fps

A few comments are in order here. The above listing for the 264 may surprise some readers who have had experience with this exceptionally flat-shooting, extremely accurate caliber. If they have experimented with this rifle "hot rod," they have noticed that it wears out barrels quite rapidly, due to the corrosive effect of those extremely hot loads. The same thing was said of the 220 Swift when it first came out, but the "thread the needle" accuracy of the Swift on a windless day earned it a place in the varminter's arsenal that it has never relinquished. The 264 is on one side of the popular 270, the 284 is on the other side. Both are effective calibers, neither has anything special over the 270, at least not on the pronghorn plains. If it does gain that lasting popularity, it will be with reduced loads, for there is really no need to belch fire and brimstone at the pronghorn; it is only necessary to place the bullet properly in the vital area — and do it on the first shot.

Obviously, I have no intention of ruling out such excellent calibers as the 280 Remington Magnum, the truly great 270 Weatherby Magnum, the very adequate 7mm-08 Remington, the 7x61 Sharpe and Hart, or even the 300 H & H Magnum, which is surely far more than adequate. However, the popular calibers listed above are commercially available almost everywhere in pronghorn country, do not need to be handloaded, and will do a fine job for the pronghorn hunter.

Pronghorn hunting requires long-range accuracy, and that is best attained by experimentation with your particular rifle, with different loads of bullet weight, powder charge, and primer model. Amazing differences in accuracy may be found with as little as half a grain of powder in the handloader's charge. Most handloaders are real gun nuts, or they wouldn't be into handloading. Such avid experimenters should not need to be reminded that:

1. The fastest velocity is not usually the most accurate velocity for that caliber and bullet weight. Sometimes backing off a bit will improve accuracy.

2. The sensible handloader who wants to keep both his eyes and all of his fingers will approach maximum loads gingerly, moving up $1/10$ of a grain at a time when nearing maximum. He will be alert for signs that he is approaching maximum

Rifle Selection

pressures. Such indications include, but are not limited to: badly flattened primers, cracks in the neck of the fired case, swollen cases, and/or difficulties in extracting the fired cases.

3. Heavier bullets will buck wind better than lighter bullets and will retain better velocity at extreme ranges. In other words, the slightly slower, heavier bullet will give more "predictable" accuracy at extreme ranges than will the lighter, faster bullet of the same caliber.

The choice of rifle for pronghorn hunting is easier than the choice of caliber. You need a light rifle, for the apparent weight doubles when you've carried it over many miles of stalking. You need an accurate rifle, so we will rule in favor of the bolt actions as compared with the lever, autoloader, or slide-operated rifle. Bolt actions are inherently more accurate, so go with them.

There are several riflemakers who produce rifles fitting these criteria. My personal choice is the Remington Model 700. Winchester Model 70s, though no longer the standard of the industry that they once were, are also excellent rifles for pronghorns. You cannot go wrong with a Weatherby, Browning, or a Ruger, either. At the time this book went to press, the Remington Model 700 was the best buy, at least in this man's opinion. I practice what I preach, and the two Model 700s that I can see from this desk are chambered in 22/250 and in 7mm Remington Magnum. With this pair I feel confident of having the right weapon for all creatures, large and small, from ground squirrels to moose or brown bear.

Since acquiring the 7mm, I have used it and no other rifle, for both deer and pronghorn. It has performed admirably. I know that a sizable portion of the shooting fraternity has no love for the Big Seven, not liking its muzzle blast and detesting its recoil. I admit that the horrendous muzzle blast and ear-banging report are conducive to flinching. When the flinch comes, accuracy goes. I do not enjoy shooting the gun from a bench rest, although that is necessary if you want to really know your gun. Once the bench-rest shooting chores are completed, the handloads selected, and the scope sight adjusted properly, I shoot the Big Seven only in the field, and there, for some reason, I don't notice either muzzle blast or recoil.

You think I'm ducking the question? You say you want a rifle for pronghorns only and you want me to name it? All right, I'll go out on a limb with the Remington Model 700 in 270 caliber. You'll be ready for pronghorn at any range.

Next question is what scope to use?

I recommend a variable, running from 2X to 7X, or even one that goes all the way up to 9X. At ranges up to 200 yards, you'll never need the higher magnification, but it is nice to have when you are just about to make the decision to pull the trigger. Is that buck really near record measurements? No time for a spotting scope? Your high magnification will help. Also, when the only shot is at a buck standing still at 400 yards (not moving)— and when you have practiced at this range, and when you know exactly where that bullet will hit, and you know that you have a much better than 50–50 chance of putting the lead into the vital area—then you'll bless that high magnification.

Why the variable rather than a fixed-power scope? Because it is difficult to find a small target in the high-magnification scope. At high power it simply does not cover a big enough field of view to allow you to find the target quickly. The high power's field of view is too small to allow you to get your sights on a running target (another good reason for not shooting at running pronghorns). If you are forced into a situation where you are crawling on your belly for 400 yards through the cactus, and you get within range, you have to at least show the muzzle to get that well-earned shot. You want to find the target quickly, because the pronghorn will find that moving muzzle quickly, and he may be off and running before you can locate him in the high-power scope. Only the lower power will enable you to find the target quickly. So, at times you need the lower power and at times you need the higher magnification—hence, the variable power scope is best.

Your rifle should be equipped with an adjustable sling, both for ease of carrying it in the field and to help you get a steady "hold" when in the sitting, kneeling, or prone position.

Okay, your equipment is ready. But there is one more thing required, and that is PRACTICE. The expert big-game hunter retains his skills by shooting every week, and he fires off about 100 rounds per month, minimum! The average hunter only shoulders his rifle once a year, during hunting season, and then he regrets his lack of practice. Target practice will do the job: Punching holes in paper at 200 yards will teach you your own limitations, and the limitations of your rifle and scope. It will also give you confidence in your ability to place the shot correctly, and confidence is a prerequisite of good shooting.

Shooting at small game—ground squirrels, jackrabbits, woodchucks, and marmots, usually referred to as "varmints"—will make you a better hunter as well as a better shooter. Shooting small varmints weekly, using hand-rolled ammunition that you prepared yourself, is the best possible way to get ready for pronghorn season.

My personal prescription for pronghorn popping is the aforementioned 7mm Remington Magnum in Remington Model 700, with a Redfield 2X–7X variable-power scope, firing the 154-grain spire point (Hornadays No. 2830) propelled by 64 grains of IMR 4831 powder at a muzzle velocity (estimated) of 2990 feet per second. Accuracy has been excellent both on the target range and in the field. The antelope I've killed with this combination were all standing stock still, and each dropped instantly and never twitched. Each shot was placed into the heart-lung area and the bullets expanded well, leaving a quarter-size exit hole. None of the bullets stayed in the animal, so you would be justified in saying that I am overgunned. Ideally, the bullet should expend all of its energy within the carcass—but that is being a bit persnickety for my tastes. All I ask is that the animal die instantly. My rifle, caliber, bullet, and scope combination does that job, and does it well.

16

Decoying Antelope

For the past 10 years, some hunters have been experimenting with decoys to lure pronghorns close enough to stick them with an arrow. The fact that it has worked so well for bowhunters should tell us that it would be near perfect for the rifleman. Only a fool would be anywhere near a decoy pronghorn during a rifle season, however. The chances of getting shot yourself are far too high. *Don't try a decoy for pronghorn during a rifle season.* Don't even try it if you are the only hunter allowed on that land. Someone may not know he is trespassing, or not care, and come close enough to try a "luck" shot at your decoy. He might hit you. Let's repeat it: Don't use a decoy in a rifle season for pronghorns.

But if you want to use a decoy for purposes of photographing pronghorns or for bowhunting, here's how some of the successful ones have done it.

Saw out a full-size silhouette pronghorn from three-eighth-inch plywood. Admittedly, this doesn't look very lifelike, although in some cases just the bare plywood will work all right. But, let's improve it. The best possible improvement is a full-body mount of a real pronghorn, of course. But that is expensive and most people don't have a spare full-body mount lying around the house. You can use the skin of a pronghorn, stretched over the plywood, to give it authenticity, or you can cover the plywood with pieces of scrap carpet of the correct colors to make it look like the real thing. If you get your carpet from end of roll remnants at the carpet house, this can be done quite inexpensively. It might be a good idea to mark off the various color areas in pencil and label them, then cut the carpet to fit your "paint by numbers" plan. Another option would be to use styrofoam blocks to flesh out the body, giving it a three-dimensional look. Then paint the styrofoam, or cover it first with cloth and then paint the cloth. If you do a good job of painting, this can be a very lifelike, durable decoy.

A nice finishing touch is to add the horns from last year's kill to the head of your decoy. If the pronghorn's eyesight is as good as we are told, he will check the authenticity of the horns and decide that it is real, all right. Some decoy users swear by the lifelike eyes, which can be purchased from your friendly taxidermist. Seems that pronghorns like to engage in staring contests. If the wild animal sees only painted black spots where shiny, luminous black eyes ought to be, it might be the difference between his losing interest and his coming into bow range.

If you make your decoy three-dimensional, it is more likely to inspire your confidence as well. In all I can learn about decoying pronghorns, it doesn't seem to make much difference to the pronghorn being decoyed if the decoy is lifelike or not. But if *you* have confidence, it will help.

Make sure that you have a system for erecting your decoy, one that will work in rocky ground, or in sand. I've seen them with a fold-out third leg that allows them to stand—free form, as it were—anywhere. The disadvantage to the tripod system is that it is easily blown over by the normal winds of the pronghorn pastures. I saw a good set-up that used a half-inch-diameter steel rod that was driven into the earth. Two conduit clamps on the inside of the decoy were slid over the rod, and the whole rig was rigid and erect.

The success of the decoying scam is dependent upon three things. One, the pronghorn is very curious. He cannot go away without knowing what sort of newcomer this is. The fact that the newcomer stands his ground, is not intimidated, and doesn't seem to know his place, just drives the wild pronghorn buck up the wall, and he comes closer to see what is going on. Secondly, there is a definite order of dominance among pronghorn males, similar to the pecking order of chickens. Every buck knows which ones he can defeat and which ones can "whup" him. How this is determined is beyond my ken, bucks seldom actually fight each other. Ninety-nine percent of the dominance questions are settled by short, bluffing charges on the part of the dominant animal. The "challenger," his bluff called, turns and runs.

Thirdly, most archery seasons run concurrently with the rut. This means that the herd sire—the largest and most desirable trophy, usually—will be anxious to defend his territory, and to keep challengers away from *his* harem. Sex-mad and jealous with rage, the herd sire doesn't think too well at this time. Sex has him set up to be a sucker, and your decoy can finish the job.

You place your decoy in a location where he can be seen for miles around. Silhouetted on the skyline near the favorite watering hole is a good spot to start your learning experience. Naturally, you have chosen a pasture that pronghorns are using, for as in every other kind of hunting, you have to go where the game is. You are hidden, either in a pit blind or behind some brush. One user of decoys simply hides behind his decoy. As long as he holds perfectly still, he will go unnoticed.

A prime requisite for decoy hunters is patience. When a pronghorn comes to investigate, he will usually come to within

200 yards and then stand and try to outstare the decoy. He may keep this up for half an hour or even an hour. If you move, that's all she wrote. After you have let the ant crawl across your eyeball without brushing him off, after your left leg has gone to sleep and the prickly sensation is spreading up into your lower back, after your mouth is so dry that you are spitting cotton — after all this, the buck may turn and walk off. He also may come running up to sniff noses and get acquainted with this newcomer. After all, no one claimed that pronghorns were smart!

Does it work? Larry Cross, an Idahoan who has seven antelope with the bow to his credit, and who has put most of them into the Pope and Young record book, uses a decoy. In fact, he has worn one out and is building a new one.

Oh, yes! One more thing. Don't put oversize horns on your decoy. Many knowledgeable pronghorn people believe that dominance depends upon horn size. You don't want to scare a buck away, so use six-inch horns — they won't scare any buck, and they might bring that record buck a-running to drive this impudent young punk away.

17

Muzzleloaders

In the past decade, there has been a great upsurge in the number of hunters who go after big game with the weapons of the pioneers, the muzzleloader long rifle. Part of this upsurge has been caused by the novelty of the blackpowder fad, but a lot of it has been the challenge of blackpowder shooting. It is much more difficult to hit and kill a big-game animal with a slow-moving ball of lead than it is with a bullet from a scope-sighted, flat shooting, modern rifle.

Muzzleloaders are heavy, difficult to swing and line up to the target, and the "lock time" of a muzzleloader is infinitely longer than it is for a centerfire rifle cartridge. Range is very limited. The lead ball will kill out to about 110 yards, but it is accurate only to about 50 yards, under hunting conditions.

The alert, quick-moving speedy pronghorn, found on the open plains, is the greatest challenge for the muzzleloader rifleman. Or, put another way, no weapon is less suited to antelope hunting than the muzzleloader. Back in the days when the market hunters were decimating the herds of bison and elk, they didn't do much damage to the antelope. Part of this is due to the fact that the hunters wanted the bigger-bodied animal with more pounds of eating meat when they fired off an expensive round from their primitive weapons. The other reason is that the wary, alert antelope simply wouldn't let them get within sure killing range of a gun that tossed a slow-moving chunk of lead in a looping trajectory.

I've never tried muzzleloading for antelope, so I asked two men who have. The following is a digest of their answers:

To kill a pronghorn with a blackpowder

If the muzzleloader hunter sits still long enough, a pronghorn may come within range, but . . .

It's still a long ways to move the gun up to the shooting position. While the muzzleloader is coming up to full cocked and aimed position, the pronghorn may move 50 feet.

gun, you sit and wait until the pronghorn comes in to drink. You are perfectly camouflaged, meaning eyeballs and glasses, everything. You are absolutely motionless, even when an ant crawls across your eyeball. Your rifle is positioned in nearly the position it will be in when you fire it. You will not have time to move the gun very far, for the pronghorn's reactions are quicker'n a cat's.

Camouflage is important in all pronghorn hunting, but doubly so with the muzzleloader, whose killing distance is relatively short.

The muzzleloader will be at half cock, which is the only safe way to carry a loaded muzzleloader. This means that you have to cock it to fire it. I know the antelope will hear that tiny click, but that cannot be helped; only a fool carries a muzzleloader at full cock, which makes it almost a hair trigger situation.

One of my successful muzzleloader friends told me that he sat in a fence corner, in plain sight, leaning back against the cornerpost in his camouflage suit, his weapon across his lap. The antelope came to drink at the windmill-supplied tank. When the buck put his head down to drink, the muzzleloader came up, being cocked as it leveled, and the shot was fired. He said that the antelope was in high gear when he fired, and that he led it almost 10 feet. The shot broke the buck's back. "Somebody up there likes me," added the hunter, "for a lot of good luck was involved."

The other successful hunter said that he hunted from a pit blind, with the rifle extended outside of the blind. The blind was covered with well-weathered burlap that had been in position for three months, to let the pronghorns get used to it. The weather was windy, and the windmill was creaking mightily, which hid the sound of the rifle being cocked. His pronghorn dropped in its tracks with a heart shot.

The odds against killing a pronghorn antelope with a muzzleloader are great. However, most antelope states provide early seasons for muzzleloaders, giving you a chance at the bucks before they know that it's hunting season again. These early seasons also give you a chance to hunt when it isn't crowded, and that is worth a lot in these days of crowded coverts and shoulder-to-shoulder hunting conditions.

To recap, muzzleloaders have killed many pronghorns . . . but it sure isn't easy. Camouflage is even more important than it is for the modern rifleman and much more important than it is for hunting deer. If you want the ultimate challenge, try clobbering a pronghorn with the ancient smokepole!

18

Hunting Equipment

Once you leave the vehicle that brought you to the place where you are going to hunt, you do not want to have to go back to the vehicle for the remainder of the hunting day. You will want to take afield the necessities for your survival and comfort during the day. That means that your pack should contain:

Binoculars
Knife to dress out the carcass.
Canteen of water.
Food for lunch.

Gamebag to cover the dressed carcass if you are going to be away from the vehicle that long.

Plastic bag to carry heart and liver, after they have been cooled out. Do not store in plastic until the body heat is completely gone.

Camera, if you want shots of your kill, of the terrain, of the watering hole, or whatever. If you are serious about your hunting, leave your camera in the daypack. Don't carry it with you. As a working photographer-writer, I learned long ago that you can hunt *or* you can take pictures, but you can't do justice to both jobs at the same time.

Nothing else! You do not need a map of the area, for you are not going to walk that far, and it is easy to keep your bearings on the wide-open plains. You do not need matches, for you are not going to start a fire. You do not need a paperback novel to read while you wait, for you are going to stay alert at all times. You are hunting—do your reading at home. You do not need a transistor radio to amuse you, for the pronghorn does not care for modern music and it is difficult to find classical music while that far from FM stations. You do not need any alcoholic beverages, not even one beer. It is easy for you to discover how much effect even one beer has on your shooting eye. Just go shoot your best 10-shot group on paper, then drink a beer or two and try it again. Your score will deteriorate remarkably.

Now that we have told you what to bring and what not to bring, let's take a careful look at the required things.

1. Binoculars. Should be the best you can afford, as small as you can afford, and as high power as you can find in a small package. I use a big, heavy pair of 8 x 50/s only because they are perfectly adjusted to work with my (necessary) eyeglasses. If you have young eyes and don't need to worry about eyeglasses, rejoice! But buy yourself a pair of those expensive (well-known trade name, such as Bushnell or Tasco), small, shirt-pocket size if possible, in at least 7X. Keep the binoculars around your neck, ready for use. Keep them from banging and bouncing around by hooking them to an elastic band around your middle. The elastic harness should be "springy" enough to allow you to bring the glasses to eye level without unhooking them, yet it should be strong enough to keep the binocs snugged against your body when not in use. This prevents them from swinging and banging, and from catching on the brush you are working through. Binoculars are no use to you unless you use them. Glass your pronghorns, find out whether that tall headgear really is as tall as it looks. Look over the body of the animal, too. I once was ready to pull the trigger on a nice pronghorn buck, whose nearside horn rose high and straight above his ears. His body was heavy, and he looked like a great trophy. But the binoculars revealed that he had only one horn; the other was a twisted, tiny thing, probably the result of an injury when the bony core was forming many years before. If you are a "world record" trophy hunter, you will probably also use a spotting scope, for that is the only way to accurately size up a real trophy. There are thousands of antelope with 15-inch horns for every one that goes 16 inches, and perhaps 100,000 for every one that goes 17 inches.

2. Knife. Pronghorns are small animals, and you do not need a big knife to dress them out. I've seen experts do a remarkably good job of field-dressing a pronghorn with a penknife boasting only a two-and-one-half-inch blade—but it was sharp, real sharp, and the expert carried a sharpening stone in his shirt pocket. I use a folding Buck knife, with a four-inch blade, and I've never been disappointed in it. The so-called "Wyoming knife," which allows you to do an expert job of opening the body cavity "from the inside," is also a worthwhile tool to carry with you when after big game. You do not need a saw or a hatchet. The average sheath knife, if sharp, will easily split open the ribcage and allow you to completely open up the carcass for rapid cooling out, which is very important.

3. Canteen of water is very much a required item during most pronghorn seasons. Use your water sparingly, so as not to run out, but drink enough to avoid dehydration. When I was a kid, we thought that it was "he-man" to go a long time without food and water. During those same years, most athletes thought that it was wrong to drink water while competing. Now all athletes know that it is wise to replace the fluids lost through perspiration, and do it as soon after the loss as is possible. Take a sip often enough to keep your mouth from drying out. But avoid

the bulky canteen that will be a handicap on the hunting grounds. For the final stalk, I usually leave a small daypack behind, holding canteen, food, gamebag, and plastic sacks. All that goes with me is the knife, and that should ride well back around the hip, if carried in a belt sheath. It can be a real nuisance, as well as dangerous, to have the knife poking you in the hip or ribs while you crawl nearer to that world-record pronghorn. It is hard to remember it in the excitement of the hunt, but it is smart to take a good drink of water just before leaving the daypack and starting your serious stalk.

4. Food. I'm not going to tell you what to carry. Your needs are different than mine. I like an apple, because it provides both food and drink. I do not want sandwiches, as they can get smashed and flattened, as well as mushy and unappetizing. But if you want something that provides quick energy, how about a candybar? I prefer crunchy granola bars to candy, but that's a matter of personal preference. If you are looking for the ultimate food value in a durable small package, and don't worry too much about the taste, try the old "C" rations. They're still hard to beat.

5. Cheesecloth or muslin light cloth bag to cover the dressed carcass. This keeps out flies, which may "blow" the carcass and contaminate the meat. This is best used on a skinned carcass, but if you have to transport the carcass a long distance before processing it, I like to use the gamebag covering a carcass that has only been gutted.

6. Plastic bag to carry bloody heart and bloody liver. Do not put the meat in the bag and close it up and leave it. This seals in the body heat and promotes spoiling, which can start in a remarkably short time. If the liver and heart are washed thoroughly before sacking, body heat should be gone. Then put them in the sack and store the sack in a shady place. As soon as possible, take the heart and liver out of the plastic sack, wash them again, and place them in the refrigerator, not the freezer. These food items are best when used fresh, not after freezing.

19

Clothing for Hunters

The only real advice anyone can give for hunting the pronghorn with a modern rifle is this: Go to where pronghorns live, find one, get close to it, and shoot it carefully so as to get a one-shot—dropped in his tracks—kill.

To which we must add: That's much easier said than done. Let's see how we can lower the odds.

First of all, what you wear is very important. If the law requires you to wear a lot of blaze orange, wear it! But pick the blaze orange material carefully. You do not want the vinyl stuff that has a high degree of reflectance. In other words, it shines and sparkles and reflects a lot of sunlight—which is seldom in short supply on the pronghorn plains. Comply with the law and don't worry about the color, as pronghorns do not seem to differentiate between colors at all. But beware of reflections, for the pronghorn is sharp-eyed and vigilant to detect any shiny object that wasn't there before.

Make sure that your clothing is tough, able to withstand crawling through the cactus and sage of the hunting grounds. It should also be neutral in color and in reflectance; sand colors are good, but camouflage brown and tan is the absolute tops. Don't wear big, floppy, dragging-on-the-ground-type jackets, for they snag in the sage and impede your crawl—and chances are good that you're going to crawl.

Be warm enough, but not too warm. That means the layer principle, which allows you to take off some outer layers if you become warm as the day progresses. Remember that it is rather foolish to wear a white shirt or undershirt under a camouflage jacket—and then have the sun force

The muzzleloader hunter is perfectly camouflaged, including a mosquito net in camo that hides shiny eyeglasses.

you to take off that outer layer and reveal yourself in all your pristine white glory. You might just as well hunt with a bright, three-foot-diameter mirror on you. I once thought that camouflage undershirts were ridiculous, until I found myself hunting in near-90°F. weather on the high, dry, and hot antelope areas in northeastern New Mexico. Then it made sense, for I did peel down to undershirt as I sat by a big rock and waited (successfully) for a good buck to come within range.

Even more important than your hunting clothes is the matter of footwear. *Don't* wear white stockings under your boots. When your pants work up a bit as you crawl, those white socks look like a pair of moving spotlights as you slink along the ground. It is not likely that the animal you are stalking will see the white socks, but it is very likely that another pronghorn, perhaps unseen by you, *will* see those white socks and will spread the alarm via heliograph rump signals and through a loud, accusatory snort. Wear wool socks, if the temperatures will permit, for they wick the moisture away from your body and allow you to stay cool and dry.

Yes, I do wear camouflage socks, but only to demonstrate my adherence to the principle of camouflage. The boots must have one prime requisite: They must be comfortable. It helps if they are made of tough enough leather to keep out spines and stickers. It also helps if they are water-resistant enough to keep out the wet of a dewy morning (a rarity in pronghorn country), or to allow you to wade across a few inches of water if the stalk leads you through a wet wash (another rarity in pronghorn country).

Pants should be especially tough, for the abrasion caused by crawling on gravel and stones can shred lighter materials. But watch out for the "canvas" pants you like to wear in the duck blinds. They are too stiff for good crawling, and they are apt to be noisier than you'd like when you are stooped over, creeping up a shallow draw in an attempt to get near to the quarry.

Long sleeves are a must, for your own protection. Pronghorn vision is so good that your white, not sun-tanned, arms shine in the sun, until the cactus and sage cover the exposed flesh with bloody scrapes. Then they don't shine so much.

Headgear is very important, too. Your eyes should be shielded by some kind of a brim or bill. The cowboy hat may look good when you pose for photos with your downed pronghorn, but leave it in the car while you hunt and while you field-dress your animal. I know a couple of expert pronghorn hunters who wear Stetsons afield, but they always seem to take them off when they begin their final stalk. I prefer a camouflage cap that fits close to my head, with nothing to move in the wind, fitted with a bill that shades my eyes when I use binoculars or a riflescope. That bill also shades my eyeglasses, (without which I cannot see to aim), and prevents the gleaming reflections that would otherwise bounce off my glasses.

Okay, you are properly clad from scalp to sole, but there is another qualification, an important one. Ammunition. I recommend carrying just two extra rounds for your rifle, after it is fully loaded. This makes you take careful aim for that first shot, as you do not have the luxury of carrying 20 or 30 extra rounds for second and third and fourth shots at each opportunity. It also makes sure that you can carry each extra round (only two, remember) in a separate pocket so that they will not click against each other or rattle if you have to trot down an arroyo. Now that you are dressed properly and carrying the right number of rifle rounds, let's see if we can find an antelope.

20

Hunting Methods

Can You Stalk Pronghorns?

About nine out of 10 stalks fail to get the hunter close enough to the pronghorn to allow him to shoot with any chance of scoring a clean kill.

Some expert pronghorn hunters stalk and kill a pronghorn every year, however.

Contradiction? No way. It's just that some hunters have learned how to stalk pronghorns, and most of us have not. As I explained in Chapter 13, I'm no longer youthfully slim. I'm no longer youthful. If you are trying to hide your bulky body behind nine-inch grass, it pays to be youthful and slim. If the grass is six inches or less, forget it.

Crawling on your belly is not fun. The most tender parts of your anatomy encounter the hardest, cruelest parts of the pronghorn pasture. Sweat rolls down your forehead in waves, and salty sweat does little to improve your accuracy when using the scope sight. Your belt buckle acts as a plow that scrapes up gravel and deposits it inside your underwear in the general location of your crotch and hips. Unseen little bits of prickly pear grab your elbows, stab stinging holes in your knees, and threaten to blind you. Springy branches of sagebrush grab your hat and rip it off you. Your breathing becomes labored and you are thoroughly miserable. The bunch of keys in your pocket gouges deeply into your thigh, and that sheath knife threatens to neuter you.

All this happens in the first 100 yards of your crawl. You still have 500 to go, and the buck might move off another 600 yards while he watches you wiggling along.

And usually, he *is* watching you. Remember, you are a part-time hunter, he is a full-time game animal, and his life has always depended upon vigilance. You have to move closer, unseen by the target animal and unseen by other pronghorns. If another one sees your wriggling rump above the cactus, that one will snort and turn on his heliograph rump signals, and will go dashing off. His every movement spells alarm, and the buck you want is also alarmed. He will usually run off first, and ask questions later.

Now that I've told you how difficult and disagreeable crawling is, I want to be honest and add the truth. You will have to crawl if you stalk pronghorns. You can avoid crawling only by using a blind, or by taking a stand and waiting.

But if you must stalk your pronghorn, here are a few tips that might make it less of a disaster, and improve your chances of success.

First of all, assume that the pronghorn has seen you. You'll be correct in that assumption at least 90 percent of the time. So your first job is to give the pronghorn the idea that you are *not* a danger to him. Take a long, careful look at the terrain you are going to have to cover. Note any brush you can hide behind. Look to see if there is a ravine or gully which might allow you to walk upright for part of the stalk, which is vastly preferable to crawling. Move slowly and deliberately, without pauses, just as you would move if you were a rancher mending fence, or performing some other ranch chore. Do NOT turn and look toward the pronghorn. Remember, he is watching you and trying to size up your motives. Walk in a direction that is not getting you closer to the pronghorn. Preferably, turn your back and walk directly away, if this is possible. Keep in mind that you want him to think you have absolutely no interest in him. Keep telling yourself, "I don't like to hunt pronghorns. I especially dislike shooting big trophy bucks." It helps if you can convince yourself, for your conviction shows in your body language as you walk away.

Once out of sight, stop and remember the lay of the land. Plan your stalk to include a lot of "stooped over" walking, even a bit of hands and knees walking, but as little crawling as possible. The human body simply is not adapted to crawling long distances. When the body tires of crawling, the rump comes up and the head comes up. When that happens, the stalk is ended by the pronghorn's sharp eyesight.

If you are breathing hard, force yourself to slow down, for you must be in control when you aim that rifle at the end of the stalk.

Move rapidly, but don't run, when you have the chance to move in the upright position. Keep you head and eyes swiveling at those moments, looking for other pronghorns which might take alarm and spook your target buck. When you are in the stooped-over mode, move slowly but steadily, and try to move silently, for pronghorns have ears as well as eyes. When out of rifle range distance, resist the temptation to lift your head over the rim and take a look. If you do, you'll be seen before you can spot the buck.

When in the hands and knees mode, try to go in as direct a line as possible, for this mode is slow and tiring. The worst, however, is yet to come.

When crawling, lie flat on your belly. Cradle the rifle in your arms. Use your elbows to hitch forward, then bring a foot up to your belt region, slowly and flat on the ground. Dig in the heel and slowly slide your torso forward through the stickers, the rocks, and the cactus. Curse silently! Then do it again. Keep your face down and look only at the weeds and rocks immediately in front of you. Do not try to sneak a look ahead, for you'll be seen. Take your time, make this torture last, so that your heartbeat and respiration rate will not be so elevated that you'll lose accuracy when aiming and firing the rifle. Naturally, your hat or cap were left behind. This does not apply to the bald-headed hunter, who should keep his cap on. A bald head shines like a mirror, and a pale face is right behind it. Here's where you're glad that you put on the camouflage grease paint. Eyeglasses also shine like signal lights in the sunshine.

When you get to the pre-selected spot from which you intend to shoot, put your face behind some sagebrush, or greasewood, or cenisa. Then, ever so slowly, raise one eyeball to the lowest position from which you can see.

Usually, the buck will have departed. But in one chance out of six, he will still be there. Do not try to assume a sitting or kneeling rifle position. Shoot from the prone position if at all possible. Use the sling to steady your hold. Take a deep breath. Let out half of it. Steady now! Aim carefully and squeeze slowly. Be surprised when the gun goes off, and the chances are pretty good that the buck will not go off. If he is lying there with his legs waving slowly in the air, congratulate yourself! You are one of a select few who have successfully stalked close enough to get a sure-kill rifle shot. You are now a pronghorn hunter *par excellence*. Go to the animal. Take your pictures, if you want them. Quickly dress out your animal. Body heat is your enemy now, so get rid of it as soon as possible.

And when you go home, brag about your stalking ability. You've earned the right!

Buck or Doe?

Usually it is easy to tell whether a particular pronghorn is a buck or a doe. Although both genders grow horns, those of the doe are much shorter, seldom longer than the ears, while the buck's horns are much longer, and may appear twice as long as the ears. But the black cheek patch, or neck patch, is a much better mark of the male.

The next distinguishing characteristic to look for is the attitude of the neck. A trophy buck almost always holds his neck and head well out in front of his body, with the neck almost horizontal. The doe almost always raises her head more, and seems to be almost up and down at times.

But how about when you are following a track in the snow and do not know whether you are wasting your time following a doe, or are on the spoor of a trophy buck? Well, the best clue is found in their droppings.

When a buck decides to empty his holding tanks, he follows a set procedure. Almost always, he will sniff a spot on the ground, as if deciding whether or not this is a good place to go to the toilet. Then he paws at the ground, with one front foot, and then with the other. He may even seem to be digging a trench with his front feet!

Next step is automatic. He takes a half step forward with his front feet, leaving his back feet in place. This puts him in the proper position, and he urinates quickly. That finished, he immediately takes a full step forward with both hind legs and squats deeply, his back bowed. This position is held, with the tail elevated out of

Bucks normally carry their heads more horizontally than do does. *Photo by Judd Cooney.*

the way, while he defecates. This procedure ensures that urine and droppings will be in almost exactly the same place. It also means that if the buck paws prior to elimination, the pawing marks will be very near to the urine and feces. This is important, because it is so very different from the system used by the doe.

The doe never paws before urinating or defecating. She squats deeply and urinates, then she stands erect and begins to defecate. Sometimes she keeps on walking while she defecates. This means that the urine marks and the feces are almost never deposited in the same place. If the feces are strung out along the walking track — perhaps for 10 feet past the urine spot — you are following a doe. If feces and urine are in the same spot, you are in all probability following a buck. If urine, feces, and pawing marks are all at the same place, you are definitely following a buck.

Remember that we said this method will help you if you are trailing a particular animal. It is of no help when there is a herd, for the feces and urine of one animal may overlap those of another, thus lousing up our system.

Curiosity

Much has been written about the pronghorn's curiosity, a curiosity that was used to lure the animal into range in the early days, but one you better not count on anymore. In the good old days, pioneer hunters used to wave a white rag atop a four-foot stick. Give it one wave, put it down, then remain motionless in your place of concealment. The pronghorns would swivel around and face this strange sight. If the hunter didn't overdo it, but just gave the flag a twitch once in a while, the pronghorns would slowly approach, trying to figure out what this strange action was all about. When the animal was within range, the hunter shot and you had another case of "curiosity killed the pronghorn."

But today, the pronghorn is accustomed to mankind and man's strange actions. The curiosity is still there, but caution is also there. Is the curiosity still really there? Well...

Once we pulled a pop-up type of tent trailer onto the pasture where we intended to hunt. We put the canvas top up and got it all ready for occupancy that night. Then we went driving across the country, trying to locate the biggest head in all the state of Wyoming. We glassed antelope for three hours, then returned to our camp, eager for tomorrow to come and bring with it the legal opening of the season. When we got near our tent trailer, we found no less than 81 pronghorns, standing motionless, staring at the pop-up trailer. One member of our party remained in camp the next morning when the rest of us went hunting. As it turned out, he shot a lovely big buck from a good rest inside the tent trailer, which he used as a blind. The pronghorn had come back to satisfy his curiosity, with fatal results.

Hunting in northeastern New Mexico with Keith Schreiner, I saw another bit of evidence. We left Keith comfortably ensconced in a pile of rocks that broke his silhouette and provided him with a good field of fire across two known pronghorn trails. My other partner, Dan, and I drove to another corner of the open area and went hunting. When we had no luck in that sector, we decided to drive back to the original hunt area. Driving slowly along on the ranch road, — it is illegal to drive off of them — we spotted a good buck standing stock-still about 250 yards away. I slid out of the driver's seat, chambered a round in my 30-06, and moved about 20 yards to the side to make it legal. Then I took a prone position while the buck stood still as a statue. I shot him — and only then did we see Keith Schreiner. He had been "tolling" that buck for more than an hour, giving an occasional flip of the handkerchief to keep the buck wondering what was over there. He said that the buck had come from three-quarters of a mile up to within 400 yards.

"If he'd come another hundred yards, I'da shot him," Keith said, "but you had to come along and blow it all."

Still another instance. We were ear-tagging and weighing newborn fawns. As we worked with the young ones, captured with a big net after a frantic chase, we happened to look up and see two mature bucks, within 150 yards of us, watching intently. There did not seem to be any suggestion that the bucks were intending to protect or rescue the fawns, for they did not snort, nor paw the ground, nor indicate anything except extreme curiosity.

Pronghorn expert Einarsen wrote that a movement will attract pronghorn curiosity from three to four miles away, but that a stationary object seldom attracts their curiosity. This squares with later observations by many behavioral scientists. If it holds still, it doesn't attract any attention, and that should tell you a lot about hunting the pronghorn.

However, the modern-day pronghorn knows how far a modern rifle can kill, and he often takes flight the minute you get out of your vehicle.

If you must move across open ground to get nearer to a pronghorn, your best chance is to move in an oblique direction, as if to pass the pronghorn, and never look directly at him, no matter how far away he seems to be (remember those binocular-like eyes). By pretending to be headed for some other destination, you can sometimes get a lot closer than you were. But don't count on it where pronghorns have been hunted heavily. They learn.

21

Advice from the Experts

Arizona

Bob Whitaker, experienced big-game hunter and well-known outdoor writer from Phoenix, gives us advice as to how to hunt Arizona.

"Arizona may not boast the biggest herds of antelope, but it is the undisputed place to go for trophy heads. Many hunters are surprised to learn the highest percentage of trophy pronghorns consistently comes from Arizona.

"For many years the Boone and Crockett record was a giant pronghorn taken in the Arizona Strip Country, north of the Grand Canyon, back around the turn of the century. Antelope disappeared from this lonely flatland until the 1960s, when animals were transplanted from Montana and Wyoming to the lush grasslands in Antelope Valley, June Tank, and the eastern side of the Strip. Trophy-sized horns soon began reappearing. According to biologists, the reason for the massive horns on Arizona Strip pronghorns is the heavy deposits of limestone and calcium in the soil.

"Hunting the vast 3½-million-acre Strip Country is no problem because 90 percent of the area is public land. This means no locked gates and no dunning for trespass fees. The country is wide open, which calls for a flat-shooting rifle to stretch out and score. Success for Strip hunters has been running close to 100 percent.

"Elsewhere, trophy bucks abound in a growing number of areas. A pronghorn taken in Chino Valley, north of Prescott,

Bob Whitaker with an Arizona pronghorn trophy. Bob claims that Arizona is THE place to try for a world record. *Photo by Whitaker.*

in 1975, beat out the long-standing world record. Many hunters claim seeing even bigger horns on antelope roaming this fertile valley of high grass and ample water.

"Good herds also exist in the St. Johns-Springerville region, with a growing band of pronghorns blossoming in San Rafael Valley near the Mexican border. You also could break a world's record stalking open grasslands atop Coconino Plateau between Highways 66 and 180 north, and west of Williams and Red Lake toward Rose Wells.

"Another possible reason for the preponderance of trophy bucks in Arizona is the short three-day season, which reduces pressure on larger animals, letting them escape to grow one year larger. For trophies, Arizona is the place to go. The problem isn't as much getting a trophy, as getting drawn for one of the limited number of permits."

For information on season dates and open areas, as well as license and permit fees and applications, write to the Arizona Game and Fish Commission, 2222 W. Greenway, Phoenix, AZ 85023; phone 602/942-3000.

California

John Reginato, well-known California sportsman, gives us the rundown on California pronghorn hunting.

"California's antelope population has grown while other wildlife is being squeezed by development and growth to take care of our 25 million people. In the past 20 years, the pronghorn population has nearly tripled to around 7000 animals. As many as 19,500 Californians annually apply for the 600-plus pronghorns that are shot annually. Doe and archery permits were issued for the first time in 1980. No nonresident antelope permits are issued. Last year, 1985, was the 22nd consecutive hunting season on pronghorns and there has been no public opposition to these hunts, not even to the harvest of does, showing that Californians recognize that their pronghorn resource is being well managed.

"Northeastern California, including all of Lassen and Modoc and part of Siskiyou and Shasta counties, is the major range of the California pronghorn. For hunting purposes, this area is divided into six zones with a certain number of either sex scheduled to be taken. The number of permits to be issued is based on herd aerial counts in early January of each year. In 1984, a seventh zone was created in Mono County for a small number of permits.

"For information as to fees, open season dates, and so on, including application forms, the prospective hunter is referred to the regional office of the Fish and Game Department at 601 Locust St., Redding, CA 96001; phone 916/225-2300.

"Application forms are also available at all Fish and Game offices including Sacramento, Yountville, Fresno, and Long Beach, as well as most license agents throughout the state.

"Drawings to determine the lucky permit holders are held in Sacramento in mid-July, and those chosen are advised by mail to forward the $35 fee. Success rates for permit holders has been averaging 80 percent. If you get a permit, make good on it, for you are not allowed to apply again for another 10 years.

"While California cannot compete with other western states in pronghorn numbers, Leo (Bud) Pyshora, wildlife biologist at Redding, states that one out of every 100 antelope taken in the state would qualify for Boone and Crockett registry.

"The California Fish and Game is trapping and shifting pronghorns to areas in northeast California to increase the range of the pronghorn and to attempt to increase the total population of this sought-after trophy. Recently, a small herd was moved to the Tejon Ranch in southern California, bordering Kern and Los Angeles counties.

"While northeast California is also feeling the "pangs of progress," the changes are not all bad. Increased farming of alfalfa is providing another food source for antelope. This, plus the fact that 1 million acres of land in this area is under the jurisdiction of either the Bureau of Land Management or the U.S. Forest Service, bodes well for continued herd increases for pronghorn in California."

For information on open seasons and area, permit, and license fees, write to the Department of Fish and Game, 1416 Ninth St., Sacramento, CA 95814; phone 916/445-3531.

Colorado

We asked Ken Heuser, well-known outdoor writer and big-game hunter of Rifle, Colorado, for some tips on bagging a pronghorn in that state. Ken says:

"Colorado is blessed with two widely diverse antelope hunting areas. The eastern plains, which is roughly half of Colorado, has an abundance of antelope, with the highest concentrations in the southeast. The antelope units south of I-70 have long had a large antelope population, and there have been many special hunts conducted there specifically to reduce populations. The unit numbers there run from A-35 to A-70.

"The northeast corner of the state, Units A-11 to A-34, have fair numbers of antelope, but not in concentrations. South-central Colorado (San Luis Valley) Units A-70 to A-86 are noted for their big bucks, but there is a lot of private land there and you have to make sure you have permission to hunt. The units in northern Colorado, A-6 to A-10, also have some excellent hunting. The northwest corner of Colorado is a high plains area with some excellent antelope hunting. The country is rolling rather than flat, and presents a real challenge as pronghorns appear and disappear like wraiths. There are two areas in the far west-central portion of the state, but they are very limited for pronghorn hunting.

"Pronghorn hunting in Colorado is by permit only, and you must apply by the first week in June. Notifications are made in August. The areas that hold the largest bucks are the most difficult to draw for, and it sometimes takes three or more preference points to get into one of them. A preference point is issued each time a license is applied for and not drawn. Permits are allotted for each area, and this assures a stable, huntable population of antelope. If you do not apply, you do not receive a preference point. Your chances of drawing a permit are best in southeastern Colorado, toughest in northwest Colorado."

For information on season dates and permit applications, open areas, and all other information, write to the Division of Wildlife, 6060 Broadway, Denver, CO 80216; phone 303/825-1192.

Idaho

My long-time friend and knowledgeable Idahoan, Jack McNeel, has the following advice for antelope hunters in the lovely state of Idaho:

"Idaho's antelope population stretches across southern Idaho in an arc from the southwestern corner of the state eastward and north to the Yellowstone country and Salmon. Largest populations are found in the more eastern and northern portions of this arc, where heavier precipitation allows for better production and survival.

"Harvests are controlled by a lottery system with quotas placed on individual hunting units. Quotas are determined annually and are publicized in the big-game regulations. Applications are due in the spring. It would be advisable to purchase a hunting license early in the year and request that controlled hunt information be mailed when it is available to avoid missing the application deadline.

"Pre-season population estimates place Idaho's usual pronghorn populations upwards of 20,000 animals. Quotas keep the harvest in the 2000 to 3000 range, three-fourths of which are bucks, although the regulations allow the taking of either sex.

"Those hunting areas with the largest number of permits generally contain the largest number of antelope. The ratios of hunters to antelope remain nearly the same in all units, and often a hunt with fewer competing hunters makes for a more enjoyable hunt. Some units contain as few as five permits while others may have 300 or more. Success rates in the 80 percent range are normal and seldom will any particular hunt drop below 70 percent. This indicates that the most difficult part of antelope hunting in Idaho is getting the permit to hunt, rather than bagging an antelope, and that hunts with fewer permits are just as successful as hunts with many permits."

For information on season dates, areas, and fees, write to The Fish and Game Department, Box 25, Boise, ID 83707; phone 208/334-3700.

Montana

Norm Strung, long-time guide and outfitter in Montana, and prolific writer on the out-of-doors, gives us some pointers on Montana pronghorn hunting:

"The eastern two-thirds, or prairie region, of the state of Montana has excellent antelope hunting no matter where you go. Harvests are controlled by a lottery system, with quotas placed on management areas. These quotas are published with the annual game regulations, so it is arguable that when you note an area with 1500 available permits, it will provide better hunting than an area with 75. Still, the ratio of hunters in the field to game in the

Jack McNeal of the Idaho Game and Fish Department is an official measurer for the Boone and Crockett Club. Here he poses with the No. 2 all-time Idaho record pronghorn, killed in 1982 by Michael Wolf of Post Falls, Idaho. *McNeal photo.*

field is theoretically the same everywhere in Montana.

"Generally, the management areas with the most liberal harvest quotas begin with a six or seven. These areas are located in the easternmost third of the state. If you are after a trophy antelope, the largest heads usually come out of those easternmost areas near Wyoming.

"Hunter success on antelope runs 70 to 90 percent, so once you draw a permit, the hunting is relatively easy. There is, however, a bit of a science in getting that permit.

"Montana's population is concentrated in the western half of the state. Much of that area has no antelope. Distances being what they are under the Big Sky, antelope hunters residing in the mountains and larger cities tend to apply for the areas nearest them, and competition is keen. On the other hand, management areas in the underpopulated northeastern corner of the state and along the North Dakota and Wyoming borders often have surplus permits. The best 'hunting' advice I can give the serious antelope hunter, then, would be to apply for permits in these geographic regions with a six or seven prefix. Once you get your permit, downing a prairie goat is almost a foregone conclusion."

My longtime friend Norm Strung writes from experience and from his home near Bozeman, Montana. Author of 14 books, and so many articles he can't count them, Norm is an associate editor for *Field and Stream* magazine, and a former president of the Outdoor Writers Association of America. He's been a college professor, a guide and outfitter, and he knows Montana's wildlife.

For season dates and other information, write to The Department of Fish, Wildlife and Parks, 1420 East Sixth, Helena, MT 59601; phone 406/449-2535.

Nebraska

Nebraska antelope herds are primarily found in the northwestern and western parts of the state, where unfenced rangelands are available. The herds are not large, and the number of permits to be issued, although varying with the year, is never large. For information as to open season areas, dates, fees, and permit applications, write to the Game and Parks Commission, Box 30370, Lincoln, NB 30370; phone 402/464-0641.

In 1985, license fees for pronghorn in Nebraska were $10 for resident landowners (restricted to their own land), $20 for residents, and $100 for nonresidents. Also, all hunters must possess a Habitat Stamp, which sells for $7.50.

Nevada

Paula J. Del Giudice, Nevada state editor for *Western Outdoors* magazine, is an avid outdoorswoman and very knowledgeable about Nevada's wildlife. We asked her advice about pronghorn hunting in the Silver State:

"Nevada has scattered antelope populations throughout the state, but for the best hunting areas, you should look to Washoe and Humboldt counties in the northwest corner of the state. Typically, the large populations of animals are centered in that portion of the state, and therefore the number of hunting permits available there exceeds the other areas where antelope hunting is permitted. The greatest percentage of trophy-sized animals taken in Nevada also come from these two counties.

Paula J. Del Giudice is Nevada editor for *Western Outdoors* magazine. Here she displays a fine buck, which she took in Nevada. The trophy scored 75⅝, which is mighty good in anybody's book. *Del Giudice Photo.*

"With hunter success on antelope running between 80 and 100 percent, getting a tag in the statewide lottery is the hardest part of hunting pronghorns in Nevada. Nonresidents were permitted to vie for an extremely limited number of antelope tags for the first time in 1984. Hunting antelope in the Silver State is a very difficult sport to become hooked on, because once you've drawn a tag, you must wait for another five full seasons to pass before applying for another chance.

"There is a special archery season available on antelope in Nevada, and if the hunter truly wanted to hunt antelope, that would be the option to take. Nearly every year, the archery hunt is undersubscribed by applicants. This hunt, alas, is available to residents only.

"Hunting opportunities for antelope in Nevada should increase in the future. Through cooperative agreements with fish and game departments in nearby states, supplemental releases of antelope have been made in various areas of Nevada where there is sufficient suitable carrying habitat. If these releases prove successful, hunters will have increased hunting opportunities in the future."

For further information concerning seasons dates, fees, and open areas, write to The Department of Wildlife, Box 10678, Reno, NV 89520; phone 702/784-6214.

New Mexico

One of my long-time friends, Jesse Williams, is eminently qualified to sketch the picture for my home state of New Mexico. A trophy hunter himself, Jesse is in the record books with a fine Coues whitetailed deer head, and has done a lot of antelope hunting. Jesse says:

"New Mexico has good antelope herds, with the best hunting in the northeast and southeast corners of the state. We do not have the large populations that occur in states to the north of us, but nimrods can find fine hunting in the Land of Enchantment. The state's management philosophy is to provide as much hunting opportunity as possible consistent with the herd's welfare and with the availability of hunting access. Hunting pressure is light due to a limited number of permits.

"Public antelope hunting is available through a drawing; however, residents and nonresidents have an equal chance for success, as all applications are treated the same. Bowhunters need only to apply, as permits in their area are unlimited. The odds average one out of four for the approximately 1000 permits that are available each year. The odds get longer in the more popular areas and those where the number of licenses is lower.

"In addition to the public drawing, certain landowners receive authority to allow additional hunting on their privately owned land. Landowner authorizations, around 2000 of them, do not go through the public drawing and hunters must deal with the landowner directly. The Department of Game and Fish has a list of these landowners available upon request. Most charge a trespass fee in addition to the state license which is required. When a hunter receives a public license he is assured of a place to hunt. This may include private land within the assigned hunt area.

"The total number of hunters, both on public and private land, is determined from yearly surveys of the pronghorn populations. The number of hunters will be higher after good years, lower when overall populations are down.

"There are hunts set aside for archers, muzzleloaders, and even handicapped sportsmen. Hunter success averages 77

Jesse Williams with a fine trophy taken in New Mexico. *Photo by Hal Swiggett.*

percent for the rifle hunters, 45 percent for muzzleloaders, and 16 percent for bowhunters."

For information on open areas, season dates, and fees, write to the Game and Fish Department, Villagra Building, Santa Fe, NM 87503; phone 505/827-7911.

North Dakota

David Jensen, with the Information section of the North Dakota Game and Fish Department, tells me that there has been quite a change since the first legal season, back in 1951. He writes:

"North Dakota has a population of pronghorn antelope that averages between 4000 and 6000 head. The biggest population is found in the extreme southwest corner of the state, along the Little Missouri River. Small herds are scattered through the Badlands and out into the Missouri slope south of Interstate 94.

"The rifle season is held in early October and is open only for residents who must wait six years between applying for permits, after once being successful in the drawing. Nonresidents and residents can buy archery licence each year. The price for nonresidents is $100, residents $18.

"The number of rifle permits runs around 1000, with about 1000 archery permits issued to residents and nonresidents. Success in the rifle hunt runs around 90 percent and for the bowmen only about 20 percent. Either-sex antelope may be taken in any season."

For further information regarding season dates, open areas, and fees, write to the State Game and Fish Department, 2222 Lovett Ave., Bismarck, ND 58505; phone (701) 224-2180.

Oregon

Ed Park, widely read author of hundreds of big-game hunting stories, provides some suggestions for antelope hunters in Oregon:

"The southeastern quarter of Oregon is mostly sagebrush desert, with scatterings of juniper. It includes extensive sage flats, rimrocks, dry lakebeds, and a few desert mountains. Most of this forgotten corner is antelope country.

"All antelope hunting in Oregon is by permit, and while a few hunts are reserved for bowhunters and muzzleloaders, rifle hunting is allowed in most units. Although most hunting is for bucks with horns longer than the ears, a few hunts are held for either sex, or for does, to help control population numbers.

"The most difficult part of hunting antelope in Oregon is drawing a permit. They are allocated under a lottery system, with the total number of permits each year ranging from about 1700 to 2200 depending upon the results of herd counts.

"The odds of being drawn are less than 20 percent in all of the rifle units and even worse in the more popular units, where odds run as low as 3 percent. The odds get longer each year as more and more hunters apply, while the antelope populations and number of permits remain about the same.

"Hunter success runs all the way from 50 percent up to 100 percent, depending on the unit and the year, and will average between 60 and 70 percent for all units.

"The best odds for drawing a permit are in the special bowhunting areas, but the hunter success is extremely low.

"The best advice I can give to those seriously wanting to hunt antelope is to apply for a permit every year; and don't plan on getting one. Make a determined hunt if

Advice from the Experts

you do luck out. But go to Wyoming if you really want to hunt these interesting animals."

Ed is a former president of the Outdoor Writers Association of America. He has hunted and fished over a very large part of the North American continent, and is known as a writer who does the things he writes about — and does them well.

For further information on open areas, season dates, and fees, write to The Department of Fish and Wildlife, Box 3503, Portland, OR 97208; phone 503/229-5551.

South Dakota

Chuck Post is my always-dependable source of information about pronghorns in South Dakota. He has been Chief of Information for the South Dakota Game, Fish and Parks Department for many years now, and is an avid hunter and angler in his own right. His advice to South Dakota pronghorn hunter is:

"The main antelope range in the state of South Dakota is west of the Missouri River, excluding the forested Black Hills area. The heaviest concentrations of pronghorns are found in the northwest quarter of the state in the four counties of Harding, Perkins, Meade, and Butte.

"We have divided the western part of the state into hunting units. Hunters must apply for a permit in a certain unit, and the number of permits per hunting units is set by quota.

"Nonresidents were allowed to hunt

South Dakota expert Chuck Post with pronghorn he took in northwestern corner of the state. *Chuck Post photo.*

pronghorns during the firearms season for the first time in 1983. The availability of nonresident licenses depends upon the antelope population.

"Hunter success runs between 75 and 90 percent. Most hunting activity takes place during the first two days of the season. Most of the huntable land is private and permission is needed to hunt it. Some large parcels of public land are available and do have some good hunting opportunities.

"South Dakota's pronghorn range contains natural rolling prairie with a mixture of croplands. Be prepared for any type of weather during the early-October season. It is usually warm, so be careful to take good care of the meat, cooling out the carcass as soon as possible after killing it.

"Our antelope will often feed and bed down in alfalfa, winter wheat, and pastureland. Try to find high ground and look the area over very carefully with good binoculars. When you find the herd, take your time—make a good stalk and take your pick of the bucks available. With South Dakota's high success percentage, you are almost guaranteed a critter."

For further information on open areas, season dates, and fees, write to the Game, Fish and Parks Department, Sigurd Anderson Building, 445 East Capitol, Pierre, SD 57501-3185; phone 605/773-3485.

Texas

Dan Klepper, long-time outdoor editor of the *San Antonio News-Express,* has hunted and fished in almost every corner of the magnificent empire of Texas. He is eminently qualified to give us some pointers on hunting pronghorns in Texas:

"Some antelope hunters in Texas have to hunt harder for money to purchase a permit than for an antelope to shoot.

"The state supports a fluctuating antelope population of around 18,000 antelope. The number generally depends upon fawn survival, and fawn survival depends upon weather and coyotes.

"Texas weather historically is unpredictable. At least that's what the locals like to say. But West Texas weather is not. Nine years out of 10 it is going to be dry. Predation by coyotes is usually predictable. If there are pronghorn fawns to be eaten, coyotes are going to eat some of them.

"The predation problem seems to be worse in the Panhandle than in the Trans-Pecos. These are the two major pronghorn ranges in Texas. The bulk of the animals, about 16,000, are in the Trans-Pecos. Since the Trans-Pecos has a healthier, larger herd and better escape cover for fawns, western Texas is the top choice for hunters.

"All a rifleman needs to hunt pronghorn in the Trans-Pecos is a permit and a license. Biologists with the Texas Parks and Wildlife Department survey pronghorn herds each year and establish the number of animals which safely can be killed.

"Since most of the pronghorns are on private lands, the department issues the permits to landowners, who then sell them to hunters. The average price of a permit is about $600. Don't be surprised if the asking price is higher.

"Most chambers of commerce in towns such as Alpine and Marfa in pronghorn country in the Trans-Pecos usually have lists of ranches where permits are available.

"If a hunter can shoot straight, he usually can get his pronghorn. The success rate is about 90 percent."

Dan Klepper, outdoor editor of the *San Antonio News-Express*, with a fine, wide trophy taken in the Trans-Pecos area of Texas. *Dan Klepper photo.*

For further information on open areas, season dates, and fees, write to the Parks and Wildlife Department, 4200 Smith School Rd., Austin, TX 78744; phone 512/479-4800.

Utah

Jim Zumbo, Editor at Large for *Outdoor Life* magazine and experienced big-game hunter, gives us some pertinent pointers for hunting pronghorns in Utah:

"Compared to other western states, Utah's antelope herds are nothing to rave about. Each year, about 600 tags are offered, most of them to residents. Recently, nonresidents were allotted 10 percent of the tags. Because a deer license has to be purchased as a prerequisite to hunting for antelope, there hasn't been much interest among nonresident hunters. The total price tag for a permit is about double that of neighboring states, and Utah's antelope aren't that attractive to warrant the increased cost.

"Despite that bleak appraisal, Utah does give up an occasional record-class buck. The most popular herds, Parker Mountain in the south and Daggett in the northeast, have some decent bucks, as do the other herds scattered around the state. The Parker herds have been the basis for most of the in-state trapping and transplanting program. The Daggett herd is cropped heavily, and is probably the most popular in the state because of its proximity to the Flaming Gorge Recreational Area. Summer vacationers and fishermen see antelope readily, and try for permits when hunting season rolls around.

"Utah's antelope are fairly well distributed around the state, with no general area being tops for trophy animals. Each herd seems to have a few outstanding bucks, but they're tough to find. Despite an abundance of roads and heavy human pressure from oil and gas activities, the Bonanza Unit in the northeast has long

Jim Zumbo with a Utah pronghorn. *Photo by Jim Zumbo.*

been a favorite, and now and then gives up a good buck. The Myton Unit produced the first official Boone and Crockett Club buck, and still has some good animals, although they're tough to find.

"Utah would have more pronghorns, but for years the United States Bureau of Land Management stalled transplant programs because the agency was reluctant to allow the forage to be shared with domestic sheep. Currently, however, antelope have been restocked in a number of Utah areas because of a change in philosophy."

For more information, contact the Utah Division of Wildlife Resources, 1596 W.N. Temple, Salt Lake City, UT 84116; phone 801/533-9333.

Wyoming

We asked Ken and Roberta Knapp, Wyoming residents and long-time hunters, guides, and outfitters, to give us their husband and wife viewpoint on Wyoming antelope:

"Wyoming is synonymous with pronghorn hunting. With half a million antelope statewide and a hunter success rate of over 92 percent, it would seem that little more need to be said. However, the picture is not rosy everywhere in the Cowboy State.

"In the far western part of the state, around Pinedale and Daniel, antelope populations have been diminishing and the number of permits given out is proportionately low. Severe winters and a tremendous demand for tags have created the problem, but it should correct itself within a few years with proper management. In the northeastern portion, between Sheridan and Gillette, most of the land is privately owned. Gaining access can be difficult or nearly impossible, even though

Roberta Knapp, who teams with husband Ken in guiding hunters in Wyoming, took this fine 17-incher off a ranch near Daniel, Wyoming. Roberta shot after a belly crawl of about 200 yards. This trophy was worth it. *Photo by Ken Knapp.*

there are many antelope in the region and plenty of licenses available. The northwest portion, around Jackson, has the smallest herds and offers the fewest licenses. In the rest of the state, and in particular the area between Cheyenne and Rawlins north to Kaycee and Casper, antelope herds are plentiful, with big bucks and lots of Bureau of Land Management land upon which to stalk an antelope.

"The future looks bright for Wyoming

antelope herds. The most challenging problem the state faces is that of too many of the critters causing crop depredation claims from ranchers and farmers . . . and not enough hunters in some areas!

"Hunters in the 1984 season harvested 98,680 head for a 92 percent success ratio, with an average of 1.85 days spent in the field for each antelope harvested. We recommend the prospective hunter apply for permits in the southern or central areas of the state. If a visit is possible before applying, come to northeastern Wyoming and make sure that you can have land to hunt upon, and then apply for that unit. It is far easier to make friends with the rancher and obtain permission before hunters descend on the area and beat down his gates.

"The chances of drawing a license are excellent in all but the north-central or northwestern portions of Wyoming. As a bonus, if you can obtain permission and a permit to hunt in northeastern Wyoming, you have the best chance of taking home a big trophy. There are many outfitters providing guided help for antelope hunters, thus greatly improving their chances. Enjoy Wyoming's plentiful herds, hunt safely, and remember to close any gates you may open while pursuing these prairie ghosts."

For season dates and other information, write to the Wyoming Game and Fish Commission, Cheyenne, WY 82002; phone 307/777-7735.

For information on land ownership (public or private) and for good campsite locations, write to the Bureau of Land Management, Box 1828, Cheyenne, WY 82003.

22

Pronghorns on the Table

In my opinion pronghorns rate above venison for palatability, above most wild game meats, but below elk and bighorn sheep.

That's an opinion which is not unanimously shared by most American hunters. In summer of 1985, a national magazine printed a lengthy article chronicling the problems met by a hunter in trying to make his pronghorn buck edible. You wouldn't believe the trouble that man went through in trying to marinate unpalatable meat into something that could be consumed without gagging.

When a pronghorn is killed cleanly, with one bullet in a vital area, and dies at once; and when that same animal is promptly gutted and cooled out, with the meat not allowed to come in contact with the hair of the pronghorn; and if that same animal is kept in a cool place for about 10 days, and is then properly cut up and packaged for the freezer; that pronghorn is excellent eating. My family, and many other families, rate it as tops.

Compare that ideal situation with what often happens on the pronghorn ranges. The animal is first chased by a "hunter" in a pickup truck. This is unsportsmanlike and illegal. The pronghorn is overheated and blood is pulsing through every inch of his tissues. He is then shot in the stomach, allowing digestive juices and bile to taint the meat. He staggers on for a quarter of a mile, doing a terrific job of mixing stomach contents with the blood that is coursing through all of his muscle tissues. He is so full of adrenaline that he dies with difficulty.

The carcass is then placed on the hood of a motor vehicle and carried for an hour or two, with the 200°F. heat generated by the motor cooking the underside, while dust and dirt blow all over the topside, mixing with blood and stomach contents that are splashed along the side of the carcass.

Then the animal is clumsily gutted, with the "hunter" cutting into the intestines and spilling their contents on the meat he intends to eat. The easily detached hair of the pelt comes off in handfuls, and adheres to the bloody sides of the carcass as it is exposed to the sun and wind. The carcass is not washed, but is rather allowed to "crust over" before transport to the proud hunter's home. Transport is often accomplished with the carcass on top of the vehicle, in the bright sunlight and in the clouds of dust that are tossed up by other vehicles on the plains of pronghorn country.

When he gets home, the "hunter" is too tired from his exertions to take care of the carcass tonight, so it is dropped on the cement floor of the garage, overnight.

The next morning, the meat is cut up into "meal-sized" portions. Only then is it washed to remove caked-on blood, bile, digestive juices, dust, and hair. By this time, spoiling has started on the still-warm inside of the meat. This process of spoiling is arrested (not stopped completely) by freezing.

Now be honest: Is it possible for that pronghorn to taste good? How would a prized Hereford steer taste if treated that way?

I think the most important part of getting good pronghorn meals is the prompt cooling of the carcass, immediately after death. If at all possible, I wash the carcass at once, oftentimes by dipping it into the watering trough out on the range, or by letting the windmill pump fresh, cool water over the *skinned* carcass as soon as possible. Water removes body heat better than anything else. It also removes digestive juices and bile that might contaminate the meat, and flushes away hair that can impart a "gamey," oily, rancid taste to the meat. As soon as the carcass is clean and cooled out, cover it with a gamebag that keeps flies off, yet allows cooling air to circulate around the carcass. Store it in the shade for transport home—*not*, however, in the car trunk, where heat builds up surprisingly quickly. Get the cooled-out meat into a shady place and let it age a week before cutting up. Perfect aging temperature is 38°F. However, University of Wyoming specialists have stated that antelope meat need not be aged at all if it is cooled out properly and placed in a freezer within 36 hours of the kill. These same specialists recommend that you leave the hide on on the way to the butcher, unless you feel it is necessary to get it off to properly cool the meat. They are the experts, but I still get the hide off as quickly as possible when I'm doing the job myself. If the carcass is to be delivered (field-dressed, of course) within three hours after killing, I do not skin it. But prompt cooling is my solution to the question of geting good-tasting pronghorn meals.

When you deliver your pronghorn to a locker plant that has a lot of pronghorns to process all at once, you will often be told, "Toss yours on the pile, we'll get to it."

Don't do it. Piling your pronghorn carcass on top of other pronghorn carcasses is an invitation to retention of body heat and quick spoiling. I'd tell the locker plant people, in no uncertain terms, that you want yours separated from the others, preferably hung up to cool better. Tell them that you'll be glad to hang it for them, if they're too busy. Do it in a nice way, but be firm. Tossing it on top a pile of rapidly heating meat is a sure invitation to spoilage and, at the very least, lousy flavor in the meat after processing.

When you cut it up, or have a butcher do the job, how much meat can you expect? According to the University of Wyoming agricultural experiment state people, the field-dressed weight of an average buck should be 76.7 pounds. When you remove the head, you lose 7.1 pounds. The skin weighs another 5.9 pounds. The loss due to aging averages seven pounds. Cutting and trimming loss ran all the way up to 12.5 pounds, leaving you with 44.2 pounds of retail cuts of meat. When you do the work yourself, you can save almost all of that cutting and trimming loss by keeping all of that meat and grinding it with pork sausage to make a fine addition to the freezer. When combining pronghorn with pork, to make salami or other cooked sausage, at least 12 percent pork fat should be added.

The weight of the heart and liver are not included in the above figures. I always carefully remove and save these two organs, for they provide some excellent eating. In our case, the liver usually disappears the same evening the animal is killed! Carefully washed to remove extra blood, thinly sliced strips of pronghorn liver are fried on a hot skillet, along with a couple of big onions sautéed in advance. Makes good eating.

Next to go is the heart, which we usually boil until tender, slice off the fat (if any, for most pronghorns are lean), and use those tender slices in the sandwiches for tomorrow's hunt. Or simply arrange the thin slices of cold heart meat on a platter with a bit of horseradish on top. Good!

If the meat is going directly into the freezer, wrap it carefully and tightly, to exclude as much air as possible. You want the freezer paper tight against the meat to prevent drying out and freezer burn. (A word of advice here: Don't put it all in the freezer. Instead, save two or three meals to be eaten without being frozen.) Do not plan on leaving any meat in the freezer until next season. Plan to eat yours in three or four months at the latest. And be sure to check the game laws in your state to see how long you are allowed to keep game meat after the end of the hunting season. That law may surprise you.

Cooking Tips

The one thing to avoid in cooking pronghorn meat is *drying out*. The meat is very low in fat, and overcooking can dry it out quickly, leaving you with stringy, unappetizing results.

How do you avoid drying out? Three ways. First, cook steaks and chops quickly, on a hot stove, without giving them time to dry out. Second, use "wet cooking" methods. Third, try meals that are wrapped in aluminum foil, which does not allow the moisture to escape.

The chops from an antelope are perhaps the best eating of all. Cook them on a very hot griddle or skillet. Do the job quickly, after the rest of the dinner is all ready. Same goes for steaks. When having my pronghorns cut up, I tell the butcher to make steaks and chops out of everything he possibly can. If you have a favorite marinade that goes well with venison steaks, it will go well with pronghorn steaks and chops, although the meat really doesn't need any marinade.

Marinades come into their own when you start working with the small roasts that are standard on the small-bodied pronghorn. Before marinating, lightly score the outside of the roast with a sharp knife, slitting the protective tissue that seems to wrap muscle bundles in the pronghorn meat. This will allow the marinade to get inside and do its work. Marinating overnight in milk (better yet, in buttermilk) will give you bland-tasting meat, something like veal—too "Milquetoasty" for my taste. A three-hour bath in a mixture of white cooking wine and your favorite herbs will give a better-tasting meal, in my opinion. A marinade of soy sauce, thinly sliced onions, and a bit of red chili powder will give you a real snappy "pepper steak" piece of meat, but don't leave it in that marinade for more than three hours.

My favorite way of preparing the usual small pronghorn roast is to use the oil and vinegar salad dressing that you usually put on your tossed green salad. Add to it a packet of seasonings (Good Seasons is the trade name, I think) which comes with the oil and vinegar recipe. Or dream up your own packet of herbs and spices to go in the oil and vinegar. Marinate overnight in the refrigerator.

Next, sauté two fist-sized onions and one large green bell pepper, cut into thin strips. Use either real butter or cooking oil, not olive oil. When the onions are soft and translucent, place the well-drained and wiped dry roast on a large sheet of aluminum foil. Place the onions and peppers on top of the meat, and pour whatever grease is left in your sautéing pan in on top of them.

Now fold the aluminum foil up and around the meat and the onion-bell pepper mixture, and carefully close it, trying your best to seal it completely. Place the foil bundle in a Pyrex dish and cook it very slowly at 250°–275°F. for about four hours, until the meat is tender to the fork. If it is getting close to dinnertime and the meat doesn't seem to be cooking fast enough, turn up the temperature, but keep the meat sealed in with the juices and onions. Slice the meat thinly, serve it hot, and eat it right away. A bit of red Burgundy goes well, I might add.

Scraps and trimmings are easily used by grinding it all into pronghorn burgers. I use this ground meat in hundreds of dishes that call for hamburger or ground beef. Remember that the meat is a little bit drier than ground beef, has less fat, and needs to be cooked less. I haven't had much luck with meat loaf, for just that reason. However, my spaghetti sauce, featuring ground pronghorn, onions, bell peppers, green olives, and a touch of garlic in the tomato paste base has found favor even with my gourmet friends of Italian ancestry. Let it cook slowly, for hours and hours. Do it in a Crock Pot for best results. Then, when all is ready, cook your pasta *al dente* and serve it quickly, ladling the sauce with pronghorn generously over the spaghetti. They'll come back for more. A bottle of Chianti helps.

When someone tells you that pronghorns are not good eating, you should use your common sense filter on their words. Filter out the nonsense, and what you'll hear is this: "I didn't take care of the meat properly." Properly cared for, pronghorn is excellent eating.

23

Guide to Trophies

If you are a head hunter, a confirmed trophy hunter, where is the best place to hunt for pronghorns with lofty horns? Perhaps the best source of information on this is the record book put out every few years by the Boone and Crockett Club. I know the situation changes constantly, as new trophies are brought to bag and entered in the listings, but the general trends continue. Some areas simply grow bigger horns than other areas. Perhaps it is the mineral content of the forage, or perhaps the vitamin content, or just the nutritional value of the forage. Differences between different parts of the same state can be startling.

But let's start out with the simplest part: Which states produce the most trophies? One would think that the state that kills the most pronghorns would have the best chance to produce the most trophies, and that points to Wyoming, where the kill is many times that of all other states combined. But when I checked the listings in the 1977 record book, I had to go to Nos. 6, 7, and 8, before I found Wyoming's top trophies. Numbers 1, 2, and 3 all came from Arizona, which has a kill of approximately 1/100 of that attained in Wyoming! The No. 4 came from Colorado, No. 5 from New Mexico.

No. 9 came from Oregon, and the 10th spot went to Arizona. But let's widen our field of view a bit. In that same edition, Wyoming had 11 of the top 25 record heads, Arizona only five. Colorado had the No. 4 head, but that was the only Colorado trophy that made the top 25.

Let's widen our scope still more. Of the top 100 heads in that listing, 39 were from Wyoming. This is still what we might expect. With the huge kill in Wyoming dwarfing that of any other state, Wyoming obviously should produce the most record-book trophies. Right?

But, Arizona produced 17 of the top 100 that were listed in the 1977 record book. That's almost half as many as Wyoming, yet the kill in Arizona in the years before 1977 wouldn't add up to even a fraction of what was taken in Wyoming.

Let's look a bit deeper. Wyoming had 34 of the top 100, Arizona had 17. Montana's eight nosed out New Mexico's seven; Nevada had four, Alberta three, Oregon two, and nine other areas had one apiece in the top 100 of the 1977 record book. These nine were Chihuahua, Colorado, Saskatchewan, Nebraska, Oklahoma, California, North Dakota, Texas, and Idaho.

Colorado had only 10 of the top 340 pronghorns in that 1977 listing. But the times, they are a-changing. Colorado now has trophy heads, and if you want proof, read Judd Cooney's Chapter 24 in this book, which tells how he took the world record Pope and Young pronghorn with the bow. It was taken in Colorado.

In interpreting the history of world-record pronghorns, remember that some states have a much longer history of pronghorn hunting than others. North Dakota, where legal hunting didn't begin until 1950, obviously has not had as many years in which to land in the record books, when compared with Wyoming or Montana where hunting began much earlier.

Also, trophy bucks take four or five years to grow those big horns. If you are hunting in a state where the pronghorn herd is cropped liberally every year, the bucks do not live long enough to grow big horns. Conversely, if you can locate an area in which hunting has not been allowed for several years, but which is now open, that area should contain some real hat-rack horns. On average, the biggest-racked bucks I have ever seen were on the Fort Wingate Ordnance Depot in New Mexico. This semi-tame herd has not been rifle hunted for many years. Bowhunters have a good crack at them, but the average buck surely lives longer than he does on the heavily hunted open areas of the same state. On my last trip out there, for the purpose of taking pictures, I drooled at the sight of bucks that surely looked like they belonged in the record book—any one of which would have been a lead-pipe cinch with the modern rifle. Perhaps I should take up bowhunting.

Although the well-known names of world-renowned trophy hunters—Elgin Gates, Herb Klein, Dr. F.C. Hibben, and others—are represented in the record books, pronghorn records are held by a widely diverse group of just plain hunters. The reason for this is that it is extremely difficult to tell a pronghorn head rating 81 points from a pronghorn head rating 83 points, yet the 83-pointer would have put its taker in 234th place in the record book in 1977, while the 81-pointer wouldn't even make the cutoff point in the records.

To score a pronghorn head, you must take a series of measurements. Measurement (A) is the distance between the tip of the left horn and the tip of the right horn. Remember that we want the shortest distance between the exact tips of each horn. That (A) measurement is called the "tip to tip" spread.

Measurement (B) is the greatest spread from the inside of the left horn to the inside of the right horn. This must be measured exactly in a horizontal plane. This is the "inside spread."

Measurement (C) is the length of the horn. It is measured with a flexible rule, around the outside curve of the horn. Record the measurement for each horn separately. If there is a difference in horn length, record that difference.

Now for the measurements which tell us how massive the horns are. D-1 measures the circumference of the horns at their base. Record for each horn, separately. If there is a difference in measurement from one horn to the other, record that difference. D-2 records same dimension of the horn one quarter of the way of the length of the horn above the base. D-3 is two-quarters of the length above the base and D-3 is three-quarters of the length of the horn above the base. D-4 measures the diameter of each horn at the top. The top is defined as the place at the same height as the bottom of the downturned curved tip of that horn. If the horns are of unequal length, you take the longer horn and divide that figure by four to ascertain where D-2-3-4 are located, marking at the same distance above the base for each measurement. If there is a difference in measurement from one horn to the other, record that difference.

Measurement (E) is the length of the prong. Now this is tricky, so follow instructions exactly. This measurement is taken from the tip of the prong along the upper edge of the outer curve to the horn, then around the horn to a point at the back of the horn where a straight edge at the back of both horns touches the horn. If there is a difference in measurement between the prong length of the horns, record the difference.

Now add up the figures for left horn, and for right horn. Then add up all the "difference" totals. Add the horn measurements together and subtract the total of the differences from that total. If the greatest inside measurement is greater than the length of the longest horn, subtract that difference from the total. That final figure is your score.

In 1977 the No. 1 trophy scored $101^{6/8}$ points!

Pertinent data are: Each horn measured exactly $19^{4/8}$ inches! Circumference at base was $7^{6/8}$ and $7^{4/8}$ inches. Third quarter measurements were identical at $3^{4/8}$ inches! Inside spread was $14^{7/8}$ inches, and tip to tip spread was $10^{7/8}$. The prongs measured 7 and $7^{1/8}$ inches.

The unbelievable, but true, part of this trophy is the length of the horns—exactly $19^{4/8}$ inches. The No. 2 animal sported horn length of only $18^{3/8}$ inches—more than a full inch shorter!

The No. 3 all-time head was even taller, with horns of 20 and $20^{1/8}$ inches. That length was offset by the smaller circumference measurements. In other words, it was taller, but not as massive. Both of those fantastic heads came from Arizona, and both were taken before 1900. After that, one 1899 head was No. 1 for nearly a century; it was topped in 1975, again from Arizona.

Let's take a look at the record book of 1981, and see what a difference four years made. In 1981, Arizona still had the top two antelope! But sheer weight of numbers has told, and Wyoming now has the fourth, fifth, and sixth all-time trophy heads to its credit. And, most important, of the top 100 heads listed by the Boone and Crockett Club, a surprising 49 came from Wyoming!

Arizona had 13 in the top 100, New Mexico eight, beating out Montana's much larger herds, where seven made the top 100. Nevada listed five in the top 100, including a tie for twelfth—which is a fine showing for Nevada with its small pronghorn population. South Dakota, which ranks third among the states in total pronghorn population, had only one listed in the top 140!

So the situation is changing to show us that Wyoming, which has the most pronghorns, also has the most trophies in the top 100. Where to go to shoot a trophy? Wyoming! Where to go to shoot the next No. 1 world's record? Arizona!

Get the latest listing of record pronghorn heads. Don't use it to pick the state, for that would mean that you are including data from 1890, which has mighty little to do with today's situation.

Take your target state and look to see which county produces the real trophies. If you narrow it down to two or three counties, that's fine. Next, take the county that offers the most permits . . . in other words, the county in which you have the best chance of taking *any* pronghorn.

Next, take only the records for the past five years, and find your best trophy area for today's hunting. This will prevent you from hunting an area that produced big heads in the 1890s but hasn't done much lately.

Now apply for that No. 1 producer of record-book-heads county first, with the second-place trophy county as your second choice, and so on. But, to avoid complete disappointment, use your third, fourth, and fifth (if available in that state) choices for the counties with the largest number of permits. That way you won't be totally left out by the results of the drawing, and you still have a good chance at your "big trophy" spot.

Now, go to the area a month before the season opener. Bring your spotting scope and a big pair of binoculars. Find out where the biggest bucks are, and glass them. When you find that trophy head, make sure that you can get access to the land. Then, you are ready to at least try for the trophy of a lifetime.

Note that in some states, your hunt area will be assigned to you. In my home state of New Mexico, for example, it does little good to know that there is a world-record book on the next ranch, after you have been assigned to hunt *only* on this ranch.

Considering the nature of the pronghorn's horns, there is a surprising number of pronghorns carrying mismatched horns. Be sure to glass both horns, and remember that the statistic "difference between right and left horn measurements" is a figure you subtract from the total.

Finding a record-book head is not an easy task. You can improve your odds, however, by studying the records and by doing a lot of pre-season scouting.

Because some pronghorns damage their horns during the jousts of the mating season (not many, but some), it is smart to pick an early season, rather than a late one. This could make the slight difference between that record-book measurement and an also-ran.

No matter what the mathematic result of your measurements, the pronghorn is a striking trophy. Many a hunter has been very proud of a good-looking head that would surely have no chance at the record book. Pronghorns simply make impressive trophies!

24

Bowhunting Pronghorns

by Judd Cooney

Hunting pronghorns with a stick and string has been going on in North America for a very long time. The early Indians knew that the pronghorn was not the easiest target to get an arrow into, however, and it consequently was not a regular item of their diet.

Antelope were taken by Indians by driving them over a cliff. One such drive in southern Wyoming in the early 1800s is reported to have taken 4000 antelope.

The Indians did take an occasional antelope by the same methods we use today. Stalking, flagging, decoying, and ambushing them at waterholes were all moderately successful for the early bowhunters, but couldn't be depended upon to keep steaks on the fire year-round.

Successful bowhunting of pronghorns has only come about in the past 15 years.

Fifteen years ago there weren't many hunters, including bowhunters themselves, who fully believed it was possible to arrow an antelope. If it happened, it was called luck. Colorado's first late-season bowhunt produced a total of three kills. That was in 1971, and the bowhunting organizations in the western states weren't pushing to get good seasons. They settled for whatever the game departments gave them, without a complaint. Remember, too, there were far fewer pronghorns in the western states 15 years ago than there are now.

As the populations increased, so did interest in bowhunting pronghorns. Coinciding with this was a very rapid and widespread improvement in bowhunting techniques and in increased knowledge of the pronghorn's habits. It didn't take long for

He is suspicious, but not enough so to raise the alarm hairs of that specialized rump patch. *Photo by Judd Cooney.*

the harvest of quality, trophy pronghorn entries into the Pope and Young Club records grew to the point where only the far more wide-ranging whitetail exceeded it. Pope and Young boosted the minimum score from 57 to 64 in 1983, but this hasn't slowed the tide of trophy pronghorns taken by the bow each fall.

Today, the bowhunter-caused mortality must be reckoned with, not ignored as "inconsequential" by the game biologists who set the seasons. In several western states the archer success rate is around 20 percent, which is higher than that for any of the other big-game species.

The basic hunting methods haven't changed much from the early days before the white man took up bowhunting, but the refinement of techniques and equipment, coupled with the great increase in pronghorn numbers, have given the present-day bowhunter a much better chance of arrowing one of these beautiful animals.

Stalking is the first method of bowhunting, although not the most successful. To successfully stalk within range of the keen-eyed pronghorn takes a tremendous amount of skill, along with planning, patience, and perseverance.

The stalker should have a good pair of binoculars and a spotting scope, because you must locate your animal without being seen yourself. They are also indispensable when you pick a stalking route that will give you a chance to get within bowrange without being observed. There will be many times when you locate a good buck in a position where your binoculars tell you that you simply cannot stalk him. Then you either wait for the buck to move to a more accessible area or give up on him and go look for another.

Good camouflage is essential for successfully stalking any antelope because their keen eyes will pick up anything that moves or anything that doesn't fit into the surroundings, well out past the 500-yard mark. Once an antelope spots you, it's all over; you might as well look for another stalk target. The key is to spot him without being seen and to stay completely out of his sight until you are within bowrange, or better yet, until you walk up to the downed animal to check your arrow hit.

The wind is of critical importance in any type of bowhunting for antelope. Don't believe those who say that the pronghorn doesn't have a good nose. His sense of smell is as keen as a whitetail or bull elk any day. If they get a whiff of you, they will snort a warning to every antelope in the country. *Keep the wind in your favor at all times* when bowhunting for antelope. An antelope's reaction to the wind is sometimes different from that of other big-game animals, though. They don't usually leave the country, but rather will stand around out of bowrange and snort at you, which is almost as bad as if they just left. At times they will circle until they get out of the scent stream and then come into the blind or waterhole, but don't count on a trophy buck doing anything that stupid. *Keep the wind in your face*.

Under certain conditions, antelope can be driven. Several bowhunters cooperate to move the pronghorns toward other hunters who are waiting in ambush along the most likely path the pushed pronghorns will take. Take advantage of the fact that antelope frequently travel along fences. A bowhunter hidden along the fence in the brush may get a shot at the passing animals. When Colorado first started an archery-only season in the northwestern corner of the state, it was held during November. We used the drive with quite a bit of success in getting shots, but had little luck in killing antelope. Hitting an antelope while the animal is smoking it down a fenceline is neither boring nor productive.

The key here is to know exactly where the antelope will go when they are pushed from a given area. Good crossings through gates or passes through a saddle in a ridge or an opening in a brushy creek bottom are all good spots to post waiting bowhunters. The key to success is found in studying their habits and having lots of patience in moving them slowly to each other. The standing hunter must be well camouflaged and hidden and have the patience to wait for the best shot, because he is only going to get one.

Decoys were used by the early Indian bowhunters when they donned antelope hides and tried to work in close enough to get a shot or to attract a jealous buck within range during the rut. Decoying is gaining in popularity among modern hunters, and in some areas, during the rut, it is very successful in getting the buck within range. During the rut, the bucks are very territorial and will try their damnedest to run off any encroaching rivals. A well-built decoy that looks like another buck will often bring the harem boss right up to the waiting bowhunter. It is important to place your decoy as close as possible to a herd with a dominant buck in it without being seen yourself. Pick a spot that will give you a good shot at the approaching buck and wait for the action. One of the best spots is on a ridge line where you can stay down out of sight until the buck is right on top of your decoy. Although I haven't tried it yet, I think that putting a decoy by a waterhole might help to alleviate some of the spookiness of the hard-hunted antelope when they are thinking about coming in for a drink.

The most effective way of taking a good buck with the bow and arrow is to use a blind by a waterhole or stock tank. Perhaps 90 percent of the bucks in the record books are taken by this method.

Water is a real factor in the antelope's daily life and is the main reason that there are more antelope in many areas of the West than ever before. The ranchers and Bureau of Land Management have spent millions of dollars putting in stock tanks to provide water for their livestock in the semi-arid lands that the antelope love to call home. With a year-round supply of water assured, the pronghorns have moved in and set up housekeeping, greatly expanding their range.

Waterhole hunting is an art in some areas, and believe me, the pronghorns are getting much smarter about coming in to water. The bowhunter who throws up a pile of brush on the bank of a waterhole and crouches down behind it, waiting for a trophy buck to walk up and drink, is going to be headed home empty-handed in a day or two unless he is very lucky and finds a really stupid buck.

There are several types of blinds used on waterholes, including windmills, pit blinds, and standing or box blinds. Windmills are effective spots from which to waylay antelope because the animals are used to the clanging and banging of the metal windmill, and they pay little attention to noises or movements near one. The second season I bowhunted in northwestern Colorado we had a windmill over a small seep that produced seven bucks in two weeks. Unfortunately, the windmill stopped working and the waterhole no longer exists, but it was one helluva spot while it lasted. Many bowhunters who don't like perching on top of a working windmill can enclose the bottom of the tower with brush or burlap and use that as

Wary and alert, but thirsty, this buck comes to the waterhole. Judd Cooney photo.

a blind. Be sure to give the antelope lots of time to get used to it before you use it.

A word of caution. Make sure you lock the blades before you climb up onto the platform, and always use a safety harness. More than one bowhunter has been knocked off a windmill by a sudden gust of wind that caused the blades and tail section to spin around. Also make sure you check with the rancher before you shut down a working windmill to hunt from it. Ranchers take a dim view of having their tanks go dry because of some careless hunter.

Solid blinds can be made on a waterhole out of posts and wire mesh covered with burlap, or even plywood, but this type must be in position long before the season to let the antelope get used to it. Keep all the covering tight and well-fastened. Nothing makes a buck edgier than to have burlap or camo netting flapping around loose when they want to come in for a drink.

My preference is for the pit blind. By far the toughest to build, it is the most

Antelope are accustomed to the noise and movement of a windmill, and this makes the windmill a good shooting platform. *Judd Cooney photo.*

Judd Cooney congratulates daughter Lisa on a fine trophy she took with the bow. Judd Cooney photo.

effective. I can always tell the neophyte hunter's blind when I see it. It is simply a hole dug deep enough for the bowhunter to sit on the rim with his feet in the hole and brush piled around it. Many hunters look for waterholes with lots of brush around them, but I prefer a flat pond with very little cover. The antelope feel much safer when they can see all around them while they drink.

Pit blinds should be placed downwind from where you expect most of the antelope to be drinking. This is easily determined by studying the tracks and trails leading to the waterhole. It also may be necessary to have two blinds, one for morning and one for afternoon hunting. I try to place my blinds where they will always allow me to remain in the shadows regardless of the time of day. The barer the area around the tank, the deeper I dig the pit with shorter brush around the top. I want enough brush around the pit to shade me and hide my bow tip when I draw—nothing more. Use brush from adjacent areas to blend in as well as possible and don't be afraid to add fresh brush every couple of days to keep yourself well hidden in the shadows. Most of my blinds are open in front to facilitate shooting in

Digging a blind is hard work, but the pit blind is the most effective way to get within bow range of an antelope. *Judd Cooney photo.*

Judd Cooney with excellent bowhunter's trophy. Note complete camouflage. *Judd Cooney photo.*

any direction. I put enough brush behind me to make sure that I'm not "skylined" against a thin background.

The bowhunter should be camouflaged from head to toe, including bow and bow quiver. I prefer the dark camo, such as tiger stripe or Viet Nam pattern with full face and hand paint or headnet and gloves. It is always a thrill to have a trophy buck walk up to within 10 feet and look directly at you in the blind, and then go calmly down to get his drink. That's the reward for all that digging and that perfect camouflage.

Antelope are light bodied, and you don't need heavy gear. Any bow in the 45-to-50-pound range, combined with balanced arrows and razor-sharp broadheads, will do the job cleanly if the arrow is placed in a vital area. Antelope country is wide open, making it easy for the bowhunter to keep the hit animal in sight at all times, making recovery much easier.

When guiding, I insist that my bowhunters do everything they can to keep a hit animal in sight until it stops moving, and then back off and just play a waiting game until help arrives.

Two years ago I spent some four weeks looking at and filming antelope as well as guiding bowhunters for the first part of the season. There were big bucks all over the area we were bowhunting and my hunters were filling their licenses with record-book animals right and left. During the early season scouting I found one of my favorite waterholes bone-dry. This particular waterhole had produced some monster bucks during past seasons because it was located adjacent to some rough canyon country where road hunters couldn't pursue their craft. This gave the bucks a chance to get a little older and grow bigger horns. During the season I checked this area for three dry weeks. Then we got an isolated "frog choker" of a rain that filled several tanks with water to entice pronghorns. I checked this particular tank just after the rain and found large buck prints in the mud.

Dave Daughtry, who was videotaping antelope with our crew, was along with me when we followed the tracks in the muddy road and spotted a small herd on a sagebrush flat. We glassed them from the

"It's a thrill when the buck comes down and looks right at your camouflaged blind and then comes in to drink anyway." *Judd Cooney photo.*

Broadside, not alarmed, a good shot for the bowman. *Judd Cooney photo.*

Complete camouflage, including painted face and hands, contributed to the downfall of this world-record Pope and Young antelope taken by Judd Cooney. Score? A whopping 85! *Judd Cooney photo.*

The Cooney family excels at bowhunting. Here's Judd's daughter Lisa with a buck she arrowed in Colorado. *Judd Cooney photo.*

A nice buck, but he'll not make the record book. Do you take him? Or do you wait? *Photo by Judd Cooney.*

Many times the best buck will hang back and let the others test the waters before he comes in to drink. *Judd Cooney photo.*

The view from the bowhunter's blind. *Judd Cooney photo.*

At the moment of release, the bowhunter is still well hidden. *Judd Cooney photo.*

Those flared rump hairs are the clue. He knows something is wrong. Judd Cooney photo.

truck, and Dave spotted a huge buck off by himself — a real keeper. As I focused in on him with the spotting scope, another buck came into view and chased that "keeper" plumb out of sight. The chaser was one of the largest bucks I had seen in five weeks of looking at antelope.

A week later I had one of my bowhunters sitting on that tank. She had a small herd come to water but couldn't get a shot at the herd buck, which she classed as a "nice" buck. Next day, she nailed a Pope and Young buck on a waterhole 40 miles away.

I finally got a chance to get out for a morning's hunt, and decided to give the big buck hole a try. I eased into the blind rather late, but there wasn't an antelope in sight, so I thought my chances were good. I had a good book to read and there wasn't a place in the world I would rather have been. I had been sitting for about an hour when a group of pronghorns appeared on the ridge above the waterhole and casually started down toward the tank. There were several does and fawns and one buck, which seemed like a very good buck through my 10 x 28 Bausch and Lombs. When they reached the water and started to drink, I decided to pass on the buck and wait, since I still had a week and a half to hunt and had both a Colorado and Wyoming license to fill.

I was casually watching the group drink

and mentally picking a spot on the big buck when I saw another buck top the ridge and start down. When I got him in my glasses, his horns looked out of proportion. They were very high, but they didn't look heavy enough to make him a really top trophy. The closer he got, though, the more my evaluation changed, and by the time he got to the top of the tank dam I had my bow in hand and my mind made up to take him. He was so tall and unusual! He watched the others drinking as he stood 35 yards from where I sat, and I had the distinct feeling that if the others left, he would too.

Without giving myself time to get more nervous, I drew the 75-pound Hoyt-Easton compound and sent a xx75 flying his

Experience has shown that the antelope will not pick out the hunter in this scene, as long as there is no movement. *Judd Cooney photo.*

way. I watched the arrow slam into the buck right behind the shoulders. As he whirled, I could see the arrow was sticking out on both sides. He ran for 40 yards and piled up in the sagebrush. To this day, I have no idea of what happened to the other antelope on the waterhole.

I hurried over to get a good look and realized this was the biggest buck I had ever been close to. Had I known how big he really was when I drew on him, I would probably have missed him entirely. The more I looked, the bigger he got! I finally had the antelope I wanted for a mount in my den. Not only was he the most beautiful animal I had ever taken with a bow and arrow, but he was also one of the largest ever taken with the bow anywhere. He tied the world-record pronghorn taken by Archie Malm in North Dakota in 1958 with a score of 85! For my money there isn't a more beautiful or exciting animal on the North American continent. He's the supreme challenge for the bowhunter.

The world-record bowhunter's antelope trophy, a Colorado buck shot by Judd Cooney in 1984, which tied the record set by Archie Malm, in North Dakota, back in 1958. *Photo by Judd Cooney.*

Location of the blind, plus camouflage, contribute to the chances of taking a world-record head. This is Judd's world-record trophy. *Judd Cooney photo.*

The time and effort you put into planning your hunt, scouting the area, and getting your blind or pit into proper shape are going to seem like the best investment you ever made when you look up and see a black-horned pronghorn buck standing a few feet away from you, just waiting for you to draw on him.

Index

Alberta
    hunting season in, 26
    license to hunt in, 26
    range-population fluctuation in, 26
Anderson Mesa Study, 118–19
Arizona
    hunting advice for, 208–10
    hunting in, 182
Autenreith, Robert E., 42–43, 118

Bailey, Vernon, 31–32
Baja California, range-population fluctuation in, 68–70
Barker, Elliott, 56
Blinds. *See* Hunting
Bowhunting for pronghorn, 231–51
    and blinds, 235–37
    camouflage, 237, 240
    first hunts, 231
    gear, 240
    methods of, 233–37
    Pope and Young scores, 233
    success rates, 233
Brazda, Art, 89, 90–91
Breeding, 99–104
Bucks
    and harems, 100–101
    managing harvest of, 128–29
Bureau of Land Management, 15, 42, 52, 222

California
    hunting advice for, 210–11
    hunting in, 182
    range population fluctuation in, 50–53
Carrying capacity, of pronghorn range, 130–31
Censusing techniques, 127–28
Charles Sheldon Antelope Refuge, 46, 48
Clothing. *See* Hunting
Colorado
    hunting advice for, 211
    hunting in, 182
    range-population fluctuation in, 61–63
Cooking pronghorn, 225–26
Coloration, 7–8, 12, 17
Competition with livestock, 28–29, 117, 138–40
Compound 1080, 31, 55, 60–70, 115–17, 119, 122–23
Cosoryx, 16
Courtship activity. *See* Breeding
Coyotes and pronghorns, 22–23, 30–32, 37, 44, 48, 55, 65, 69–70, 74, 115, 117–24
Cud chewing. *See* Rumination
Curiosity of pronghorn, 206–7

Decoys, use of, 189–91
Del Giudice, Paula. *See* Nevada, hunting advice for
Description of pronghorn. *See* Pronghorn
Diet of pronghorn. *See* Pronghorn
Diseases of pronghorn. *See* Pronghorn
Does
    managing harvest of, 43, 129–30
    See also Breeding
Drought, 64

Fawning. *See* Breeding
Fawns, 105–7
Fences, affect on pronghorn, 14, 160–67

Index

Glands. *See* Pronghorn
Golden Eagle predation, 124
Greenwalt, Ernie, 50

Hailey, Thomas L., 122, 138–39
Harems. *See* Bucks
Hart Mountain Refuge, 44–45
Hawaii, stocking in. *See* Trapping and transplanting
Heliographic rump. *See* Pronghorn
Heuser, Ken. *See* Colorado, hunting advice for
Homestead Act, 45
Hooves. *See* Pronghorn
Horns. *See* Pronghorn
Hunting
    advice from experts, 208–22
    from blinds, 169–78
    clothing for, 199–201
    equipment for, 196–98
    methods of, 202–4
    rifles for, 183–88
    scopes for, 187–88
    season for, 130
    where to go, 179–82
    See also Bowhunting; Muzzleloaders; specific states

Idaho
    hunting advice for, 211–12
    range-population fluctuation in, 39–43
Imprinting, 106

Jensen, David. *See* North Dakota, hunting advice for

Kansas, range-population fluctuation in, 74–76
Klepper, Dan. *See* Texas, hunting advice for
Knapps, Ken and Roberta. *See* hunting advice for

Land use, changes in, 27–28, 40, 45, 131
Lemm, Walden, 37
Lewis and Clark, 30
Locoweed, 160

Management of pronghorn, 125–32
    basic questions about, 125-26
    censusing, 127–28
    and landowners, 131
    and livestock diseases, 159
    and parasites, 159–60
    and poisonous plants, 160
    and range capacity, 130–31
    and supplemental feedings, 131
    and transplants, 132
    and trapping, 126–27
    water used in, 131
Manitoba, lack of pronghorn in, 26–27
Market hunting, 21, 62
McBratney, Cliff, 89–90
McLucas, Jim, 93, 127
McNeel, Jack. *See* Idaho, hunting advice for
Meat, care of, 223–25
Megafauna, extinction of, 9
Mexico, range-population fluctuation in, 66–68
Montana
    as best pronghorn state, 27
    and Charles M. Russell National Wildlife Refuge, 28–29
    hunting advice for, 212–13
    hunting in, 180, 182
    range-population fluctuation in, 27–29
    and transplanting pronghorn, 89–95
Mortality factors, 155–67
Muzzleloaders, 192–95

Nebraska
    hunting advice for, 213
    range-population fluctuation in, 37–39
Neff, Don C., 118–19
Nevada
    hunting advice for, 213–15
    hunting in, 182
    range-population fluctuation in, 45–50
New Mexico
    hunting advice for, 213–15
    hunting in, 182
    range-population fluctuation in, 56–61
North Dakota
    hunting advice for, 216
    range-population fluctuation in, 29–34

Oklahoma, range-population fluctuation in, 72–74
Oregon
    hunting advice for, 216–17
    hunting in, 182
    range-population fluctuation in, 43–45

Parasites. *See* Pronghorn
Park, Ed. *See* Oregon, hunting advice for
Population numbers, 21–23
    Autenreith research of, 42–43
    See also specific states
Post, Chuck. *See* South Dakota, hunting advice for
Pronghorn
    bones, 149
    breathing, 107
    communication of fear, 147–48
    description of, 7, 8

diet of, 31, 34, 74, 157, 159
and drinking, 108–14, 170–71
eyesight of, 12
and forbs, 135–38
glands of, 148–49
heliographic rump, 147
as herd animals, 14
hooves, 10
horns, 10–11, 149–54
jumping ability, 98
migration of, 76, 96–99
and parasites, 156–57, 159–60
and running, 8, 13, 107, 141–46
size of, 11
sounds of, 11–12
speed of, 12–13, 141–45
winter effects on, 25–26, 32–34

Range-population fluctuation. *See* specific state
Reeve, Archie F., 126
Reginato, John. *See* California, hunting advice for
Rumination, 108
Running. *See* Pronghorn

Sagebrush, 130
Sans, E. R., 46, 48–50
Saskatchewan, range-population fluctuation in, 24–26
Shedding of horns, 151-52
Sheep, competition with, 139–40
Sodium monofluoroacetate. *See* Compound 1080
South Dakota
    hunting advice for, 217–18
    hunting in, 182
    range-population fluctuation in, 34–37
Strung, Norm. *See* Montana, hunting advice for
Supplemental feeding, 131

Taxonomy of pronghorn, 8

in fossils, 9, 16
peninsularis, 18, 68
sonoran, 17
Texas
    hunting advice for, 218–19
    range-population fluctuation in, 63–66
Trapping and transplanting, 57–60, 76–82, 126
    failed attempts in Florida, 87
    Hawaii, stocking in, 83
    in Louisiana, 87
    by McLucas, 93
    in Montana, 54, 89–95
    in New Mexico, 23
    in South Carolina, 87–88
    timing of, 132
Trophies
    measurement of, 228–29
    where to find, 227–30
    world record with bow, 250
Twins, birth of, 104

Utah
    hunting advice for, 219–21
    hunting in, 182
    range-population fluctuation in, 53–56

Whitaker, Bob. *See* Arizona, hunting advice for
Wichita Mountains Refuge, 73
Williams, Jesse. *See* New Mexico, hunting advice for
Woolsey, Norman G., 118–19
Wyoming
    hunting advice for, 221-22
    hunting in, 179–80
    range-population fluctuation in, 70–72

Yoakum, James D., 117

Zumbo, Jim. *See* Utah, hunting advice for

*Some other fine hunting books
from America's Great Outdoor Publisher*

Badge in the Wilderness
My 30 dangerous years combating wildlife violators.
by David H. Swendsen

Grouse Hunter's Guide
Solid facts, insights, and observations on how to hunt the ruffed grouse.
by Dennis Walrod

Art and Science of Whitetail Hunting
How to interpret the facts and find the deer.
by Kent Horner

Hunting Rabbits and Hares
The complete guide to North America's favorite small game.
by Richard P. Smith

White-tailed Deer: Ecology & Management
Developed by the Wildlife Management Institute. Over 2,400 references on every aspect of deer behavior.
edited by Lowell K. Halls

Bowhunting for Whitetails
Your best methods for taking North America's favorite deer.
by Dave Bowring

Deer & Deer Hunting
The serious hunter's guide.
by Dr. Rob Wegner

Elk of North America
The definitive, exhaustive, classic work on the North American elk.
ed. by Jack Ward Thomas and Dale E. Toweill

Hunting Ducks and Geese
Hard facts, good bets, and serious advice from a duck hunter you can trust.
by Steve Smith

Spring Turkey Hunting
The serious hunter's guide.
by John M. McDaniel

How to Plan Your Western Big Game Hunt
All you need to know to plan a do-it-yourself or guided hunt in the 11 Western states.
by Jim Zumbo

Available at your local bookstore, or for complete ordering information, write:

Stackpole Books
Dept. PH
Cameron and Kelker Streets
Harrisburg, PA 17105

**For fast service credit card users may call 1-800-READ-NOW
In Pennsylvania, call 717-234-5041**